DOROTHY PARKER
IN HOLLYWOOD

DOROTHY PARKER

IN HOLLYWOOD

GAIL CROWTHER

GALLERY BOOKS

New York   London   Toronto   Sydney   New Delhi

G

Gallery Books
An Imprint of Simon & Schuster, LLC
1230 Avenue of the Americas
New York, NY 10020

First Gallery Books hardcover edition October 2024

GALLERY BOOKS and colophon are registered trademarks
of Simon & Schuster, LLC

Simon & Schuster: Celebrating 100 Years of Publishing in 2024

For information about special discounts for bulk purchases,
please contact Simon & Schuster Special Sales at 1-866-506-1949
or business@simonandschuster.com.

The Simon & Schuster Speakers Bureau can bring authors to your live event.
For more information or to book an event, contact the Simon & Schuster Speakers
Bureau at 1-866-248-3049 or visit our website at www.simonspeakers.com.

Interior design by Davina Mock-Maniscalco

Manufactured in the United States of America

10   9   8   7   6   5   4   3   2   1

Library of Congress Cataloging-in-Publication Data is available.

ISBN 978-1-9821-8579-4
ISBN 978-1-9821-8581-7 (ebook)

In memory of my best boy, my life and writing companion,

My George (2011–2022)

And what do you do, Mrs. Parker?
Oh, I write. There's a hot job for a healthy woman.
I wish I'd taken a course in interior decorating.

—Dorothy Parker, "In the Throes: The Precious
Thoughts of an Author at Work," *Life*,
September 16, 1924

CONTENTS

Out There

My name is Dorothy Parker. I'm not very important.
I'm a woman who writes and tries to live by writing.
I don't know quite what anyone wants to hear about me,
but Lord knows I don't want to hear about myself.[1]

By all accounts, Dorothy Parker's two favorite words were *fuck* and *shit*. Coming from such a small, genteel, quietly spoken woman, these words often made people do a double take and wonder if they had misheard. Yet this mismatch so accurately sums up what we know about Dorothy Parker, a woman who exploited the incongruity of her appearance against what came out of her mouth, and sometimes onto the page. Many words are often used to describe Parker: *irreverent, witty, mocking, uncontrollable, derisive, drunk, world-weary, deadpan,* and *wry.* Words less often used to describe Dorothy Parker are *subversive, political, a fearless activist,* and *a writer with an unresolved legacy.*

Parker, known for her wit on and off the page and for her brief time as part of the Algonquin Round Table, dismissed those early years as "dingy," a group of people showing off and drinking too much. In 1959, when an interviewer asked her to describe the so-called brilliant excitement of those times, Parker was having none of it: "I give you my word, it wasn't."[2] Although the Algonquin Round Table cemented itself as a legendary part of literary history, Parker apparently "forgot" about it and claimed that nobody there was really *that* special and all they needed to do was grow up and grow out of it. Which she did. Looking back, she judged her younger self harshly: "Dammit, it *was* the 'twenties' and we had to be smarty. I *wanted* to be cute. That's the terrible thing. I should have had more sense."[3] By the late 1960s, Parker's attitude toward the Round Table had hardened even further: "Just a bunch of loudmouths showing off, saving their gags for days . . . 'Did I tell you what I said?' And everybody hanging around, asking, 'What'd he say? What'd he say?' The whole thing was made up by people who'd never been there. And may I say they're still making it up?"[4] For all the fame attached to that infamous Manhattan hotel table, Parker spent just a small slice of her life there. Perhaps more significant, but often overlooked, is her long-standing love-hate relationship with Hollywood, where from 1929 she spent almost thirty-five years of her life on and off, working on film scripts, becoming politically engaged in left-wing causes, and leading a chaotic personal life of marriage, miscarriage, alcoholism, divorce, blacklisting, unemployment, and remarriage. Her work on the script for *A Star Is Born* (1937) led to her first Academy Award nomination. She worked with Alfred Hitchcock on his high-profile spy thriller *Saboteur* (1942). She cowrote, with Frank Cavett, the script for one of the first Hollywood films to tackle the subject of women and alcoholism, *Smash-Up: The Story of a Woman* (1947), which earned her a second Academy Award nomination for best writing. Along with these successes, she also collaborated on numerous other film scripts (credited and uncredited), partied hard, lived in huge mansions, bought spectacular clothes, and earned vast amounts of money. When her older sister, Helen, visited her in Beverly Hills, she was impressed that everyone seemed to know Parker. And Parker knew everyone. Her friends and colleagues included Orson Welles, James Cagney, F. Scott Fitzgerald, Harpo Marx, Fredric March, and Sam Goldwyn. She even started work on an (unrealized) script for Marilyn Monroe. Yet despite this surface glamour, Parker had real reservations. "Out there," she called Hollywood with some derision, as though it were in the alien beyond. In a 1956 interview, Parker claimed: "I can't talk about Hollywood. It was a horror to me when I was there and it's a horror to look back on."[5] Yet by the early 1960s, she was back there again. It was a town that captured her for decades and repeatedly drew her in.

It does seem easier to attach Parker to the urban chic of Manhattan. In the sepia loveliness of photographs, her bobbed hair and floppy hats make the Roaring Twenties flare into life. There is something about the wildness and potential of that decade that promises hope, the emerging from a darker time into the light. But even the most cursory look at Parker's life during those years shows that far from being carefree and happy, she was dogged by depression, creative blocks, and romantic disasters. Battling through all of this, she began to perfect a persona, the early emergence of "Dorothy Parker" as she is most famously known—her quips, her asides, her cutting reviews. Nobody was safe from her tongue-lashing, and she was, rightly, feared. During her years working for *Vogue*, *Vanity Fair*, and the *New Yorker*, Parker established herself as a girl-about-town, knowing and droll. This distinctive voice became her trademark, and the Hollywood studios were willing to pay her a lot of money for it. But ultimately, she got trapped in a persona that became destructive and limiting. Today many people can probably name a Parker quip; in fact, they appear in popular culture all the time. They may even be able to recite one of her better-known poems or infamous reviews. But how many of the eighteen film scripts she worked on are known?[6] The scholar Faye Hammill points out that "Dorothy Parker is primarily remembered for her public personality, evolved through her journalism and disseminated via the sophisticated magazines of New York."[7] Even as early as 1941, Parker could see where her legacy was going: "I am serious about my writing. The reputation I didn't earn and don't want has been embarrassing and harmful."[8] As much as she tried to break away from those early New York years, there was a public desire to hang on to the wisecracking young woman and freeze her in time. But in Parker's eyes, those days were short-lived and insignificant. She longed to write the perfect short story, a novel, a brilliant play. She wanted to be taken seriously: "I am not witty, and I am not funny."[9] While this seems a little disingenuous (she was clearly both), she had the perception, and dread, to know that something amusing she might or might not have once said would outlast any of what she called the "blood sweating" she put into her serious writing. In 1956, even with a string of literary awards behind her and successful published collections, she never felt she had achieved her best and regarded writing as a tough, lonely business: "But if you write—there you are—there's you and your paper and that's all. But let us pray God you put someday something on your paper you won't be ashamed of." When her interviewer expressed incredulity that Parker could be ashamed of anything she had written, her response was kindly but firm: "Well, that's darling of you, but of course I am."[10] Yet caution is needed when it comes to trusting Parker as judge of her own work. While she was seemingly happy to dismiss her film work in Hollywood ("I never did a picture I was proud of and there was never a picture that was proud of me"), a closer revision of her Hollywood film work reveals a completely different story.[11] Parker tackled many political and social issues that were important to her, such as capitalism, the role of women, and the insidious nature of racism, and included them in a subversive but radical way. Her ability to write snappy and witty dialogue saved many pictures from being tossed completely, and reviewers often singled her out as one of the talents who created certain successful films. Parker seemed unable to see this for herself and regarded her work in Hollywood as a cautionary tale for all writers: "But oh my dear, if you want to be just a simple writer, doing the best you can, I plead with you—don't go there!"[12] Ultimately, Parker felt as though she had wasted her talent out there.

This blunt honesty and self-searching meant Parker was a woman who paid the price for somehow never quite fitting into her time. At first, in 1920s New York, she was ahead of it. She was the city's only female drama critic when she worked for *Vanity Fair*. Her reviews and verses poked fun at the untouchable wealthy elite. Collections such as *Enough Rope* (1926) and *Sunset Gun* (1928) were, for poetry, unusual bestsellers. And these continued to sell in large numbers throughout the 1930s and '40s. In 1944, a collection of short stories and verses called *The Portable Dorothy Parker* was much lauded and another commercial success. In the late 1940s, she came to the attention of the FBI, which put her under close surveillance and began to question exactly how involved she was with communist activities in Hollywood. Somehow, by the late 1950s and '60s, she got left behind, perhaps partly connected to her informal blacklisting for her left-wing political allegiances. Work dried up in Hollywood. In 1956, with her usual acerbic insight turned on herself as much as others, she claimed: "Let's face it, honey, my verse is terribly dated—as anything once fashionable is dreadful now. I gave it up knowing it wasn't getting any better, but nobody seemed to notice my magnificent gesture."[13] The only surprise many people expressed in 1967 on hearing about Parker's lonely death in a Manhattan hotel room was that she hadn't died years earlier.

Parker is a classic case of the misunderstood woman. She was a problem, and a problem that simply didn't fit in one way or another. All too often, women who refuse to conform must live and die with this temporal displacement. At the start of her career, Parker's stinging barbs and biting bons mots were seen as shockingly modern—indeed, ahead of their time—and most "unlady-like." By the end of her life, Parker was regarded as a relic of a time long gone, her verse anachronistic, her witticisms haunting popular culture and the rooms of the Algonquin as though she were a ghost long before she had even died.

During her life, this *out-of-timeness* made Parker feel rootless and restless. She never settled; she constantly moved around, from apartment to apartment to hotel to house, city to country, state to state, and then back again. She was looking for roots, for a time that, sadly, she never found. In her own words, in contrast to the Hollywood dream, there are no happy endings. Yet from what we know about Dorothy Parker, it seems unlikely that she would ever have had a happy ending. At certain moments in her life, joy flared and then quickly died, a promise almost within reach but never quite fulfilled. Some of this was down to circumstance; some of it was down to Parker's life decisions. Parker's hopelessness with money, her incapacity for any sort of domestic life (according to her second husband, Alan Campbell, she would eat raw bacon rather than learn how to cook it), as well as a series of romantic disappointments and seemingly perpetual writer's block were all wrapped up in a knot of desires, hopes, and wishes, but, most destructively, with her self-hatred. The playwright Lillian Hellman, who knew Parker for many years and would act as the executor for her estate, best described her as "a tangled fishnet of complications."[14] Just as Parker became well-known for the superficial put-downs of the century, she wrote a devastating short story unpacking and exposing racism at the heart of high society ("Arrangement in Black and White,"

1927). Just as she breezed around the city bouncing from one love affair to the next, she wrote a verse pondering the best way to kill oneself ("Resumé," 1926). Just as she cooed and showed delight at being introduced to a new friend at a dinner party, she ripped them to shreds when they left the room (throughout her life). And just as her name became synonymous with New York, she upped and moved to Hollywood. Dorothy Parker seemed to be a woman who was unknowable. Her friend the writer Wyatt Cooper famously wrote that whatever you think Dorothy Parker was like, she wasn't.

But if Dorothy Parker was unknowable to her friends, she is even more elusive to her biographers. Initially, looking at some of the obstacles, such as her lack of a paper trail, may make writing about Parker appear impossible. But in a curious twist, these obstacles often result in forging new, creative, innovative pathways. If we can't reach her by one route, we'll just have to use another. Each problem has a solution.

One of the first challenges is that none of her friends ever really felt as though they knew her, so any existing interviews or memoirs stress this unknowability. She may have been *this*, but then she wasn't really. Second, she has no dedicated archive. Upon her death she left no manuscripts, no poem drafts, no personal copies of screenplay scripts. Nothing. With her nomadic lifestyle of moving from one place to the next (sometimes even within the same hotel), she had very few possessions. Seeing her signature is rare. Few letters she wrote still exist and most correspondence is one-sided (not hers). Scraps can be pulled together from holdings at Columbia University and institutions in

Michigan, Maryland, Boston, Texas, Indiana, Pennsylvania, Los Angeles, and Cambridge, England. These scraps are telegrams, just a few lines long; signed checks; and inadequate grocery lists, as one might expect from the not very domestically minded Parker ("eggs" / "dogmeat" / "drugs"). One archive collection sounded promising, listing telegrams and phone messages from Parker, but turned out to be a single-line telegram stating, "Certainly wish to sign manifesto please use my name."[15] Which manifesto? Where?

Every potential lead seemed to slam into a dead end. In January 1959, Parker appeared on a TV show called *Open End* with David Susskind. Her fellow guests were Truman Capote and Norman Mailer. The promise of seeing footage of Parker was an exciting one, offering the prospect of being able to examine her mannerisms, her interaction with others, how she responded to questions, her clothes, just her physical presence. Weeks of searching finally revealed that all the *Open End* episodes from 1958 to 1966 had been erased. From those years, only ten episodes survived. Parker's interview is not one of them. No known copy exists.[16]

Wyatt Cooper revealed in his memoir of Parker that he carried out up to twelve hours of recorded interviews with her on reel-to-reel tapes in anticipation of her writing an autobiography. Because she often sounded drunk and was clearly stretching the truth, recording Parker became so uncomfortable that Cooper stopped the sessions and suppressed the tapes. After his death, his estate (and presumably the tapes) was passed on to his wife, Gloria Vanderbilt. After her death, all her possessions were inherited by their son, Anderson Cooper. Although they've been searched for, their location is unknown. The Parker tapes are nowhere to be found.[17]

At the time of her death, Parker's hotel apartment in the Volney in New York City was quickly stripped of its few belongings. These comprised mostly books, but also some uncashed checks, her clothes, a small model set of Napoleonic soldiers, and some letters. The scholar Marion Meade managed to speak to the maid who cleaned Parker's apartment and discovered that most things had been thrown immediately into the trash. In correspondence, Lillian Hellman confirmed that there were no professional manuscripts left in the apartment.[18] However, in 1971, in her role as estate executor, she admitted in a letter to Thomas J. Hughes, a New York lawyer, that Parker did leave some letters, but that Hellman had no intention of parting with them, and that she would prefer Hughes tell people they no longer existed. In an odd parenthesis, Hellman then claimed that in truth she did not think they existed any longer.[19] There is no trace of these letters, and it is unknown whom they were addressed to, why Hellman did not want to share them, or what became of them. More mystery, more silence.

When Dorothy Parker described the money she made in Hollywood as "like small ice in your hand. It all vanishes. That's all,"[20] she could well have been describing herself. Just when you think you have captured her, she slips away again, like a maddeningly elusive ghost. But although there is a peculiar challenge in writing about her, it is far from impossible. It is simply a case of throwing the net a little wider and looking in more unusual places. There are audio and published interviews, fragments in archives here and there, all her verses, stories, reviews, and plays, memoirs by friends containing facts and stories, contemporaneous newspaper articles, hundreds of pages of her FBI file, transcripts of political speeches, photographs, recordings of her reading her own work, archival material belonging to her friends and colleagues in which she sporadically appears, along with existing scholarship to draw on.[21] In some ways, coming at Parker from this multi-angled approach allows a fuller, more honest picture of her life and work, her achievements and her flaws.

Several features become evident when exploring Parker in this way, not least that she was not only "out there" geographically in Hollywood. She put herself out there in all sorts of other ways too. Certainly, operating unapologetically as a woman in a man's world made her unusual. The language, wisecracking, and subject matter in her published work was uncommon. So was her lifestyle of excess: fashion, exquisitely expensive lingerie, parties, drinking, staying out till dawn. Her romantic life of marriage, divorce, remarriage (to the same person), and a string of spectacularly unsuitable younger lovers was unconventional. Her commitment to left-wing politics, supporting communist causes and the Spanish Civil War, was bold and brave, both in the 1930s and a decade later when Hollywood fell under the suppressive gaze of Senator Joseph McCarthy and the FBI. This didn't stop her from helping to establish the Screen Writers Guild and the Hollywood Anti-Nazi League. Neither did she hesitate to fight for the underdog and use her position of privilege to platform causes she truly believed in. Temporally, Dorothy Parker was always out there, ahead or behind, rebel or relic.

When Dorothy Parker left Hollywood in 1964 for the last time, she returned to New York and died alone in her apartment in 1967. She left her estate and assets to Martin Luther King Jr., a man she had never met but whose causes she spent much of her life supporting and campaigning for. Upon his death less than a year later, her estate passed into the hands of the National Association for the Advancement of Colored People (NAACP). In Lillian Hellman's papers, a 1970 letter written by Oscar Bernstien, from Parker's law firm, almost three years after her death, pointed out that Parker's ashes were still in the funeral home, and that her estate was being billed for the storage, which didn't make any sense. He asked, somewhat callously, what they should do. Have them scattered, "or what?"[22] There is no reply in Hellman's papers. But when Marion Meade began her Parker research in the 1980s, the ashes were found in a filing cabinet in the firm's office on Wall Street. The crematorium had mailed them there in July 1973. Parker's ashes were eventually moved to the headquarters of the NAACP in Baltimore, and in 2020 were returned to New York to be buried alongside her parents and grandparents in Woodlawn Cemetery in the Bronx.

The fate of Parker's ashes reflects so much of her life: shelved, alone, and yet simultaneously, not quite forgotten. While Parker's remains were sitting in the drawer of an office or being shipped from New York to Baltimore and back again, very few people stopped to ask where they were. Yet plays were being written and performed about Parker on Broadway and in London's West End: The film *Mrs. Parker and the Vicious Circle* was released in 1994, starring Jennifer Jason Leigh. "Resumé" is recited by Angelina Jolie in the 1999 film *Girl, Interrupted*. A character in season 3, episode 7 of the long-running show *Desperate Housewives* quotes Parker's well-used quip "What fresh hell is this?" In 2018, the drag queen Miz Cracker played Parker in the season 10 "Snatch Game" episode of *RuPaul's Drag Race*. The New York Distilling Company, based in Brooklyn, produces a Dorothy Parker gin, with the label featuring a semi-silhouette of Parker's head. How many writers would be so recognizable from a small, cameo-shaped picture? It is all classic Parker. Both there and not there, both famous and hidden, both forgotten and remembered, both known and unknowable. In death as in life she blasts us with her elusiveness. She is long gone but still with us and ever-present in popular culture. What people do not know, they are happy to make up.[23]

Faced with all this, how can a book possibly capture Dorothy Parker and her years in Hollywood? Is it possible to separate the myth from the reality, the persona from the woman? Is it even important to try? Perhaps the guide should be Parker's own playful words. She doesn't mind at all what anyone writes about her, so long as it is not the truth.

CHAPTER 1

Getting There

Come, curb the new, and watch the old win,
Out where the streets are paved with Goldwyn.[1]
—Dorothy Parker, "The Passionate Screen Writer
to His Love"

Dorothy Parker didn't like films. She didn't like Hollywood and she didn't like the people who ran Hollywood. Evil, she called them. She claimed to have rarely watched movies, and she disliked the way film studios treated writers with indignity. She hated palm trees and wished that the whole film industry would collapse. Coming from New York, she found Hollywood to be too "small townish,"[2] and found writing there to be a "strenuous bore."[3] "For Hollywood," claimed Parker, "the place where they manufacture moving pictures, is as dull a domain as dots the globe."[4] Yet, on and off, Dorothy Parker spent almost thirty-five years associated with Hollywood. The obvious question to ask is why. And her answer is quite simple—money.

When she was offered her first three-month contract, in

1929, her salary was $300 a week (the equivalent of around $4,700 today).[5] By the time she moved to Hollywood on a more permanent basis in 1934, she had signed a contract for $1,000 a week (today about $20,000). Parker was open and honest about this move: "I went out there for possibly the reason many people go out there, because I was broke. I wanted to make money there."[6] But Parker's association with Hollywood is not quite so straightforward. True, she may have initially gone there lured by the high writing salary and to join the increasing number of friends and writers from New York who were moving from the East Coast to the West. But Parker's relationship with Hollywood studios was symbiotic; she needed them, and they wanted her. In fact, they wanted her so badly they were willing to pay large sums of money to be associated with the prestige of her name and trademark voice. In return, Parker was introduced to a whole new way of life: vast wealth, huge mansions, famous friends, parties full of beautiful people, and a subterranean political world that reflected sensibilities that had been brewing in her from childhood. Parker understood this trade-off, selling her talent for "things." But she also understood the emptiness of things: "I stayed there because if you stay there, you can have the most remarkable house. You could have a pool if you wished. I don't swim."[7]

But the fascinating question to consider is why did Hollywood executives in a booming movie industry want so badly to buy Dorothy Parker? What was it about her that captivated them? If this were a Hollywood film, it is the moment when the frame would freeze just as Parker breezily steps off the train from New York to Los Angeles for the first time in late 1928, to begin her contract in 1929. After a perceptible pause, the film would shift into reverse as we whiz backward, the train traveling back to New York. We whiz farther back, through a dizzying string of unsuitable lovers, an abortion, several suicide attempts, a divorce, endless smoky nights in the speakeasy clubs of Prohibition Manhattan, back to her being the only female theater critic in New York, back to a first marriage to Edwin Pond Parker II, where she gets and keeps her surname, back to working in the offices of *Vanity Fair* and *Vogue*, wisecracking in the Rose Room each lunchtime at the Algonquin Hotel, hanging around with fellow writers Robert Benchley and Robert Sherwood, getting paid and published for the first time in *Vanity Fair*, teaching dance lessons to make money. Faster, we regress to the death of her father and a family member dying on the *Titanic*. And back we whiz into childhood, to Miss Dana's School, where Parker is introduced to radical political ideas, back to her expulsion from a New York Catholic school for insulting the Virgin Mary, back to the difficult relationship with her stepmother, back to the death of her mother, Eliza, back to August 22, 1893, when Parker enters the world, two months prematurely, in West End (part of Long Branch), New Jersey, during a hurricane, "the last time I was early for anything."[8] Here the film freezes as we catch our breath standing outside a summer cottage on Ocean Avenue facing the sea.

Dorothy Parker appears for the first time as Dorothy Rothschild in a seaside town during a hurricane to her well-to-do parents, Eliza (née Marston) and Henry J. Her mother was of Scottish descent, while her father had a European Jewish heritage. Not *those* Rothschilds, Parker was keen to stress, but still a comfortable family with their own garment business ("a fairly prosperous cloak-and-suiter")[9] and a home in Manhattan on West Seventy-Second Street filled with Irish servants brought straight from Ellis Island. This was the world Dorothy Parker was born into. And in the coming years it was where several experiences ignited in her life that in many ways would make Hollywood the natural place for her to end up. These were her early education, her formative years working on developing a public persona in high-profile Manhattan publications, and a personal life that rivaled any Hollywood melodrama.

Parker's childhood was not easy despite the comfortable financial and social position her family held. Little is really known about these years because Parker rarely spoke about them, and any paper trail is sparse and incomplete. A large home with servants and regular vacations to the seaside did not prevent tragedy. In 1898, one month before Parker turned five, her mother died from "diarrhoea with colic followed by weakness of the heart."[10] Parker's biographer Marion Meade explained that her reaction upon hearing about her mother's death was to scream and scream and to somehow blame herself for it. The rain fell hard on the day of the funeral as young Dorothy Rothschild watched her mother's coffin be lowered into the ground at Woodlawn Cemetery. Judging from comments that she made later in life, if she felt somehow responsible for her mother's death, she equally felt abandoned. "My mother went and died on me," Parker told Wyatt Cooper, and then hinted that the rest of her childhood had been an unhappy time of isolation and dis-appointment.[11] When she was born, her sister, Helen, was six. The age difference between her and her two brothers was even greater; Harold was twelve when she was born and Bertram nine. So great was this gap that Parker believed it was impossible to bridge. If her brothers saw her in the street, like classic elder siblings, they would ignore her. "All those writers who write about their childhood! Gentle God, if I wrote about mine you wouldn't sit in the same room with me."[12] As she grew older, however, she did develop a closer relationship with Helen, al-though she remained relatively distant from her brothers. Indeed, Harold simply disappeared at some point, and nobody in the family ever knew what became of him.

This early trauma seems to have been the spark for Parker's life sensibilities: always expecting the worst and never really being disappointed because the worst tended to happen. This was compounded by the arrival, on January 3, 1900, of a step-mother, a retired teacher named Eleanor Frances Lewis, whom Parker hated and refused to call anything other than "the house-keeper" or "hey, you."[13] The second Mrs. Rothschild was, accord-ing to Parker, crazy with religion and asked her every day if she loved Jesus ("Now, how do you answer that?").[14] Parker was sent to the Blessed Sacrament Convent just a few blocks away from the new family home on West Sixty-Eighth Street near Central Park, a school so evocative that fifty years later she could recall with some clarity the smell of oilcloth and the nuns' garbs.[15] The building, still standing today, is a double-fronted brownstone, with three imposing columns at the top of a short split-stone staircase to the front doors. Above the first floor, an ornate frieze runs the length of the building. It was here that something resembling the later manifestation of "Dorothy Parker" would begin to emerge: irreverent, mischievous, wisecracking, and wry. She found herself a sidekick in the shape of Mercedes de Acosta, the daughter of a wealthy Spanish-Cuban family, and the two became the terrors of the school. They joked, they taunted, they misbehaved, they caused trouble, and they were so diabolical that one of their teachers suffered a breakdown.[16] Perhaps this was the first sign of a more unpleasant side of Parker that her lifelong friends struggled with—her cruelty. She had moments when she did not flinch from inflicting malice on her victims, whether it was warranted or not. And this cold eye was turned with equal brutality on her family. With cinematic attention to detail that would serve her well years later in Hollywood, Parker noted the eccentricities and absurdities of her father, who would take the family out to the cemetery on Sundays to visit their mother's grave. Hanging around the family plot, he would wait until he heard people approaching, then quickly whip out a large handkerchief and start crying and wailing, "We're all here, Eliza! I'm here. Dottie's here. Mrs. Rothschild is here—" and put on quite a show for the approaching audience. "Some outing," Parker noted with cold disdain.[17]

But what this seemed to instill was a habit of observation. Often, Parker appears like some silent presence in her childhood, standing back and watching it unfold. Listening to conversations, mocking, taking it all in, and mentally recording dialogue for future use. Perhaps it is little wonder that in 1959 she admitted, "I think narrative stories are the best, though my past stories make themselves stories by telling themselves through what people say. I haven't got a visual mind. I hear things."[18] This early skill of Parker's, the skill of being able to effectively regurgitate the nuances and quirks of conversation, is exactly what Hollywood wanted from her. When a film script was floundering, Parker would be engaged to spruce up the dialogue and give it a kick. She rarely failed.

This was also the time when she started to hone her wit, usually at the expense of others, though she was not averse to turning it on herself. The nuns at the convent school were subjected to a fair amount of wisecracking, and as it turned out they had their limits. When Parker told them that the Virgin Mary's immaculate conception was likely a case of spontaneous combustion, they expelled her. Parker was unrepentant: "Boy did I think I was smart! Still do."[19] Unexpectedly, this turned out to be a good thing for Parker because she was then sent to Miss Dana's in Morristown, New Jersey, a first-rate private boarding school set on spacious grounds with the main building a four-story Victorian mansion housing rich and fashionable daughters from all over the country. The approach to teaching and learning could not have been more different. Parker complained that the convent school simply did not teach her how to read. Dickens was not allowed because he was too vulgar. In fact, she went so far as to say, "The convent taught me only that if you spit on a pencil eraser it will erase ink."[20] Miss Dana's, however, took almost the opposite approach, exposing pupils to a wide range of reading, politics, art, and social justice issues. Parker found herself with a choice of botany, music, studio art, and psychology. Evening and weekend talks and debates covered racial issues, socialism, Darwinism, challenges to religion, the plight of the poor, and critiques of the encroaching consumerist culture. Parker's first biographer, John Keats, interviewed some of Parker's classmates from Miss Dana's, and they noticed that Parker never complained about the school. Their description of her differs wildly from the glimpses we saw at the convent school. Here she was well-behaved, brilliant, never bored. They found her to be outstanding in schoolwork (but not games) and most attractive—petite, with large, soulful eyes, and "preppy."[21] There seems little doubt that this was the moment when Dorothy Parker began to engage with certain ideologies (anti-capitalist, anti-racist, and anti-fascist) that would get her into trouble decades later in Hollywood. If Miss Dana's wish was to turn out well-educated, well-informed young women, she likely did not anticipate that some of them would end up under FBI surveillance and hauled in front of the House Un-American Activities Committee.

Parker left Miss Dana's in 1908, and her next few years become rather vague, with sketchy records and mostly silence. We do know that between 1911 and 1913 a series of tragedies struck. While Parker was still at the convent school, her much maligned stepmother died of a cerebral hemorrhage. Having previously wished her dead, Parker once again felt somehow responsible for this loss of life, and "now she had two murders on her conscience."[22] But this was just the start of family loss. In 1911 her paternal uncle Samuel went insane and was committed to an asylum, where he died shortly after. Six months later, her aunt Hannah Rothschild Theobald died of a brain hemorrhage. Then, in April 1912, her beloved uncle Martin booked passage back from a European vacation in a first-class cabin aboard the world's newest, most luxurious ocean liner, the *Titanic*. He did not survive. This series of tragedies simply seemed too much for Parker's father, who on some level gave up on life. Although only sixty years old, he took to staying at home and expecting everyone to take care of him. Since his eldest daughter, Helen, was married with a young child, the person he was most dependent on was Parker, who, having left Miss Dana's, was now stuck in an apartment with her father, looking after him and an increasing number of dogs. When Henry Rothschild died just after Christmas 1913, he was buried next to his first wife, Eliza, in Woodlawn.[23] We do not know how Parker felt about the death of her father, though her biographer Leslie Frewin claims she did not bother to go to the funeral. Suddenly she found herself in a somewhat precarious position. "After my father died, there wasn't any money. I had to work, you see . . ."[24]

From the age of twenty onward, Dorothy Parker began to perfect the persona "Dorothy Parker" that would make her name. According to Faye Hammill, "the creation of Dorothy Parker as celebrity was begun through her own cultivation of an identifiable style . . ."[25] It began with her teaching dance lessons, "about which I knew nothing," and playing single notes on the piano with one finger.[26] But Parker, in her own words, "fell into writing, I suppose, being one of those awful children who wrote verses."[27] In 1914, age twenty-one, she submitted her first poem to Frank Crowninshield, the editor at Condé Nast's new magazine, *Vanity Fair*. He accepted it and paid her twelve dollars. The poem was called "Any Porch" and immediately displayed classic Parkerisms that she would perfect over the coming years. It was a poem based entirely on dialogue poking fun at society women with their gossipy irrelevance and flightiness: "So she's got the children? That's true; / The fault was most certainly his—" / "You know the de Peysters? You *do*? / My *dear*, what a small world this is!"[28] Already evident is the snappiness that Parker would take with her to Hollywood, her absolute precision at capturing conversational characteristics and idiosyncrasies.

Emboldened by this acceptance, Parker dressed in her best suit and headed to the offices of *Vanity Fair* to ask Crownin-shield for a job. Although he had nothing available then, within a few months he contacted her to say a vacancy for a picture caption writer had opened up at their sister publication, *Vogue*, which he offered to Parker with a salary of ten dollars a week. Parker accepted immediately. In 1956, her older self reflected on this career break with some fondness: "Well, I thought I was Edith Sitwell. I lived in a boarding house at 103rd and Broadway." She paid eight dollars a week for her room, including breakfast and dinner.[29] She began a love affair with another writer living in the boardinghouse, Thorne Smith, and although money was tight, she found herself having fun and enjoying a certain amount of freedom. At work, though, she struggled to fit in at the *Vogue* of-fices. "Funny, they were plain women working at *Vogue*, not chic. They were decent, nice women—the nicest women I ever met—but they had no business on such a magazine."[30] Parker regarded *Vogue* as being much more conservative than *Vanity Fair* despite both being owned by Condé Nast. Faye Hammill offers an in-depth look at the differences between the two publications during Parker's time there, and it is easy to see why Parker felt a more natural home for her talents might be *Vanity Fair*. First, Hammill points out, *Vogue* concentrated on women's clothes and dress-making along with features on interiors, gardens, and entertaining etiquette. Its coverage of the arts was limited, and it published no fiction or poetry. "The ideal *Vogue* reader would project her image through clothes, accessories, quiet good taste, and correct behavior . . ."[31] Into this culture of quiet sophistication came Parker and her mischievous caption writing, trying to slip double entendres under the watchful and increasingly suspicious eyes of the copy editors. In contrast, *Vanity Fair* offered extensive coverage of the arts, reviews, photographs, serious and comic articles, satires, and fiction pieces. But perhaps key here is the point that Hammill makes regarding the associations of each magazine. *Vogue* was very much about European style, French haute couture. *Vanity Fair* quickly established itself as a magazine all about New York. It did not require the wide readership of *Vogue*; rather it aimed for a readership based on exclusive, urban sophistication.[32] It also employed a certain skeptical wit, casting an eye over cultural events with a healthy dose of humor and a metaphorical raised eyebrow. Hammill notes that the regular feature The Hall of Fame was often replaced with The Hall of Oblivion, nominating celebrities who deserved to be forgotten.[33]

Enter Dorothy Parker, with her already-established dry view of the world, irreverence toward her elders and betters, and a deep love of Manhattan life. During her two and a half years at

Vogue, Parker wrote picture captions for underwear—"Brevity is the soul of lingerie, as the Petticoat said to the Chemise"[34]— fact-checked, copyedited, and was allowed to produce the odd longer article (the privilege was soon revoked when her mocking piece "Interior Desecration" enraged interior designers across the city). She volunteered to test any new beauty products, diets, and exercise regimes, but most importantly, she continued to submit verse to Frank Crowninshield for publication in *Vanity Fair*. Many pieces were overlooked, but in 1916 she submitted the first of what would become known as her "Hate Verses," sassy and witty and poking fun at, well, everyone and everything. The first, "Women: A Hate Song," begins with "*I hate women / They get on my nerves*," and proceeds to pull apart domestic women, married women, intelligent women, nervous women, and cheerful women—"They ask me what they would do without their sense of humor? / I sometimes yearn to kill them. / Any jury would acquit me."[35] Over the next eight years, Parker would continue with her hate verses, tackling subjects such as men, actresses, bores, parties, books, college boys, Bohemians, and movies. The latter reveals a certain level of prescience with the opener "*I hate Movies; / They lower my vitality*."[36]

In 1917, *Vogue* editor Edna Woolman Chase spoke to Frank Crowninshield about "Dorothy Rothschild." Insightfully, Chase realized that *Vanity Fair* would be better suited to this up-and-coming writer, and Crowninshield agreed. Much to Parker's delight, she switched publications and immediately became a staff writer with more scope and the prospect of writing the occasional review. "You have made me very happy," she told Crowninshield.[37]

Work was not the only area of Parker's life that was going well. The previous summer she had met and fallen in love with Edwin ("Eddie") Pond Parker II, a stockbroker who had recently established himself on Wall Street. They increasingly spent most of their evenings together, and since he was reasonably wealthy, they spent time at the theater and about town eating and drinking. Although at this stage Parker rarely touched alcohol, Eddie was a heavy drinker, often joking about his hangovers, and never really taking them seriously. The two made a good-looking pair. Eddie was handsome and well-dressed. Photographs show a lively, intelligent face despite his nickname of Spook, his legendary hangovers having left him pale as a ghost. At this time Dorothy Parker was admiringly described by Crowninshield as wearing horn-rimmed glasses that she quickly removed if anyone spoke to her and having "a habit of blinking and fluttering her eyelids." She wore smart shoes and suits, and hats that turned up at the brim. "Green, as a color, seemed to appeal to her greatly, whether in dress, hat, or scarf."[38] Her apparent femininity did not go unnoticed by others, either. The writer Donald Ogden Stewart recalled: "Dottie was attractive to everybody—those eyes were wonderful, and the smile! It wasn't difficult to fall in love with her . . . She was both wide open and the goddamndest fortress at the same time."[39]

As the Parker courtship intensified, world events began to take over. The conflict in Europe, which previously had seemed so far away, suddenly loomed larger when President Woodrow Wilson declared war on Germany on April 2, 1917. In May, Eddie enlisted as an ambulance driver, preferring the thought of saving lives rather than taking them. He quickly proposed, and the wedding took place in June. Dorothy Rothschild was now officially Mrs. Dorothy Parker, the professional name she would be known by for the rest of her life. After what seemed to her merely five minutes of matrimony, Eddie shipped off to France.

The structure of society was changing as more men headed off to war in Europe. As Eddie nursed increasingly problematic hangovers on both sides of the Atlantic, in America the early rumblings from the Prohibitionists who were attempting to end the trade in alcoholic drinks died down as the war took over. At this stage, though, they were only three years away from banning the sale of alcohol nationwide in their attempt to heal what they saw as communities beset by alcohol-induced violence and immorality. In Hollywood, films were beginning to take off, the industry still not really making use of many writers, but already establishing a reputation as a seductive place of corruption. Some of the first writers had started to trickle from the East Coast to the West despite the suspicion—perhaps even the hope—that they were heading to a sinful land of transgression. When William DeMille (brother of Cecil) left New York in 1914 to work as a writer in Hollywood, he claimed that "my friends unanimously agreed that I was committing professional hari-kari, that I was selling my pure, white body for money, and that if my name were ever mentioned in the future, it could only be . . . by people lost to all sense of shame and artistic decency."[40]

While the world was fractured and disrupted, Dorothy Parker continued her work at *Vanity Fair*, missing her new husband, but working hard to establish herself. She was frequently invited to the home of businessman and publisher Condé Nast, often accompanied by Crowninshield, and her verses and snappy articles were gaining an increasingly admiring readership. These were the years when Parker began to hone her trademark celebrity. Culturally it seemed the perfect time to be gaining notoriety, making her name, and establishing herself as a wit and writer. Perhaps importantly, Parker both embraced and rejected the agenda of the publication she worked for. Hammill points out that Parker refused to fully collaborate with certain commercial messages, and rather than promote a product or a play, she promoted herself. In 1918, when she temporarily replaced P. G. Wodehouse as *Vanity Fair*'s theater critic (thus becoming the only woman theater critic in New York), reviewing a bad play would be more about the agony *she* suffered having to watch it than the play itself, so that "interacting with her own celebrity image in complex ways, she became a mistress of self-satire, yet even this became a way of consolidating her trademark persona."[41] Often her reviews were biting, tart, and cutting. Even when she enjoyed a play, she somehow managed to present herself as a world-weary critic putting herself out there to save people from the horrors of the stage: "My life was a long succession of thin evenings."[42] It was this persona in its early infancy that would develop over the next ten years and catch the eye of Hollywood.

But for the earlier part of that year, Parker continued writing reviews and patriotic pieces for *Vanity Fair* and publishing more of her hate verses, some taking aim at certain sections of society, such as "Slackers": "There are the Conscientious Objectors, / They are the real German atrocities."[43] When news reached her that Eddie's ambulance had been hit by an enemy bomb, killing all occupants except her husband, she became desperate for his return. For Eddie, who lay in a ditch for a day and a half surrounded by his dead compatriots, the trauma brought about a marked change in his behavior. His heavy, jovial drinking soon turned into something much more serious, and by the time he did eventually return to New York he was not only addicted to alcohol but also to the morphine that had been stored in his ambulance and the field hospitals.

Life was about to change for Dorothy Parker too. In May 1919, *Vanity Fair* hired a new managing editor, Robert Benchley, a freelance writer who was known for various humorous pieces he had published over the previous five years. Middle-class and a teetotaler, with a wife and family in the suburbs, he hardly seemed on paper to be the dazzling personality needed to become Dorothy Parker's soul mate. Despite introducing themselves as "Mrs. Parker" and "Mr. Benchley" when they first met (names they used for each other for the entirety of their friendship, though sometimes Parker referred to him as "Fred"), they eventually established a deeply platonic but intense bond. Four years older than she, Benchley immediately displayed irreverence toward work and society people, and generally treated life as a big joke. This was perhaps their meeting point, along with gallows humor and a liking for bad behavior.

Shortly after the arrival of Benchley, Crowninshield hired a new drama editor, Robert Sherwood, and the three of them formed a trio of rogues. With Sherwood almost seven feet tall, Parker and Benchley would walk down the street, passing the

Hippodrome in Midtown Manhattan, a venue famous for hosting circuses. Parker later recalled, "The midgets would come out
and frighten Mr. Sherwood . . . they were always sneaking up
behind him and asking him how the weather was up there."[44]
They messed about, they joked, and, Parker admitted, "I must
say we behaved extremely badly."[45] Within a decade, all three
would be working in Hollywood together. But in the meantime,
they subscribed to two undertakers' magazines, the *Casket* and
Sunnyside, and decorated the office walls with such delights as
color instruction plates on how to embalm a corpse. Parker said
that she "had this hung over my desk until Mr. Crowninshield
asked me if I could possibly take it down. Mr. Crowninshield was
a lovely man, but puzzled."[46] Crowninshield, for his part, appeared to show a certain level of bemused indulgence toward his
younger employees: "I dared suggest that they [the corpse pic-
tures] might prove a little startling to our occasional visitors,
and that, perhaps, something by Marie Laurencin [a French
Cubist painter] might do as well." The proposal was met by
Parker with "the most palpable contempt."[47] The *Casket*, far removed from French Cubism, advertised itself as "devoted to the
higher education of funeral directors and embalmers" and contained information about a variety of coffins, draperies, chemi-
cals, and fluids, plus a mortician's advice. It also advertised
newfangled devices such as reusable pull alarms for those who
were terrified of being buried alive. (After seven days these con-
traptions could be removed from the grave and reused for other
poor phobic souls.)

Parker, Benchley, and Sherwood played practical jokes on

others in the office, made deadlines by the skin of their teeth, and, although they were due to start work at eight thirty, generally sauntered into the office by about ten, plotting the day's antics. The only time Parker arrived early to work was to play a joke on Albert Lee, one of the editors, who had a map above his desk with little flags showing where American troops were fighting. She would sneak in and move the flags around. Crowninshield remembered, "Mrs. Parker[,] in recalling her tactical direction of the Allied armies[,] has reminded me that Mr. Lee finding his 'soldiers loused up overnight never failed to go crazy. It was,' she added[,] 'a considerable hardship for me to get up in time to be at the office so early, and after all it didn't do any harm as Mr. Lee became convinced it was the work of a German spy in the *Vogue* organization'..."[48]

When Crowninshield and Condé Nast went on a two-month trip to Europe in June 1919, they made the extraordinary decision to make Benchley, assisted by Parker and Sherwood, responsible for bringing out two issues of *Vanity Fair*. The three of them turned up to enthusiastically wave off their bosses, who were aboard the *Aquitania*. Then they returned to the office for two months of mayhem and farce, which involved working when they felt like it, Benchley giving Sherwood a promotion, paying each other higher salaries for articles than even the best-known contributors, and finishing half-completed columns with utter gibberish. It was also around this time that the three miscreants started strolling down the street to take prolonged lunches at the Algonquin Hotel, where other writers and critics also began to informally gather. It was here that Parker met a whole array of people, some of whom would become lifelong friends and all of whom would eventually be regarded as members of the Algonquin Round Table. There was Franklin P. Adams (F.P.A.), columnist at the *New York Tribune* and author of the Conning Tower, a gossipy weekly piece summing up New York happenings and sometimes including poetry. Alexander Woollcott, drama critic for the *New York Times*. Heywood Broun, sportswriter at the *New York Tribune*. Harold Ross and Jane Grant, who in 1925 would found the *New Yorker*. Donald Ogden Stewart, the author and playwright who, along with Dorothy Parker, in years to come would be blacklisted by the FBI. Neysa McMein, a painter and magazine illustrator who would produce a striking portrait of Parker. And many other writers, actors, and critics who dropped in and out over the years.

Parker's relationship to the Round Table was complicated. Although at the time she was regarded as presiding over the lunchtime sessions and word games with her wit, she downplayed her involvement as she got older. "I wasn't there very often—it cost too much."[49] She complained that most people present were nothing special, except for Haywood Broun, and that the meetings were a vehicle for people to spout witty comments that they had spent all week thinking up and rehearsing.[50] Although the Algonquin Round Table remains a legendary part of American literary history, for Parker it was a few years of lunching with some people she tolerated but subsequently claimed she didn't particularly like. However, Parker is not always the most reliable narrator of events. Even if her enjoyment of those lunches was limited, she *did* make some friends, and the

Round Table became a vehicle through which to further her fame, make connections, spend weekends out of the city at debaucherous parties on Long Island, and bring her to the attention of an even larger group of people beyond the readership of *Vanity Fair*.

While the Round Table wisecracked their way through the early 1920s, other events were taking place "out there" in Hollywood. Most movie production had moved to the West Coast, and all the well-known studios were in business there: Fox, Universal, Warner Bros., Columbia, and Metro Pictures (soon to be MGM). A financial alliance soon formed between East Coast money on Wall Street and West Coast creativity in the movies: "Financiers like the idea of an industry that could reap big profits even as it lulled the masses into a cheerful, not to say grateful, acceptance of the status quo."[51] Ian Hamilton, who documented the history of writers in Hollywood, noted that as early as 1919 the movie mogul Sam Goldwyn had distributed a thirty-two-page brochure to be included as an insert in the leading Hollywood papers, advertising not forthcoming films or even stars, but eminent authors who were working for him. The idea was, according to Goldwyn, to use "classy writers" to inject "verbal eminence" into his films.[52] They were offered vast advances against the film's profits, and this showed confidence in the ability of writers to elevate the quality of movies even during the silent period (talkies had not yet taken over). This experiment ultimately failed because writers were annoyed at how sloppily their work was handled and the lack of respect shown toward their creativity, and actors were suspicious of Goldwyn promoting writers above them. It created feuds, discord, and power struggles, resulting in Goldwyn's skepticism toward writers despite his ongoing desire for his films to have some sort of literary class. He lamented, in somewhat sexist language, that "the great trouble with the usual author is that he approaches the camera with some fixed literary ideal and he cannot compromise with the motion picture viewpoint."[53] These initial skirmishes between the film industry and writers would resonate and amplify in the coming decades. As talking pictures took off and more writers moved from New York to Hollywood, how their work was treated and how their talent was valued became a point of contention. It also had a psychological impact on writers' self-worth. So many who went there for money, including Dorothy Parker, ended up asking themselves, "Am I wasting my talent?"

In January 1920, Dorothy Parker was fired from *Vanity Fair*. Her theater reviews, although garnering a devoted readership, had become increasingly outspoken and scathing. Her write-up of Oscar Wilde's *An Ideal Husband* spent as long eviscerating the audience—"'Look at us,' they seem to say, 'we are the cognoscenti'"—as it did the play.[54] Her piece on Edward Knoblock's *Tiger! Tiger!* began lamenting the dreadful life of a theatergoer: "We go heroically to the theater, hoping always, with piteous faith, that maybe it won't be so bad after all—yet ever dreading, with the bitter fear born of cruel experience, that probably it will be worse."[55] But it was when she criticized Billie Burke in Somerset Maugham's *Caesar's Wife*, likening her performance to that of a hammy exotic dancer, that Parker really got herself into trouble. Burke was the wife of Florenz (Flo) Ziegfeld, who happened to be one of the biggest advertisers in both *Vogue* and *Vanity Fair*.

Taking umbrage at Parker's insults, he said if she wasn't fired, he'd be taking his business elsewhere. In later years Parker bluntly said: "*Vanity Fair* was a magazine of no opinion, but *I* had opinions. So I was fired."[56] In an impressive act of solidarity, Robert Benchley resigned his position in protest, and a week earlier Sherwood and *Vanity Fair* had, in the words of the *New York Times*, come to a parting of ways. When the two men went to the office to collect their belongings, Benchley left a sign reading CONTRIBUTIONS FOR MISS BILLIE BURKE. Nobody donated.

From this moment on, Dorothy Parker remained freelance for the rest of her life. Sherwood became assistant editor at *Life*, and he employed Benchley as drama critic. Parker picked up work here and there as well as reviewed theater monthly for *Ainslee's* magazine. By February she was renting a small office with Benchley in the Metropolitan Opera House studios: "He and I had an office so tiny that an inch smaller and it would have been adultery."[57] They registered "Parkbench" as their cable address. Retrospectively, this seemed a pivotal moment in Parker's life. She had been fired, her husband had returned home from Europe an addict, and Prohibition had been introduced, banning the sale of alcohol. The journalist Josephine van de Grift interviewed Parker for the *Bisbee Daily Review*, beginning her piece with, "Miss Parker wouldn't specialize in words at all, she says, were it not for the howling of the wolf immediately outside the door of her little office in the New York Metropolitan House."[58] It seemed as though Parker was suddenly under both professional and personal strain. Publicly she began to underplay her own achievements: "Everything I've ever written looks wretched to me," she wrote, and described the process of writing as "pure un-alloyed blood sweating."[59] Even commissioned pieces were a challenge. But if the office rent was due and "B'rer Wolf opens his teeth," then she was prepared to sit down and write something "bright and snappy about bed springs."[60] The interview was accompanied by an ink portrait of Parker with dark bobbed hair looking wistfully to the side of the frame and ended with a despairing quote about her agonizing writing process: "And you sit down before your typewriter—and sit and sit and sit. And the moon goes up and the stars come out—and you sit and sit and sit."

This was the beginning of certain financial strains that would, by the end of the decade, see Parker boarding a train for Hollywood. But in the years she had left in New York, she began to frequent smoky speakeasies, such as Tony Soma's and what would eventually be known as 21 (originally called the Red Head when it opened in 1922), staying out all night drinking, and initially trying to save her floundering marriage. A verse titled "Fragment" (1922) lamented the loss of love but ended on a note of conciliation: "Why should you dare to hope that you and I / Could make love's fitful flash a lasting flame? / Still, if you think it's only fair to try— / Well, I am game."[61] She took holidays with Eddie as he tried to curb his drinking, sending ridiculous letters and postcards back to Benchley describing their exploits, one signed "Flo and Billie." A five-page letter in verse from somewhere called the Birches in Maine is a rare surviving handwritten letter by Parker to Benchley. Using rhyming couplets, she describes how they are roughing it in the country: "Kindly forgive our writing in pencil; / It's too much trouble to get the other utensil." And with her usual wit she projects the horror of being away from her beloved, sophisticated Manhattan: "There are some people right next door / Who turned out to be a terrible bore. / There always seems to be some kind of a hitch / Isn't Nature a (finish this line for yourself, and get a year's subscription to the Boston Post)."[62]

The Parkers moved to a brick building on West Fifty-Seventh Street mostly occupied by creative types, and they acquired a dog, Woodrow Wilson, and a canary, Onan (so named because he would spill his seed on the ground).[63] Another resident there was fellow Round Tabler Neysa McMein, and soon informal gatherings took place in her studio. If the crowd were not at the Algonquin or a speakeasy, they were drinking at McMein's. Parker was central to the happenings, quipping, tongue-lashing, and making rude comments about people when they left. Although many found this amusing, others found her uncalled-for cruelty uncomfortable, and they wondered what she said about *them* when they left. Indeed, some found themselves staying longer than they wanted to because they were too scared to leave before Parker. But during these long afternoons and evenings the studio would be filled with writers and critics, actors and musicians, drinking homemade wine. A small band even formed for musical afternoons. Dorothy Parker played the triangle.

The coming years saw the end of the Parker marriage, which would result in divorce in 1928. But in the meantime, Eddie, deciding he needed to leave New York and dry out in the country, went home to his family in Hartford, Connecticut. Parker stayed in the city. Realizing that her marriage was over, she began to get involved with several unsuitable lovers and started drinking heavily herself. The agony she felt about writing, and the caustic eye she turned on others, was turned inward as she appeared to become increasingly depressed, and with the depression drank more and more. Muriel King, a fashion designer, remembered Parker as "charming, darling, and loathsome. No, not really loathsome, disappointing. When you thought you were friends, you didn't expect her to slap you down."[64] Yet if she left others feeling deflated, King noticed that Parker "had as little use for herself."[65] George Oppenheimer, who would publish her first poetry collections, referred to her as "a masochist whose passion for unhappiness knew no bounds."[66] This self-hatred seemed to have been carried with her from childhood, and as much as she sometimes hurt others, she always seemed harsher with herself than anyone else. During events that were about to unfold, it became clear that Parker did not quite have the support network she needed.

An ill-advised affair with newspaperman (and inveterate womanizer) Charles MacArthur ended extremely badly for Parker. She was still married; MacArthur was married, though like the Parkers estranged, and as she became besotted with him, he remained indifferent to her. Though her "friends" rolled their eyes and speculated why Parker allowed MacArthur to treat her so badly, none ever stopped to switch the onus and ask why MacArthur thought it was acceptable to treat Parker this way. Somehow the blame was always laid on her, when it seemed all she did was simply fall in love. When Parker realized that MacArthur was seeing other women she was heartbroken, and even more so when she discovered that she was pregnant. Predictably, MacArthur wasn't remotely interested, and Parker was paralyzed with indecision. Since the 1880s, abortion had been criminalized nationwide. Illegal abortions did occur but there was a discriminatory element to them; wealthy white women could arrange safe terminations, while poor women and many women of color faced dangerous back-alley abortions. When it came to ending pregnancy, this was "the century of silence."[67] Distraught and consequently perhaps leaving it longer than she should have, Parker eventually found a doctor willing to carry out the procedure, though he was brutal and judgmental. Some sources suggest that he insisted Parker view her aborted fetus and told her what a terrible person she was.[68] Understandably, this left Parker traumatized. One feature of this trauma was to repeatedly tell her story and talk about what had happened until her friends, lacking the required empathy, grew tired of her narrative and suggested she stop going on about it. This only resulted in Parker sinking further into "the isolation and stigma of illegal abortion."[69] For all the silence, according to Meg Gillette, in the early twentieth century illegal abortion was estimated to be a $250 million industry. One drugstore near Grand Central Terminal carried a selection of thirty-four preparations, such as quinine, slippery elm, and rubber catheters, which were at best ineffective and at worst life-threatening. Forty-five percent failed to induce an abortion.[70] For as much as Parker quipped about the experience, "It serves me right for putting all my eggs in one bastard,"[71] she was clearly deeply unhappy. Shortly after, she failed to turn up for an evening at the theater and was discovered on her bathroom floor with slashed wrists. Her Round Table friends, again ascribing the worst possible intentions toward her, treated this as an attention-seeking act. Parker complained that Eddie couldn't even leave a sharp razor behind. If she had struggled with the shame and stigma of abortion, she could now add a suicide attempt to the list, along with an increasing dependency on alcohol. Some of these issues brewed away inside her and would make further appearances when she started writing for Hollywood.

If Parker's life seemed chaotic, and it was, she worked hard. Despite struggling with her output, it was nevertheless rather impressive as she freelanced for magazines such as *Ainslee's* and *Life* as well as writing her own verse and short stories. She dipped a toe into some film work in New York, but nothing significant, writing captions for silent films, and it only lasted a matter of weeks. Out in Hollywood, Sam Goldwyn continued his problematic partnership with writers, finding himself being rejected by such names as H. G. Wells and George Bernard Shaw. Undeterred, he pursued his quest to "secure the greatest creative brains from the world's literati."[72] This became increasingly desirable as talkies took over at the end of the decade, and by the mid-1920s what studios were looking for in their films was "the gilded quotable one-liner."[73] The obvious place to look for this was from members of the infamous Round Table. Sadly, for Goldwyn, movies were at the top of the hit list during those Algonquin lunches. Happily, for Goldwyn, most of the writers were broke, and he had lots of money to offer.

The first writer to be tempted "out there," by Walter Wanger at Paramount, was Herman Mankiewicz in 1926 for a salary of $400 per week (today, about $6,000). This was a significant increase over what he had been earning as a reporter, critic, and assistant editor in New York. He was given his own Hollywood office suite, rented himself a huge house, bought a convertible, played high-stakes poker games, and lunched with Charlie Chaplin.[74] He missed his East Coast friends, though, and worked hard to persuade Paramount to hire more of them. This was the beginning of the east-to-west shift as more writers were drawn to what Hollywood had to offer. As many of Parker's close friends, such as Benchley, were tempted out there, it seemed increasingly inevitable that she would join them.

Parker was now thirty-two and had already gathered many life experiences—love, loss, death, trauma—but the final two significant things that happened to her before she left New York for Hollywood were travel and political activism. In many ways these two things were connected. In 1926, fleeing from another failed love affair, she sailed to France. She was also trying to leave behind increasing alcohol dependency, and a second suicide attempt, this time using Veronal (sleeping pills), that landed her in the hospital for a significant spell. Accompanied by Benchley, who decided to escort her across the Atlantic, she set sail aboard the *President Roosevelt* during a blizzard. Parker quickly realized that all the scotch she had smuggled on board had been stolen, and Benchley quickly realized that he was accompanied by a bad case of pubic lice he had picked up from a Manhattan bordello. A fellow traveler was Ernest Hemingway, who soon befriended

Parker and Benchley, and the three ate all their meals together and played bridge in the afternoons. During the crossing and subsequent time spent together in Paris, Hemingway shared his political sensibilities and love of Spain. Although Parker made a brief visit to Barcelona, Seville, and Madrid over the summer, when she was taken to witness a bullfight she found matadors so detestable that she took a dislike to the whole country. In the coming years this would change as she supported Hemingway's activism during the Spanish Civil War and even visited in the 1930s to report back to Americans what was occurring under Francisco Franco's reign. She also spent time over the summer in Paris working on her first volume of verse, which was published later in the year under the title *Enough Rope*. It included poems such as "Unfortunate Circumstance," "Resumé," and her much-cited "Comment": "Oh, life is a glorious cycle of song, / A medley of extemporanea; / And love is a thing that can never go wrong; / And I am Marie of Roumania."[75] Much to everyone's surprise, for a volume of poetry, it became an instant bestseller. Dorothy Parker was officially a literary celebrity.

This first trip to Europe was important for the connections Parker made both politically and personally, which would follow her in subsequent years to Hollywood.[76] But it also seemed to spark her into some sort of political activity when she returned to New York. In 1927 she traveled to Boston to protest the impending execution, by electric chair, of two Italian American anarchists, Nicola Sacco and Bartolomeo Vanzetti. In 1921 they had been found guilty of murdering a guard and a paymaster in Braintree, Massachusetts, during a shoe factory payroll robbery a year earlier and sentenced to death. Opposed to the death penalty, Parker was further incensed when Benchley was told by a close friend that the judge involved had vowed he would "show them and get those guys hanged."[77] Press photos reveal that Parker turned up for the demonstration wearing heels, an embroidered dress, a scarf draped elegantly over one shoulder, and a cloth hat, and holding a stylish black clutch bag. As she strolled down the street singing "The Internationale" and "The Red Flag," people called out her name. Indeed, the next day, the Boston newspapers would devote as much attention to Parker's presence as they did to the protest itself. This was a sign that her reputation and fame were spreading well beyond New York as she increasingly became a national celebrity. When she was arrested for loitering and sauntering—surely the most Parkeresque charges possible—she was roughly walked to the police station, where she complained about her treatment. Although her fingerprints had not been taken, "they left me a few of theirs. The big stiffs!"[78] After pleading guilty and being charged a five-dollar fine, she returned to New York and continued campaigning and fundraising for the cause. But the political apathy of her Round Table companions infuriated her. "Those people at the Round Table didn't know a bloody thing. They thought we were fools to go up and demonstrate for Sacco and Vanzetti."[79]

This was the start of Parker's politics beginning to impact her friendships as she became more committed to left-wing activism. In later years she would even cool toward Benchley, who did not embrace issues of social justice with the same dedication. Publicly, Parker also started to become more politically outspoken. In October 1927 she took a job with a newish publication called the *New Yorker* that had been established in 1925 by two of her Round Table associates, Howard Ross and Jane Grant. Her role was to review books under the pen name Constant Reader. On December 10, in a piece titled "A Socialist Looks at Literature," Parker openly declared, "My heart and soul are with the cause of Socialism."[80] Three months later, on March 17, 1928, she began to speak out about racism and the insidious nature of what we would now call white privilege. Reviewing *Home to Harlem* by Claude McKay, Parker wrote: "We needed, and we needed badly, a book about Harlem Negroes by a Negro. White men can write, and have written, Heaven knows, such tales, but one never loses consciousness, while reading them, of the pallor of the authors' skins."[81]

As Parker's celebrity grew, she published a second book of verse, *Sunset Gun*, in 1928, which again was a commercial and critical success. Many of the poems deal with the hopelessness of love, including "Fable," "Mortal Enemy," and "On Being a Woman," which ends with the lament: "And why with you my love, my lord, / Am I spectacularly bored, / Yet do you up and leave me—then / I scream to have you back again?"[82] This was the year she divorced Eddie after a four-year separation and began to drink so heavily that many of her friends grew concerned about her health and behavior.[83] She would often look bloated and exhausted. She had blackouts, treated those close to her poorly, and went from one unsuitable lover to another, the relationships mostly fueled by alcoholic arguments and fights. A friend recalled that she "was half-soused a good deal of the time, and that's when her worst qualities came out."[84] Parker even built her hangovers into her book reviews, suggesting that somehow this cycle of drinking and feeling terrible the next day was now a central part of her life. She referred regretfully to this as having "the rams," which "are much like the heebie-jeebies except they last longer, strike deeper, and are, in general, fancier." Using the old joke of "it must have been something I ate," Parker blamed it on a bad stick of celery, "because you can't tell me that two or three sidecars, some champagne at dinner, and a procession of mixed Benedictines-and-brandies, taking seven hours to pass a particular point, are going to leave a person in that state where she is afraid to turn round suddenly lest she see again a Little Mean Man about eighteen inches tall, wearing a yellow slicker and roller skates."[85] Friends disliked how drinking made her meaner, and some found her boring and repetitive when she reached a certain stage of drunkenness. Although Benchley encouraged her to see a therapist, nobody really seemed to question why Dorothy Parker was drinking herself into oblivion most nights.[86]

For many alcoholics there is a desire to forget. We cannot know for certain the reasons why Parker preferred to blot out her days, but there are surely events she would have been happy *not* to remember. The trauma of her abortion, her depression, her suicide attempts, being treated badly by uncaring men, the pressure of being freelance, her hopelessness with money that saw her drinking it away, and the existential angst that comes from caring about social issues that seem far out of one's control. The writer Ellen Lansky explored the alcoholic figure of Dorothy Parker, placing her in the male-centered personal and professional worlds she inhabited. For all her success, Parker was operating deep within a patriarchal setup. Perhaps this is why Lansky argues that Parker often wrote stories about women and the troubles they encountered "as they try to negotiate a life for themselves in a culture that asks them, as heterosexual women, to subordinate their bodies, desires, and aspirations to their male partners."[87] One such story, "Big Blonde," written in 1928 and published in early 1929, was the story of Hazel Morse, an animal-loving, divorced, big-drinking suicide survivor. The autobiographical aspects are unmistakable. Morse begins as an anxious observer of her husband's drinking, only to become dependent on alcohol herself: "She could not recall the definite day that she started drinking, herself. There was nothing separate about her days. Like drops upon a window-pane, they ran together and trickled away."[88] But as Lansky points out, a key aspect of Hazel Morse is that she is constantly being watched, scrutinized, and judged by men who subsequently punish and ridicule her for transgressing gender boundaries with her drunkenness. The story catapulted Parker to literary fame, winning her the O. Henry Award for best short story of the year and establishing her more serious literary reputation.[89]

At this point, Parker was well-known as a wit and a writer with a unique voice. Having shaped herself into this combination of humorist with literary credentials made her highly attractive to Hollywood studios. She perfectly met their desire for a classy writer who could give films some cultural credence but could also turn out snappy dialogue and memorable one-liners. By the end of 1929, there were more than twenty thousand movie houses in the United States, and nine thousand of them were wired for sound.[90] By 1930 the silent-movie era was dead, and the talkies needed dialogue and scripts. Writers such as F. Scott Fitzgerald were already out there, "confident to the point of conceit" that he could churn out film scripts with no effort on his part. His plan was to not only make plenty of money but also to use it to subsidize his novels.[91] He was in for a shock. Writing fiction was a totally different craft from writing a script. "The scripts Scott Fitzgerald wrote just wouldn't play," claimed one of his contemporaries, the screenwriter Anita Loos.[92]

On January 4, 1929, the journalist Mollie Merrick wrote an article titled "Movies and Movie People" for the Washington, DC, *Evening Star*. She noted that there were "new lights" in Hollywood, "a fresh wallop, infusing new spirit into Hollywood whoopee . . ."[93] Two of them were Robert Benchley and Dorothy Parker. Parker was singled out and recognized for her wit and talent. With her $300 a week for three months, Parker had been persuaded with excessive flattery to head "out there" toward the end of 1928. Years later she described her experience as "a thing that just came down on me."[94] The article, viewed in context, shows exactly how out there Parker really was as a woman heading off to Hollywood to earn her own salary. The adverts surrounding the piece are all about January sales offering housewives the chance to buy new color tablecloths "that allow the far-sighted hostess the opportunity to work out unusual and delightful color schemes for the table." Below are adverts assisting women with menu ideas, such as ground beef on toast, fried liver and bacon with brussels sprouts, and chop suey in a can, "a most tempting substantial meal."[95] Had Parker seen the article in situ she likely would have been amused by the piece below hers about personal hygiene, pronouncing that if you bathe daily, changing your underwear twice a week is more than "sufficient." Unable to cook for herself or anyone else and completely disinterested in domesticity, Parker boarded the train in New York and headed to Hollywood.

And here we are, back where our film started. The railway station in LA is filled with train smoke and luggage. As Parker stepped out onto the platform, she was about to join the movie industry. It was a monumental decision for her, both personally and professionally. But it was also just the start of the story.

CHAPTER 2

Hollywoodland

STUDS TERKEL: *Do you want to speak on a subject that has bothered you a great deal, perhaps just to add a little sauce here, because you're so gentle. Hollywood. This is a trigger word isn't it?* [laughter]

DOROTHY PARKER: *Would you mind if I leave the room when you speak that word?*[1]

—"Dorothy Parker Discusses Her Plays and
the State of Literature," February 6, 1959

A week after arriving in Hollywood, Dorothy Parker realized that she hated the place. Sadly, for her, she had signed a three-month contract, so it was not possible for her to board a train and return to New York. Everything about the town annoyed her: the non-native palm trees that had been shipped in—"poor dears, they died on their feet"—wonderful exotic flowers that smelled of old dollar bills, vegetables tasting like they had been "grown in old trunks." Even the weather was not to her liking. "That way of having no seasons . . . it's just terrible, you can't have any dates. They haven't Easter."[2] Worse than that, she found herself transplanted from a city where everyone knew her to a town where even the most important people who hired her had no idea who she was. When she met the head of production at MGM for the first time, Irving Thalberg, he inquired what it was she wanted to do for them, having put out a publicity release getting the name of her best-selling book wrong, miscasting it as *Too Much Rope*. Like Scott Fitzgerald before her, Parker assumed that film writing would be easy money: "Why I could do that with one hand tied behind me and the other on Irving Thalberg's pulse."[3] Also like Scott Fitzgerald, she was about to find out that writing for the movies was nowhere near the breeze she anticipated.

Her surroundings seemed to symbolically sum up what she thought of the town, for although she found her office in Culver City rather large and lovely, with a huge, deep-drawered desk, however much she opened the window, the air in it remained oppressive. A little investigation uncovered that the previous occupant had been using the desk to grow mushrooms. "And he was raising mushrooms by a correspondence system, a system that raised them anywhere. So, they had to be in liquid manure."[4] She felt lonely sitting at her large desk, isolated from other writers, and this loneliness still resonated in the last year of her life. When she was interviewed by Richard Lamparski in 1966 about this first assignment in Hollywood, she sounded sad and wistful: "I wanted to see *someone* . . . They can leave you so alone."[5]

She was supposed to start work on a script for *Madame X* (1929) starring Ruth Chatterton, who played a "fallen" woman longing to be reunited with her son. But after two months Parker was still waiting for instructions on what they wanted her to do. This was to be Parker's brutal introduction to how writing for Hollywood worked. The same script would get passed around to several writers, even producers would get involved, until it became almost impossible to know whom to credit for what. The culture shock of moving from fast-paced Manhattan publications like *Vanity Fair*, with short, sharp deadlines, to movies, where nobody really knew who was writing what for months on end must have been hard for Parker to deal with. No longer was she familiar with the editing process. No longer did she get authorial approval. No longer was her name attached to the work in a prominent position. Even though she excelled at never meeting deadlines and was the queen of procrastination, full of wily excuses, not knowing what she was supposed to be doing unnerved her. Professor Richard Fine, the author of *Hollywood and the Profession of Authorship 1920–1940*, noted that many of the authors who went to Hollywood prospered financially, but almost every single one was "disquieted or unnerved by the experience" because the profession of authorship as they had known it was under attack.[6] Writers were not really respected, they had no creative control over the films they worked on, and often their scripts would be rewritten or tampered with by somebody else.

But there was not just the professional contrast between New York and Hollywood; there was the geographical difference too. The history of the area was no different from that of any other western frontier. Initially occupied by native residents, the Gabrielinos, toward the end of the nineteenth century, the town had no particular name, and was a landscape of farmers, cowboys, bandits, and prospectors. All land north of Sunset Boulevard was used for grazing. In 1887, Mrs. Daeida Wilcox, wife of the Los Angeles real estate developer Harvey Wilcox, met a woman on a train who mentioned her Florida summer home, "Hollywood." Mrs. Wilcox loved the name so much, she mentioned it to her husband, who bought a tract of land filled with apricot and fig trees and named it Hollywood. He subdivided the plots and sold them for $1,000 each, then registered the subdivision of "Hollywood" with the Los Angeles County Recorder Office.[7] In 1923, Harry Chandler, the *Los Angeles Times* publisher, decided to invest in a real estate development called Hollywoodland, with one myth claiming this was named after the nearby Holly Canyon. The famous white sign was erected, but the development never happened. For the rest of that decade, Hollywood still had dirt roads. Barley fields surrounded central buildings. Melons were grown commercially on Sunset Boulevard. In essence, Hollywood was a sleepy farming town until moviemakers started moving in and leasing orchards and land to build their production companies. The native residents hated the newcomers, whom they perceived as bringing their East Coast ways with them. Then as actors and writers increasingly moved there, they were regarded as bringing debauchery, too much money, and, somewhat tragically, broken dreams.

It is true that most of the companies had moved from the

East Coast, mostly New Jersey and Florida, and there were a few reasons for this. First, back east most motion picture patents had been bought by the inventor and businessman Thomas Edison, who, having developed a motion picture camera called the Kinetoscope, wanted the monopoly on making films. Using his ownership of these various patents, he would shut down film productions by other companies or, worse still, sue them. By moving west under the jurisdiction of California law, Edison could not take legal action against them. Second, Hollywood had good, reliable weather, which allowed outdoor filming year-round, and a diverse terrain that could act as a backdrop for just about any film scenario, from cowboys charging around the Wild West to Rudolph Valentino creating mass swooning in Morocco. Crucially, everything was cheaper, not only land, but since there were no unions established in the 1920s, wages were low too. As early as 1924, moviemaking was the seventh largest industry in America, employing fifteen thousand people and with the moviegoing public spending $500 million a year on tickets.[8] It seems safe to say that Dorothy Parker, however, wasn't one of them. On the rare occasions when she watched a talkie, she was overwhelmed with the desire to yell at the screen, "Oh for heaven's sake, shut up!"[9]

Upon arriving in Hollywood, Parker stayed at the Ambassador Hotel on Wilshire Boulevard. If she felt isolated at work, it is likely she felt less so in the hotel, which had been designed by the architect Myron Hunt and opened in 1921 to be the center of LA social life. Although this section of Wilshire Boulevard was supposed to be the equivalent of Manhattan's Fifth Avenue, one feels it would have stretched the imagination to equate the two, since in 1921 it was still surrounded by bean fields. However, since film companies were pouring in from the East, it was felt that the city needed a grand, spa-like hotel. The Ambassador offered 444 luxury guest rooms and 76 bungalows set on almost twenty-four acres of land containing fountains, a courtyard, and sculpted gardens, all with Mediterranean styling. The Hollywood journalist Adela Rogers St. Johns explained the importance of the hotel: "There was absolutely no other place to go . . . back then the film stars and producers didn't have the large and beautiful homes they have today . . . so this is where we all came to meet one another, to be seen, to be coddled, amused, and entertained."[10] But no amount of West Coast luxury was good enough for Parker, who claimed that her ten-dollar room was worth no more than three.

The real significance of the Ambassador, though, lay not in the accommodation but in its nightclub, the Cocoanut Grove, which rapidly became known as *the* premier nightspot in LA. Over the years everyone performed there: Frank Sinatra, Judy Garland, Sammy Davis Jr., Nat King Cole, and Bing Crosby, with an audience comprising the likes of Marilyn Monroe, presidents, and movie industry executives. The club was Moroccan styled and decorated with leftover papier-mâché palm trees used on the set of Rudolph Valentino's *The Sheik*. Swinging from their fronds were stuffed monkeys with amber electric eyes that would light up and flash. The ceiling was blue and filled with twinkly stars, and one full wall sported a mural of a Hawaiian moon shining over a splashing waterfall. The club hosted theme nights. Fridays were the Charleston competition, where Joan Crawford and Carole Lombard would battle it out on the dance floor. When she wasn't sweeping the boards with her dance moves, Crawford would keep a close eye on her competition entering the club. Any night that Loretta Young arrived left Crawford especially seething, since she regarded her as more beautiful and charismatic. One hotel resident, the actor John Barrymore, would let loose Clementine, his pet monkey, to join the stuffed creatures swinging from the palm trees. Although this was the age of Prohibition, the Cocoanut Grove paid absolutely no attention to the law, and on one infamous night, Scott and Zelda Fitzgerald arrived atop a taxi swigging champagne. They proceeded to pile all the furniture in their suite into the middle of the floor, balanced their unpaid bill on top, and set the lot on fire. They made a quick getaway in the dead of night.

Dorothy Parker enjoyed nights out at the Cocoanut Grove, both in the 1920s and in later years, when she was photographed there slightly worse for wear at a lively-looking party with James Cagney. The nightclub and hotel were regarded as bringing about the modern era in LA and even hosted six Academy Awards ceremonies. Sadly, in 1968 it became famous for a much more tragic event, as the site of Bobby Kennedy's assassination. Today the Cocoanut Grove no longer exists, having been mostly demolished in 2005 and rebuilt as a school. Somewhat incongruously, a few remains of the club now form part of the school's gym. The only remnants of the hotel's illustrious past are the original, beautiful art deco entrance gateway posts reading PARKING and HOTEL still standing in the busy rush of Wilshire Boulevard.

Dorothy Parker moved out of the Ambassador as soon as she received her first paycheck. Instead, she went to live with the Romanian American screenwriter Arthur Caesar and his wife, Dira Platts.[11] In December 1928, Robert Benchley also arrived in Hollywood and decided that he also hated the place. This resulted in the two partners in crime sitting around moaning profusely about everything. From Parker's recollections, one feels that however surreal her behavior may have been in the New York offices of *Vanity Fair*, nothing prepared her for the ludicrous nature of the film industry. An early movie she became involved with starred Greta Garbo. Parker listened incredulously as the plot was outlined for her. Essentially Garbo and her leading man are lost in a desert for five days without water. Eventually crawling on her hands and knees, Garbo says she will give herself to the leading man if he lets her drink some of the water (except it's really spirits) in the flask around his neck. "Now I don't know about you gentlemen," Parker sniffed in a 1953 speech looking back on those early days, "but I should think a man five days in a desert without water, that's the last thing he would want."[12] Another film produced by Cecil B. DeMille, *Dynamite*, was even more bizarre. "It was so long and so involved I couldn't possibly remember it to tell you," she said, but it appeared to involve a hero wrongly convicted of murder sitting in his prison cell waiting to die. Luckily, he had a guitar, and DeMille wanted Parker to write the song he would sing. Overwhelmed by the level of detail, Parker exclaimed to DeMille that it was all truly staggering. He replied cryptically, "Ah yes, zebras, in the *King of Kings*." Completely thrown as to what this had to do with a condemned man in a cell, she scuttled back to her office and pulled out a Bible ("I felt in heaven's name what are zebras doing in a film about the life of Christ? I thought maybe he said 'Hebrews'?"). But no, he had said zebras, which had been used to pull the chariots of the Magdalene. "I should have known this," said a quietly wry Parker, though she still had no idea why this was a response to her original comment, or even what he was talking about.[13] Rising to DeMille's challenge, she wrote a song for the condemned hero called "Dynamite Man, I Love You," which was promptly rejected. One can only lament that no copy has survived of this masterpiece. Instead, Parker worked with the composer Jack King and produced the exquisite song "How Am I to Know?," which would later famously be recorded by Billie Holiday and opens with the beautifully wistful words "Oh, how am I to know / If it's really love / That's found its way here?"

In Ian Hamilton's study of Hollywood writers, he noted that during the years 1928–1931, Hollywood was "photoplaying" just about everything—novels, stories, and plays. He believes that it was the "beginning of the great era of Hollywoodization."[14] Movies were churned out, and dialogue was bought by the ton, leaving the studio executive Joseph M. Schenck to conclude that "the trouble with the whole industry is that it talked before it thought."[15] The result was that writers were expendable, with their work discarded or going uncredited. Although Parker had been open about taking a job there just for the money, she still appeared shocked by the disposable way in which talent was treated, claiming, "You don't need any talent—the last thing you want is talent."[16] Professionally she felt wasted. Socially she seemed impatient at house parties full of overly polite people, bowing and scraping, and dithering around the dining room door. The journalist Mollie Merrick witnessed Parker ("the lady from New York") losing her temper when guests ignored the hostess urging them to go and eat. "Come on you So-and-Sos! Get a little action on this!" yelled Parker, herding them toward the food.[17]

After three months of this, Parker had had enough. Curiously, there are very few details of her first months in Hollywood. Most emerge from her later remembrances, or the odd glimpse in contemporaneous newspaper reports. But a clear enough picture emerges of Parker as deeply unimpressed and homesick for New York, wondering why she was squandering her talent in a place that turned out to be even more ridiculous than she could have imagined. She'd known she would hate Hollywood, but she left the town with this feeling confirmed and offered a devastatingly acerbic goodbye to MGM: "Metro-Goldwyn-Merde would be a better name for that shit heap . . . I hoped the whole industry would collapse . . . It looks, it all feels as if it had been invented by a Sixth Avenue peep-show man."[18] She demanded that Irving Thalberg pay for her train ride home, and she left without even a goodbye to her housemates, Arthur and Dira.[19] On her four-day journey back to Manhattan, it seems unlikely that Dorothy Parker was aware that her relationship with Hollywood was only just beginning and would last another thirty-five years.

The year now, though, was 1929, and Parker did not head back "out there" until 1934. America was heading for catastrophic change with the Wall Street collapse and the start of the Great Depression. Hollywood found itself in the unique position of making films to sell to people who had no money to go and see them. Oddly, though, for the first two or three years of the Depression, audience figures held up. Despite times being hard, in 1930 alone 110 million people went to the cinema.[20] Films offered meaning and escape for many whose lives were suddenly without hope or reason. Movies were not just fluffy moments of relief, either. Hollywood turned to subjects for gritty realism, such as wronged heroes, scoundrels, and gangsters. The movie palaces offered sanctuary with showy, over-the-top décor and warm upholstered seats. The discovery in 1922 of Tutankhamun's tomb led to Egyptian Revival architecture, with movie theaters embracing this style and filling themselves with statues of pharaohs, temple facades, hieroglyphics, chandeliers, and, in some cases, giant organs that were played during intermission.

But in 1929, Dorothy Parker was well removed from all of this. At the request of Viking Press she rashly agreed to write her first novel, scheduled for spring 1930 publication. Deciding to complete this task away from New York, she sailed to Europe in April, which had the added advantage of allowing her to escape yet another disastrous love affair that had ended when she moved to Hollywood. She stayed briefly in Paris, where she took ill and was diagnosed with an enlarged liver, no doubt connected to her increasingly heavy alcohol intake. Writing home to her sister, Helen, she lamented the "rotten ugly" affair she had been caught up in with a young cad named John Garrett and spoke with horror of her medical troubles, "a dainty complaint too, —something the matter with my liver."[21] Barely leaving her hotel room, she saw only Ernest Hemingway and his second wife, Pauline, but found she was able to "stagger dizzily out once or twice to get some of the most ill-advised clothes ever assembled. They were just what somebody with an afflicted liver WOULD have picked out."[22] From here, in June, she traveled to Antibes in the South of France, where she stayed for almost five months with a wealthy couple she had met through New York acquaintances, Gerald and Sara Murphy. The Great Depression seemed a whole other world away. The Murphys were both from exceptionally rich backgrounds, his in the leather goods trade, hers in an ink and varnish company. In the 1920s they moved from New York to the French Riviera and became famous for throwing lavish parties and being the center of a large group of artists and writers. Rumor had it that they were the model for F. Scott Fitzgerald's Nicole and Dick Diver, in his novel *Tender Is the Night*. Parker had her own guesthouse on the grounds of their villa, "exquisitely furnished, and set in the midst of fig trees all full of purple fruit—except I hate figs in any form."[23] Here she planned to work long days on her novel, but instead found herself swimming more than a mile each day in the sea and having wild nights out in Cannes getting, in her words, blotto. On one occasion, after a one-night stand with a sporting type, she dismissively wrote to her sister, "I can't tell you how little I think sex means to me now. And polo players wouldn't count anyway."[24]

By November she was in Montana-Vermala, Switzerland, accompanying the Murphys to a sanatorium where their son, Patrick, had been admitted with tuberculosis. They asked for Parker's support during this worrying time, and she was happy to help in any way, feeling heartbroken over what they were all facing. Writing a long letter to Robert Benchley back in New York, she breezily asked, "And is there any news? I understand there has been some little trouble in Wall Street . . . Anyone we know wiped out . . . ?"[25] She remained unimpressed with her surroundings, admitting to Benchley, "Well, Fred, I have always thought of Switzerland as the home of horseshit, and I see no reason to change my opinion now. For what does anyone want with a country that has no history except William Tell, and I don't know to this day whether he was a legend or not?"[26] Although she struggled with homesickness, feeling trapped on the top of "a God damn Alp," she still felt lucky. "Well, Fred, if you had told me last year that this November I should be in a sanatorium for the tubercular in Switzerland, I should have said—well, I should have said 'That's great!,' because last November I was in Hollywood, and any change would have been for the better."[27]

Yet change was coming to Hollywood, and not necessarily for the better. There had always been concern about the immoral nature of movies, and indeed the industry itself. Hollywood was sometimes referred to as "Sodom by the Sea."[28] A few off-screen scandals, including the death of the young, aspiring actress Virginia Rappe after attending a party with the screen star Fatty Arbuckle and the murder of actor/director William Desmond Taylor, stirred up condemnation from a number of different pressure groups. Combined with the switch from silent to talking films, where people could now actually *say* things rather than merely imply them, producers began to fear that federal control was about to be imposed on them. To ward off this interference they took preemptive action and formed the Motion Picture Producers and Distributors Association of America in 1922. This self-imposed organization was to ensure the highest moral standards were upheld in the industry, and its head was brought in from the government—Will H. Hays, former chairman of the Republican National Committee. For the first few years, Hays worked alongside producers, placating pressure groups, and in turn the industry made a show of seeking moral guidance from Hays. In 1927 he consulted with studio executives and issued a series of "Don'ts" and "Be Carefuls" that moviemakers were expected to consult and follow to maintain a moral compass. These consisted of eleven "Don'ts" and twenty-five "Be Carefuls." Subjects covered under "Don'ts" included no profanity, no nudity, no white slavery, no children's sex organs, and no ridicule of the clergy. Among the topics that needed careful handling were scenes of a man and woman in bed together, surgical operations, sympathy for criminals, the use of firearms, and methods of smuggling.

The problem was, writers were not used to having their work restricted in this way, and now that bad language could be—and was—heard in picture palaces, religious pressure groups became very twitchy indeed. To try to stave off even more trouble, producers invited Martin Quigley, a Catholic publisher, and Father Daniel A. Lord, a Jesuit priest, to redraft the loosely formed "Don'ts" and "Be Carefuls" into a more comprehensive list. What resulted was the infamous Hays Code, whose rather grand purpose was to suggest the moral unity of Western civilization. On

March 31, 1930, this code was accepted by the movie industry—though *accepted* is perhaps too strong a word, since most films ignored all features of the code for the next four years. Sadly, there is no existing record of what Dorothy Parker thought about the Hays Code, though looking at the various prohibitions, one can imagine her raised eyebrows and searing commentary, particularly in the years to come when she would have to work within its restrictions.

Divided into three sections, the code dealt with General Principles, Working Principles, and Plot Material. The main messages were that evil must not be presented in an alluring fashion and, most importantly, must always be punished. Adultery should be avoided. There should be no lustful kissing or prolonged embraces. Male and female organs and the breasts of women should *never* be uncovered. Murder should not be brutal (quite a challenge). Criminals should not be glamorized. The name of Jesus Christ should never be used unless in reverence. Dances such as the can-can and belly dancing were simply deemed to be *wrong.* Topics that faced an absolute ban were sex perversion (which was essentially anything relating to same-sex relationships), interracial sex, venereal diseases, and scenes of childbirth either in fact or in silhouette. Hollywood's response was to make movies that were tougher, more lurid, and sexier than ever before.

While the code was coming into being—and being ignored—back in New York, Dorothy Parker was finally having to admit that work on her novel, tentatively titled *Sonnets in Suicide,* had pretty much amounted to nothing. Later in life she realized that this genre was not one of her strengths. She was not, in her words, a long-distance writer, however much she wanted to be. In 1930 she grew increasingly anxious and panic-stricken that she had nothing to show for almost a year's work on a novel that was clearly going nowhere. Always restless, Parker had just experienced an especially chaotic two years as she moved from New York to Hollywood back to New York, then to Paris, Antibes, Switzerland, and back to New York. Despite her liver complaint she continued to drink heavily, and despite her publisher eager for her work, she struggled to write anything of any length. Two years divorced, and after a series of entanglements with hopeless men, professionally shaken, and presumably not seeing a way out of her troubles, she made a third suicide attempt by drinking shoe polish. Though it did not kill her, it made her sick enough to be hospitalized. Once again those around her did not take the attempt seriously, and Parker's biographer Marion Meade referred to it as "a foolish gesture," speculating that it allowed Parker to break her publishing contract with Viking while being able to keep the advance.[29] Yet dismissing a third attempt on her life seems to potentially miss exactly what Parker was doing. Psychiatric studies have found that the risk of a subsequent suicide attempt increases by about thirty-two percent for each prior attempt.[30] If Parker was not able to own up that her novel writing had failed, and if she was turning her failed love affairs inward, then perhaps her risky behavior was an act of self-sabotage rather than manipulative attention-seeking. Indeed, the professor of psychiatry Ronald W. Maris studied suicidal behavior in the context of suicidal careers and noted that in this context suicide attempts are rational, "an effective means of resolving common life problems."[31] He concluded that often in this context a person is ambivalent about living, but if their tolerance thresholds have been repeatedly breached and if they experience negative interpersonal relationships, then this can result in suicidal behavior. Parker was at the end of her tether with her writing and was sick of being lied to and cheated on by men. Maris claims that if non-suicidal alternatives are unavailable or seem unacceptable, then an attempt on one's life seems rational. Perhaps for Parker drinking shoe polish was the desperate act of a woman who felt she had nowhere else to turn.

Realizing that a novel would not be making its spring publication list, Viking Press opted instead to produce a collection of Parker's stories called *Laments for the Living*. This contained some of Parker's best work, such as her award-winning story "Big Blonde" and other successful pieces, including "Mr. Durant" and "Just a Little One." Once again, Parker's bold voice was speaking out in her short stories about female alcoholism, abortion, and the shoddy treatment of women by men. In her poems, which would be published the following year, she covered the hopelessness of love and the cruel nature of men. In "Ultimatum," her narrator begins, "I'm wearied of wearying love, my friend, / Of worry and strain and doubt; / Before we begin, let us view the end, / And maybe I'll do without."[32] And in "Sonnet for the End of a Sequence," dealing with the end of a love affair, another of Parker's narrators claims that being on her own is for the best: "Therefore, I am immeasurably grateful / To you, for proving shallow, false, and hateful."[33]

With the panic and pressure of her novel removed, one may have expected Parker to give herself time to recover from the emotional upheaval of a suicide attempt and hospitalization. Instead, in May, her response was to travel back to the Murphys' home in Switzerland, where she stayed for six months. Despite visits from Robert Benchley and other friends such as F. Scott Fitzgerald and Donald Ogden Stewart, by the time October came around Parker was sending forlorn telegrams to Benchley in New York saying she was "almost gone with loneliness and discouragement"[34] and that traveling to Europe had been "a bad mistake."[35] Whether she was in New York or Hollywood or across the Atlantic, she simply could not settle. This dissatisfaction was not just in her day-to-day life, but in her writing too. Every word seemed at times to be a chore and she was never happy with the finished product. Yet there seems little evidence to explain why she was so hard on herself professionally. Her first two poetry collections had been bestsellers, and when *Laments for the Living* was published that year, it went through four editions in the first month.

This insecurity about her writing made Parker possibly one of the worst candidates to be a Hollywood screenwriter. Even the most mediocre writers who had more confidence in themselves than was warranted felt undervalued by the film industry. The dismissive nature of movie executives was simply not good for Parker's morale. Some writers were able to better deal with this than others. In 1930, P. G. Wodehouse was taken to Hollywood by MGM and given $2,000 a week and Norma Shearer's house to live in (she no longer needed it, having married Irving

Thalberg in 1927). Wodehouse's attitude seemed to be bemusement and a determination to make the situation work to his advantage. He negotiated being able to work from home instead of an office and noted, "When I get a summons from the studio, I motor over there, stay for a couple of hours and come back. Add incessant sunshine and it's really rather jolly."[36] Work that he claimed he could complete in a morning the studio assumed would take six weeks, and since he was earning $8,000 a month, he was happy to go along with their time frame. At the end of his contract, he gave an interview to the *Los Angeles Times* about the movie industry that highlighted just how different his mindset was from Parker's: "I have twenty novels, a score of successful plays, and countless magazine stories to my credit. Yet apparently, they had the greatest difficulty in finding anything for me to do."[37] Wodehouse, secure in his talent, placed the onus back on Hollywood; the failing was theirs, not his. Parker, much more inward looking and less sure of her talent, somehow seemed to blame herself. It may be reasonable to see a gender disparity here, as Parker fought her way to survive in a world that was much kinder to confident men. But there was also Parker's lifelong lack of belief in her own work. In 1959 she admitted, "About my work. My work is not important. I do the best I can. I wish to the Lord in Heaven it were better."[38] Yet Parker did succeed in Hollywood for decades, making vast amounts of money, and the industry was one area in which certain women could match, or even surpass, the salaries of men. When Parker returned in 1934, she was one of the highest-paid writers out there.[39] In fact, in 1930 *Fortune* claimed the film industry employed "more members of the literati than it took to produce the King James Bible."[40]

When Dorothy Parker returned to New York from Europe in 1931, she entered almost immediately into another unsavory relationship, this time with a journalist named John McClain. At twenty-seven, he was eleven years younger than Parker and regarded by her more astute friends as a social climber and hanger-on. He had the classic good looks that Parker favored in her men, and she assumed he was genuinely in love with her. She was soon to discover her mistake when he increasingly began to dodge her attempts to set dinner dates with him. She was also to discover that she was mistaken about being the only woman in his life. He would openly arrange other dates in her hearing, and he repeatedly complained to his friends that Parker was smothering him, while simultaneously bragging that he had a famous woman on his arm. During one embarrassing public fight in the lobby of the Algonquin, where Parker was temporarily living, McClain yelled at her that she was a "lousy lay" before storming off. Parker concluded, "I'm afraid his body went to his head."[41] Yet his cruel and humiliating behavior was still not enough for Parker to get rid of him. It was as if her low self-esteem made her feel lucky that any man was interested in her, however appallingly he behaved.

While Parker was being treated badly by men in New York, writers who had headed out to Hollywood also felt as though they were being treated badly and rapidly realized that they would never be afforded the name status they received on Broadway. By the mid-1930s over a thousand were working in Hollywood, many of them from Manhattan and many of them deriding the movie industry, claiming they were saving their talent for projects back east. The playwright and journalist Ben Hecht felt that too many of the writers were not working the system to their advantage, mainly because they were "incompetent thickheads."[42] Instead of caring about formal dinner arrangements that seated people in order of importance (writers were at the end of the table just above hairdressers),[43] they needed to understand that screenwriting was about endlessly collaborating and ultimately not caring about attribution. Being a vociferous complainer didn't hurt, either, with Hecht explaining, "My own discontent with what I was asked to do in Hollywood was so loud that I finally received $125,000 for four weeks of script writing."[44] This may well have worked for Hecht and Wodehouse, but other writers disliked what they saw as the devious nature of studio executives. Irving Thalberg, for example, was notorious for secretly setting different writers to work on the same project, since he regarded their output as interchangeable. To secure a fortune as a writer in Hollywood meant giving up so many aspects of authorship that had previously been taken for granted—editorial approval, accreditation, pride in one's work.

Discontent seemed to be in the air. While some writers were earning vast amounts of money out west, the full impact of the Great Depression was creating devastating financial and emotional trauma. In the years following the Wall Street crash, unemployment peaked at twenty-five percent in the early 1930s. Hundreds of thousands of people had lost their jobs. Those who were lucky enough to continue working had to take wage cuts. There were so many defaults on loan payments that more than five thousand banks failed. Without enough money for food, grocery stores could not afford to stock their shelves. People went hungry, shortages hit everywhere. Droughts exasperated the problem, causing crops to fail and creating the need for food rationing. Evictions soared, causing overcrowding and visible homelessness. Suicide rates were at a high, and as people tried anything to survive, crime and prostitution also started to rise. It was almost as if the Roaring Twenties had disappeared overnight. Given that many had barely enough money to buy food, it was no surprise that by 1933 audience figures in cinemas were down by forty percent and would not recover until the late 1930s.[45]

For Dorothy Parker, the start of 1932 was terrible. Even though she seemed relatively untouched in her material life, living through the national trauma of a depression, seeing poverty and homelessness around her, left her feeling ground down by just about everything. On February 23 she made a fourth attempt at suicide, this time taking an overdose of barbiturates. She was taken to Presbyterian Hospital to recover as the news hit the national press. The *Evening Star* reported that the sleeping medicine had been taken accidentally, though this was clearly not the case. Once again, Parker received little compassion from those around her, most notably John McClain. Marion Meade notes that "[a]fter her suicide attempt, he announced to many that he considered it a typical female scheme, staged in the hope that she could tie him to her. He professed to have lost respect for her."[46] Whether Parker's overdose was a genuine attempt to die or a desperate cry for help hardly seems the point, for either way, she was clearly deeply unhappy and despondent enough to gamble with her life. Unsurprisingly, the relationship with McClain ended shortly afterward, and in April a wounded Parker gave a revealing interview to the *Bismarck Tribune*.[47] She claimed that women ought to leave writing alone—"There is something ridiculous about a woman who writes"—and that the act of writing was a lot of work for her, she hated it, and was never satisfied with what she produced. In what seemed an extraordinary claim, and what at first glance may seem typical Parker mischief, she announced, "The only full life for a woman is marriage and babies . . . Really!" She informed the journalist that she would be willing to give up her reputation as writer, her cynicism, and her wit "for a family of kids." These words, which at the time seemed like biting sarcasm, would be reevaluated four years later when Parker's life took an unexpected turn. But in 1932, Parker, with her hurt openly on display, declared, "A woman can bear physical pain, but she can't bear mental pain," and even more revealingly, "The cleverest woman on earth is the biggest fool on earth with a man." Concluding that she only wrote because "of the wolf you must have stumbled over at the door," she ended by claiming that her chief devotion was to Robinson, her dachshund, "now in a hospital having lately been chewed by a larger dog."[48] Some of the themes in this interview were old ground for Parker—her dislike of writing and continual dissatisfaction with her work. But the openness with which she tackled mental pain and the agony of love was new. Her verse, of course, deals with these issues, but there is a difference between being able to hide behind the authorial voice and giving an interview where it is "you" speaking unfiltered.

Despite her creative struggles, Parker did begin to work and completed some short stories throughout that year, including one of her best, "Horsie" (about another cruel man and his critical gaze that only values attractive women) and the possibly semi-autobiographical "Lady with a Lamp" (the dialogue of an unsympathetic woman visiting her friend ill in bed with nerves following an implied suicide attempt and recovering from a relationship breakup). By October, Parker was once again restless and keen to escape. Her dissatisfaction with life seemed to create an inability to stay still, as if running away might get her to a better place or a happier time. She headed across the Atlantic on the *Europa* with her friend Sara Murphy to spend a month in Paris. It was on this crossing that an encounter happened that would become significant for Parker's later years in Hollywood. Aboard was Mary Mooney, who was traveling to Russia with a delegation of American communists. Her son, Tom, a labor leader and political activist, had received a sentence to hang in 1916, which was then changed to a life sentence in 1918, after being convicted of carrying out a bombing at the San Francisco Preparedness Day Parade.[49] This conviction, however, was based on falsified evidence, perjured testimony, and quite frankly ludicrous claims (one witness said it was her astral body that was at the scene). In the years following his conviction, a whole campaign was underway to secure his release and bring about a pardon. Mary Mooney was one of his most vociferous supporters, but so were many Hollywood celebrities, politicians, and activists. The renowned photographer Dorothea Lange photo-graphed Mooney in his cell at San Quentin and used the images on posters demanding his release. For Parker, this had shades of the 1927 Sacco-Vanzetti protests she had been involved in in Boston. But it was also the second time she became involved with the Communist Party, attending their meetings on board the ship and agreeing with the speeches they gave. She believed Mooney to be innocent and fully supported the actions of his mother.[50] Professor Milly S. Barranger credits this 1932 encounter aboard the *Europa*, along with the Sacco-Vanzetti case, as being the two events that sparked and secured Parker's subsequent political activism.[51] Although these miscarriages of justice may seem isolated events in Parker's life, what they brought about was the introduction to not only on-the-ground activism but also a political ideology that she would cross paths with in a much more sustained way once she returned to Hollywood.

In the 1930s, the stirrings of this ideology were growing within the movie industry, especially regarding writer exploita-tion. Despite paying vast sums to well-known writers, film studios often used any excuse to cut wages, or even to suddenly stop the employment of lesser-known writers. This financial in-security led writers to believe it was time that they unionized. Unsurprisingly, this did not go down well with industry execu-tives. Joe Cohn, production manager of MGM, explained that with so many pictures being made it was essential that studios have a reservoir of writers they could draw on at any time. Pro-ducers needed to pull in writers as and when they needed them, and they worried that unionization would bring about an end to this. On the other side of the coin, the precarious nature of this employment was brutal. Dorothy Parker, who would get involved in this struggle when she returned to Hollywood the following year, explained why a writer's union was so important: "It was extremely badly needed because there were people who . . . were coming in and getting nothing. The greatest money they could have was $40 a week and then bang, it would stop. A screenwriter might be employed, say, for two weeks in a year and then they can say, 'the hell with him.'"[52] Parker was not the only prominent writer who would take up this cause in the coming years, for although they were financially secure, their aim was to protect up-and-coming younger writers. In 1934, fifty percent of screenwriters earned less than $4,000 per year, forty percent less than $3,000, and thirty percent less than $2,000, with only ten percent earning more than $10,000 per year.[53] In other words, it took over half the screenwriters in Hollywood one year to earn what Dorothy Parker was being paid for one week. By anyone's standards this discrepancy was huge, but Parker with her socialist heart found it completely unacceptable.

Fortunately, Hollywood did not have to wait long for Parker to return and join the agitating. When she landed back in New York from Paris, she was merely months away from meeting the person who would transform her life. Having spent her time in Europe doing nothing at all apart from spending her money and once again becoming broke, she did settle down to do some work at home writing reviews. But she continued to party hard at the usual hangouts and attended parties at friends' homes. As ever, drinking too much brought out Parker's nastier side and she became increasingly notorious for causing awkward scenes at gatherings if she decided to turn on another guest. Almost always remorseful the next day and quick to apologize, she didn't stop her behavior, and her fearsome reputation left some people around her nervous. The humorist and screenwriter S. J. Perelman, who met Parker in the fall of 1932, recounted a typical example of this. He described his first encounter with Parker as a "scarifying ordeal,"[54] at a party thrown ostensibly to try to come up with a name for a new revue show for which he had written some sketches. Parker, who was glamorously dressed but exceptionally drunk, made a couple of suggestions that Perelman rejected. This went down badly, and Parker proceeded to lay into him. While everyone around them fell into an embarrassed silence, Parker wound up her diatribe with, "I wonder though if Mr. P. realizes that he's a great big etcetera. Because he is you know. In fact of all the etceteras I've ever known—"[55] Perelman left the party devastated, and the following evening a dozen magnificent roses were delivered to him with a contrite apology from Parker. He accepted, and their friendship lasted for thirty years. They would even work together on a script in Hollywood six years later.

If Parker's social skills were somewhat acerbic, her book reviewing in the *New Yorker* was equally caustic. Her take on the latest sex novel by the writer Tiffany Thayer pulled no punches: "He is beyond question a writer of power; and his power lies in his ability to make sex so thoroughly, graphically, and aggressively unattractive that one is fairly shaken to ponder how little one has been missing. Bewildered is the fox who lives to find that grapes beyond reach can be *really* sour."[56] Mabel Dodge Luhan's memoir *Intimate Memories: Background* received similar treatment: "But *Background* is to me as dull, and with that same stuffy, oppressive, plush-thick dullness, as an album of old snapshots of somebody else's family group."[57] Overlooking how devastating it would be to receive a review like this from Parker, it is difficult not to be impressed by the beauty of her writing, which manages to capture the exquisite boredom certain books can inspire. That year also saw Viking Press publish *After Such Pleasures*, a collection of stories including "Horsie" and "The Waltz." If there was no particularly new material in the edition, readers did not seem to mind and, as ever, it was received with critical praise, described as amusing, poignant, sparkling.

In the spring of 1933, Dorothy Parker met Alan Campbell. Campbell was a part-time actor, part-time writer, and like Parker came from mixed parentage, being of Scottish descent on his father's side and Jewish on his mother's. His father was deceased, and his mother, Hortense, would soon—and rather amusingly—become Parker's nemesis. Campbell had appeared in numerous Broadways plays and had several stories published in the *New Yorker*. At twenty-nine he was eleven years younger than Parker, and rumors swirled around Manhattan that he was gay, or at the very least bisexual. Whatever the truth, Campbell and Parker fell deeply in love. She enjoyed his classic, clean-cut good looks and sharp humor, and he claimed Parker was "the only woman I ever knew whose mind was completely attuned to mine ... No one in the world has made me laugh as much as Dottie."[58] More importantly, Campbell immediately took on the role of Parker's lover-nurse-stylist-manager, realizing that she was hopeless at organizing herself, her life, and her work. He encouraged her to buy new clothes, took her for a restyle at a salon where she was given flattering bangs, freed her of any boring domestic tasks, and tried to straighten out her finances (which by this stage were quite far gone). Parker not only spent her money until she was broke but was also generous to a fault with her friends. If they ran into trouble, she'd hand out checks, and in the years to come she'd give large amounts of her earnings to various political causes. There was something wonderfully bewildering about a woman who would spend hundreds of dollars on one piece of elegant lingerie while equally funding several socialist campaigns. In a rather empowering way, she saw no reason why she should not benefit from her wealth (however sporadic) so long as she never lost her desire to level things up for everyone else.

Campbell and Parker spent most of the year together, and in December 1933, Prohibition was repealed. Although alcohol was once again legal, the previous ban on it had made no difference to Parker's drinking, which was now so heavy that she began, again, to suffer blackouts. Campbell took care of her, put her to bed when needed, and nursed her through hangovers. Perhaps it was this level of care that she was unwilling to give up when he landed an acting job in Denver early in the summer of 1934. Unusually, for Parker, rather than be left in New York, she decided to go with him, and they packed her dogs and belongings in a car and drove for four days to Colorado. Miraculously, two letters written to Alexander Woollcott survive from Parker's stay in Denver. They are wonderfully rich and describe her

day-to-day life, her feelings about Campbell, and her bemusement at ending up in North Denver, "which is like one of those
places you pass when the train starts slowing down, and you say
to yourself, 'Well there's one thing anyway, —I don't have to live
in a dump like that.'"[59] They arrived to a gaggle of reporters who
had discovered their whereabouts after Donald Ogden Stewart
showed a telegram they had sent him to a Hollywood journalist.
Media reports began to emerge speculating that they were living
in sin, and Denver appeared to have a much less relaxed attitude
toward this than Manhattan. Rather rashly, Campbell told reporters that he had married Parker the previous October on
Long Island, and Parker backed this lie up, telling the *Evening
Star* (which referred to her as "the Queen of punsters") that they
had been married by a justice of the peace: "We didn't care who
knew about our marriage and we made no special effort to keep
it secret."[60] They certainly didn't, because no such marriage had
taken place. And when journalists went poking around and
could find no marriage certificate, some awkward questions were
raised. On June 18 Parker and Campbell drove to New Mexico,
where they were married just before midnight before turning
around and driving straight back to Denver. Movingly, Parker
wrote about married life: "It is lovelier than I ever knew anything could be, and we are in a sort of coma of happiness . . ."[61]
They found a "darling" house with three servants, got to know
some of the locals, and Parker discovered that "[d]rinking here is
quite an interesting experiment, because of the altitude. Two
cocktails and you spin on your ass."[62] Sounding ecstatic, Parker
declared that she thought she would hate it there, but she loved

it, she loved being married, she loved living in a bungalow, she loved pottering around her garden. One drawback was that she did not see much of Campbell because he was tied up in long rehearsals, but this gave her the opportunity to cast her judgmental eye over the rest of the theater group, and she was able to observe that the leading lady "looked like a two-dollar whore who once commanded five."[63]

Alas, this idyll was not to last. Although Campbell was earning money from his acting and Parker was drawing in royalties, her debts by this stage were monumental. In the second letter to Woollcott, she declared that Campbell worried "about finances— as, he points out, I should have been doing all these years."[64] A solution, however, had been reached, with Parker writing somewhat dramatically, "Dear Alec, I am afraid it is only too true about Hollywood. The Paramount contract, or Kiss of Death, has come."[65] Campbell had negotiated a ten-week contract treating them as a dynamic husband-and-wife team; he was to create dialogue and act for $250 per week, and Parker was to write for $1,000 per week. She admitted to feeling flat about the arrangement and described it as horseshit, remembering only too well how much she had detested the place five years earlier. But the thought of clearing her debts was pleasing, and showing just how much value she placed on her husband, she believed that this time around Hollywood would be different because "Alan will be there."[66] Hollywood was indeed different, but perhaps not for the reasons Parker anticipated. Since she had left, political unrest had been brewing, more and more writers had streamed into the movie industry, and the Hays Code had been introduced.

September 1934 brought about the end of the theater season in Denver. Parker and Campbell once again loaded up the car with their dogs and belongings, and this time headed to California. "It is for ten weeks," Parker wrote optimistically to Woollcott, as though such a short amount of time made it more bearable. Except it wasn't ten weeks. As they crossed the state line out of Colorado heading west toward Hollywood, they would end up staying there, intermittently, for almost thirty years.

CHAPTER 3

A Star Is Born

It's a state of mindlessness.[1]
—Dorothy Parker on Hollywood

L ike many other writers, Dorothy Parker spent quite a lot of time complaining about Hollywood. Though she and Robert Benchley had always excelled at bemoaning what life threw at them—whether it was their own fault or not—when it came to Hollywood, Parker took her discontent with the place and some of the people there to a scathing new level. In her case, it was less to do with feeling that she was squandering her talent—since she believed she didn't have any—and more to do with the level of interference in her work. She was not used to being told what to do. Her last job working "for" somebody, at *Vanity Fair*, had seen her fired. From then on she had been freelance, able to do and say what she liked, achieving success that led to her becoming a national literary celebrity. But out in Hollywood, she soon observed that, as a writer, very few people cared what she thought. Buying the cachet of her name was key, less so the contents of her mind. But even worse than that, *everybody* thought they were a writer: the directors, the producers, the actors. "Everybody wrote. I never saw such a thing. The nice man at the gates would write. The producer would write—that was much worse. But everybody wrote."[2] She complained that you were simply never left alone to write a film. Somebody somewhere would interfere. Often what Parker did write went uncredited, or what she did not write was attributed to her. The whole process seemed to her a mess, with way too much unnecessary fiddling: "I tell you; nobody can do anything alone. You are given a script that eight people have written from a novel four people have written." But that wasn't all—the interference continued at every stage. "You then, they say, write dialogue. What a curious word. Well, you know you can't dialogue without changing scenes. While you are doing it, eight people back of you are writing beyond you. Nobody is allowed to do anything alone. I think that's most of the trouble with the movies."[3]

Parker's friend Donald Ogden Stewart, who was also working in Hollywood, noticed that there were certain things to learn as a screenwriter. It was better to hold off writing until shooting had started, because it was always the third or fourth writer who got credited. Subterfuge was not beneath some, either. Deliberately messing up the original writer's script increased the chances of a later writer getting their own version accepted. It didn't do to work too fast. Executives thought that if something was produced quickly, it couldn't possibly be any good, so taking three or four months on a job impressed studio bosses much more than anything they perceived as being churned out. Finally, Stewart understood that you had to accept there would be mysterious credits; family members of studio executives or people who had been kept on the payroll might be listed as a cowriter despite never having been near the project.

This disregard for intellectual property ownership had always been a standard feature of Hollywood, but when Parker returned there in 1934, new Hollywood writers wanted their film work treated like any other form of writing and seen as belonging to the author. This lack of accreditation went hand in hand with other long-standing unsatisfactory features: no minimum wage; no minimum periods of employment; material scrapped, passed on, rewritten, or attributed to somebody else. Ian Hamilton notes that if a writer's work "got made into a profitable film, the writer took no share of the profits. The credit system worked to the whim of the employer."[4] This simmering dissatisfaction was the working environment that Parker entered, for although she was highly paid, she could see many were not.

But immediately upon her return, she was greeted with the front page of the *Los Angeles Times* calling her "the most dangerous woman in the country" and introducing Alan Campbell as her bridegroom who had enjoyed that title "for about ten months" (it had been three): "I'm sure he has enjoyed it as there's a the-world-is-mine air about him."[5] Their first task was to find somewhere to live. After a brief spell staying in the house of her publisher, George Oppenheimer, who had moved there the previous year to work as a screenwriter, Parker and Campbell moved into the only Hollywood place that anyone from New

York moved into—the infamous, the outrageous, the preposterous Garden of Allah.

The history of this place is worthy of a melodramatic movie of its own. In 1918, the highest-paid actress in Hollywood, the Russian-born Alla Nazimova, bought a mansion and three and a half acres of land at 8152 Sunset Boulevard. Having made her name in silent films, she decided that a splendid house was required to befit her status as star of the town. She remodeled the main villa, built a swimming pool, planted exotic bushes and trees, and renamed her new home the Garden of Alla (no *h*). Although Nazimova was married, this seemed to be a nominal setup to disguise the fact that she was a lesbian, or certainly bisexual. Her home became the center of all things happening in Hollywood— wild parties, affairs, and literary salons comprising a collection of intellectuals, writers, and actors. Since by 1918 she was approaching middle age, Nazimova realized that her time as a leading lady was limited. As an alternative, she became keen to produce and direct movies. Unfortunately, her skills as a producer did not match those of her acting, and she began to invest much of her fortune in projects of her own that ultimately cost more money than they generated. As a result, by the mid-1920s she was in financial trouble. A couple of outside investors suggested that she turn her mansion into a residential hotel and add twenty-five bungalows to the grounds so they could be rented out to ensure a steady income. Nazimova poured the rest of her savings into the renovation and left Hollywood while the work was undertaken. Sadly, too, her investors saw the renovations completed and then left Hollywood with the rest of Nazimova's savings.

Although on January 9, 1927, the Garden of Alla opened with a wild eighteen-hour party and a band of trombonists playing in the pool, by 1928 Nazimova's finances had not recovered. She sold her shares and retained a home for life in one of the bungalows, and the new owners changed the name to the Garden of Allah (now with an *h*, much to Nazimova's disapproval). It became *the* place to stay. In fact, the gossip columnist Sheilah Graham, who lived there briefly while having an affair with F. Scott Fitzgerald, noted, "The famed celebrities who lived there are the supporting players although very important to the story."[6] This is perhaps because the Garden of Allah bore witness to what the writer Martin Turnbull described as the Golden Age of Hollywood. He notes that it opened just prior to the advent of the talkies and eventually closed in 1959 at the end of the Hollywood studio era.[7] Within that thirty-two-year period it witnessed murder, drunkenness, robbery, despair, divorce, orgies, suicides, fights, pranks, games, and if tales are to be believed, an awful lot of naked swimming.[8] It was, in fact, the precursor to a hotel directly across the road that would soon develop a similar reputation of its own: the Chateau Marmont.

If Dorothy Parker was going to live anywhere upon her return to Hollywood, of course it was going to be the Garden of Allah. Partly because that's where everybody went to live who was in transit, but mostly because it was where her partner in crime Robert Benchley stayed. Indeed, not just Benchley, but many of her old acquaintances from New York. So many that Sheilah Graham said, "The Garden of Allah was the Algonquin Round Table gone west and childish."[9] Benchley's bungalow was usually the center of activities. Having left his wife and children back east in the suburbs, he started parties every night at cocktail hour, when word would spread around the gardens that Benchley's bar was open for business. Everybody who knew him would turn up, as well as many who didn't. The mansion house was mostly deserted, with a dreary décor, a dingy restaurant, and terrible food. Immediately across the parking lot was the famous Schwab's.[10] Any liquor, sandwiches, or snacks could be delivered from there at any time of day or night. The Garden of Allah also had Ben the Bellboy, who would supply whatever was needed—alcohol, girls, food. He made it his business to know everything about everyone. One evening when Parker asked him to go to Schwab's to bring back some scotch, he replied, "But you have some. There's scotch in your underwear drawer."[11] Invitations to afternoon "tea" comprised dry martinis served from a glass teapot, and "most of the time it was not necessary to leave the Garden of Allah to find entertainment."[12]

Dorothy Parker and Alan Campbell moved into a bungalow near the pool and immediately entered into the spirit of life there. Parker was usually the first at Benchley's for cocktails, and she would lead "the Game," which featured convoluted rules about wordplay, and often saw Benchley crawling about on his knees. The bungalows were so close together that once a party started, everybody knew about it. But worse than that, the bungalow walls were so flimsy that everybody could hear everyone else's conversations. A story that made the rounds was that one night Robert Benchley, half-asleep, got out of bed to get a glass of water at the request of his bed companion. It was only when he returned to an empty room that he realized he had heard the woman in the bungalow next door.

One reason that the Garden of Allah was so perfect for Dorothy Parker, the ultimate observer of life, was that anything could happen, and nobody blinked an eye. Sheilah Graham described how, throughout history, it was so absurd there, people could be themselves. Whether Ernest Hemingway was giving an impassioned political speech, or the Fitzgeralds were raging drunk, or men in white from the local asylum came to take people away in a van, "no one paid any mind."[13] When a married Humphrey Bogart moved in with Lauren Bacall, this resulted in much entertainment. His wife, Mayo, would turn up and storm into his bungalow, shortly followed by the sound of crashing furniture and flying bottles, with Bacall running out the back door, and Bogart running out the front pursued by his irate wife brandishing a kitchen knife. Orson Welles, whom Parker would become friendly with over the coming years, was living in a bungalow with two other writers trying to update the Lord's Prayer, which he wanted to adapt into a movie. When he was told he shouldn't do that because it was God's word, Welles roared, "Don't tell me about God's word. I am God!"[14] Other residents over the years included Greta Garbo, Katharine Hepburn, David Niven, Errol Flynn, Lillian Hellman, Ginger Rogers (with her mother), and Gary Cooper. It had, quite simply, according to Dorothy Parker, "a kind of superb idiocy."[15] No one received any special treatment, and Parker recalled one day strolling the grounds with Benchley (almost certainly moaning about Hollywood) when they came across Frank Sinatra surrounded by "yelping girls."

Benchley casually nodded at Sinatra and said, "What you up to these days, Frank?"[16]

Parker herself was an object of interest for other residents living in and around the Garden of Allah. Sheilah Graham studied her with intensity, and a slight wariness. Being friends with Parker, she claimed, was like living on a volcano. She was "the most unpredictable woman I ever met."[17] Graham's descriptions bring Parker vividly to life, depicting her round smudges of black, doleful eyes, slightly sticky-looking bangs, and unusual combination of clothes—tennis shoes with black stockings, skirt, and blouse. She was like "a tired Renoir."[18] Most of Graham's caution came from Parker's habit of being extremely nice to somebody's face, then eviscerating them the moment they left the room, or indeed sometimes while they were still in it. The writer Wyatt Cooper recalled witnessing Parker at her best (worst?) when he observed an unfortunate-looking young man espousing his Hollywood dreams to Parker, who replied sweetly, "Oh, they've been *searching* for a new Cary Grant."[19] It was one of the many paradoxes of Parker, who managed to be both sentimental and brutal. One moment she would be singing songs popular in Manhattan, such as "I'll Get By," and openly weeping, the next she would be rude, ignore people, and deliberately hurt them.[20] With some perception, Graham wrote, "I realize that she was a very unhappy woman. She inhabited a vale of tears, and the only way she could live with herself was to murder everyone else with her biting words."[21] Parker was, according to the Hollywood biographer Fred Lawrence Guiles, always invited to parties out of fear of what she might say about a hostess who excluded her.

But then when she attended, she could be unkind and ungrateful. Graham witnessed this at one Garden of Allah gathering where the hostess had been cooking for days in preparation. Parker, who had been holding a tray of hors d'oeuvres, greeted a friend by saying, "Will you hold this shit for me?" Yet Parker also directed this level of nastiness at her own parties, often welcoming guests with, "It's so nice of you to come, isn't this a lot of shit?"[22] It is difficult to know whether it is better or worse that however rude Parker was to other people she was equally as hard on herself.

Another onlooker at this time was the screenwriter Anita Loos.[23] Unfortunately, she'd heard the rude things Parker had said about her (Parker dismissed Loos—"She's all out to improve herself"),[24] so her observations are somewhat colored by this. But Loos provided an evocative portrayal of how different Hollywood was in the 1930s compared to Parker's first visit in the late twenties: "Hollywood may have been uncouth, but from being the remote outpost it was at the beginning, it was now in the mainstream of life."[25] Loos observed the wild parties and offered some Parkeresque takes on the celebrities around town and at the Garden of Allah. She liked the Fitzgeralds well enough when they were sober, but this was all too seldom. "Zelda had a habit of stripping in public . . . of which the rule is, 'If you've got it, flaunt it.' But to flaunt something you haven't got can be a mistake." There was no doubt in Loos's mind that Zelda "should have kept her bosom strictly under wraps."[26] Poor Zelda had already caught the critical eye of Dorothy Parker a few years earlier and was considered an ordinary, gum-chewing

Kewpie doll: "She was very blonde with a candy box face and a little bow mouth, very much on a small scale and there was something petulant about her." It would seem sisterhood wasn't high up on the agenda in the Garden of Allah.

For all Loos's descriptions of Hollywood being in the mainstream of life, the Garden of Allah was still surrounded by dirt roads when Parker and Campbell moved in. Situated right on the boundary of Hollywood and the unincorporated section that would become West Hollywood, the Garden was perfectly placed to fall between the cracks of policing. Those not-quite-in-one-place-or-another estates were often overlooked by the city police, which, given what went on there, is just as well. It being advertised as "California's Finest Summer Hotel in Hollywood" rather glossed over the Garden's debauchery and copious amounts of illegal activity. Yet despite its relatively remote location, the area was still busy enough to have a cab rank outside Schwab's and enough traffic to scare Robert Benchley. If he wanted to cross the road to get dinner, he would take a taxi and make it turn around to drop him off on the other side.

Life was not all parties and drinking games, though. Parker and Campbell had moved to Hollywood to write, and in late 1934 they began immediately working on the dialogue for two films, *Here Is My Heart* and *One Hour Late*. Both were suited for Parker's wit since they were comedies. *Here Is My Heart* starred Bing Crosby as a famous singer who pretends to be a penniless waiter to win the woman of his dreams. She just happens to be a European princess. As Parker and Campbell got to work on the script, she wrote to Alex Woollcott wryly that they had been "summoned to labor" on the story but Paramount was not quite sure whether the male lead would be Tullio Carminati or Bing Crosby, so they were instructed to "just sort of write it with both of them in mind."[27] On December 22, the *New York Times* reviewed the film, describing it as bright and funny entertainment, so presumably Parker had injected some life into the screenplay, though both she and Campbell went uncredited for their efforts.

It seems likely that in the same letter to Woollcott, Parker also mentioned their work on what would become *One Hour Late*. The film, set over a twenty-four-hour period, starred Joe Morrison and Helen Twelvetrees in a farce about a romance that goes sour due to a series of misunderstandings. The farce appeared to continue off-screen too. Parker described the film as a "little opera." She explained that it had begun life as *Twenty-two Hours by Air* but had been lying around the studio for so long it was now called *Eleven Hours by Air*. "By the time we are done, the title is to be, I believe, 'Stay Where You Are.'"[28]

From their large joint office in the Paramount building, Parker and Campbell settled into a way of collaborating that was extremely effective. Professional photos from the time show them working closely together. Parker, no longer in tennis shoes, was always impeccably dressed and accessorized for the press. Campbell, as ever, was smartly turned out and movie-star handsome. Even if the scripts they had received so far were light, frothy musicals, they both took their work seriously. Campbell was the driving force keeping Parker on track in his organized, dedicated, and caring manner. He was keen to learn the trade and became skilled at constructing and pulling a scene together. Parker was unable to do this, but her strength lay in adding dialogue and wit. She would sit in the corner of the office, somewhat improbably knitting, and respond to Campbell's requests of "Okay, so what does he say next?" She would then speak the dialogue while Campbell typed her answers. What this process created was well-constructed and snappy screenplays. She was not, however, above trying to insert some of her favorite colorful words into the script. A screenwriter in the office next door would hear Campbell reading aloud what he had just typed, asking Parker for contributions, followed by a shocked "Dottie! If you use that word once more, I'm walking out of this office and never coming back!"[29]

When the script meetings included larger numbers of people, observers were never quite sure to what extent Parker was listening. Equally, her demeanor could be somewhat unexpected. Far from the wisecracking New Yorker, she would turn up, knitting bag under her arm, glasses on the end of her nose, and proceed to clack away, creating from her needles "a gray artifact seven feet long that looked like a stair runner."[30] This seemed a surprisingly domestic side to Parker that would increasingly develop over the coming years. S. J. Perelman, who would collaborate with Parker and Campbell in 1938, recalled that everyone in the meetings wanted to get her attention and was keen to meet with her approval, but she appeared to be completely zoned out in relation to what was going on around her. In one meeting, the producer Hunt Stromberg was espousing his ideas and views and kept glancing at Parker to see if she was listening. She had her head down, seemingly at work on her stair runner creation. To gain her attention, Stromberg resorted to cajoling her in a jolly voice, "I'd say we were making pretty good progress on the story, eh, Dorothy?" Perelman observed that Parker looked up, "plainly retrieving her attention from very far away, and replied with a hint of breathlessness, 'Oh I <u>do</u> think it is altogether marvelous, don't you?'"[31] Perhaps what is more interesting about this story is how Parker had created a personality from her own insecurity that not only intimidated much more powerful men but also made them desperate for her approval. It is not clear whether she realized this strength she wielded, and she was always one to underplay her achievements, but it was a feature that occurred again and again.

There is no doubt that Parker hated the work she was doing, and she was aware it prevented her from concentrating on what she might have regarded as her real writing. She hated screenwriting at the time, and she hated it looking back. In 1966, thirty-two years after she had begun her life out west with Campbell, she recalled in a radio interview, "I stopped writing short stories because I went to Hollywood to make some money, a very odd reason for going . . . [voice fades] . . . and I was there for a long time. Alan and I would go out and wrote together. We both hated Hollywood. I more than he did."[32] Yet there is a sense in which Parker is not being entirely honest here, because there *were* aspects of Hollywood she did like. She may have needed regular breaks from it, but her work there brought her wealth, a luxurious lifestyle, and friends with similar political sensibilities. Not long after arriving she admitted this to Woollcott, writing, "Aside from the work, which I hate like holy water, I love it here."[33] She lists her likes as better weather (having previously disliked the heat in 1929) and being able to own a large house with a big garden, and suddenly she found everywhere pretty to look at (having previously disliked all the trees and vegetation). She didn't like some of the people— "any number of poops," apparently—but admitted this was true of people in New York, too, and that in fact in Hollywood, "there are some nice people here—who would be anywhere, of course . . . James Cagney is, I should say, the best person here, or, for that matter, just about anywhere."[34]

All in all, life was as good as it got for Dorothy Parker. She was married to a man she adored, who adored her in return; she was making enough money to clear her debts; and she had plenty of work offers. With the ten-week contract fulfilled and a new one signed, in 1935, Parker and Campbell moved from the Garden of Allah into a large rented house at 520 North Canon Drive, situated just behind the famous Beverly Hills sign. A red-brick path ran up to the front door, which was surrounded by an ostentatious four-column portico. Four bedrooms were spread across a one-story L shape. The living area was open plan and spacious, with several glass doors opening onto a garden that wrapped around a large paved area containing a pool. Even today, the house is listed as perfect for entertaining, and back then Parker threw a huge housewarming party, to which a hundred people were invited but three hundred showed up. Her subsequent hangover was so epic, she declared it could easily be referred to as "we."[35] This would be the first of two house moves that year, continuing the usual dizzying pattern of Parker being unable to stay in one place for very long.

The garden was soon filled with an increasing number of dogs. Along with the two that had traveled from Denver, Wolf and Cora, both Bedlington terriers, Parker added a four-month-old dachshund named Fraulein—"pure enchantment"—and a mixed-breed dog called Scrambles, "the one dog in the world you couldn't love."[36] The presence of these four hounds made the purchase of plush white carpets throughout seem a bad idea, but practicality was never at the top of Parker's mind. Earning large amounts of money each week, she saw no reason not to make the most of it. Her expenditure was extraordinary. She ordered two $35 hats from John Fredrichs and an $86.36 hat in the same week from Bullocks Wilshire, spent $628.45 on handmade lingerie from New York, and ordered $80.03 worth of perfume from Cyclax of London. The hats of the French-born American milliner Lilly Daché tempted Parker into spending a further $176.39. Having listed these extravagant purchases, it is puzzling that her biographer John Keats then ponders, "One wonders how she succeeded in doing it, but she did: her bank account was frequently overdrawn."[37] Spending money at that rate along with rent, travel, entertainment, parties, and repaying debts, it seems quite easy to see how Parker might end up overstretching herself yet again. And she realized the cycle that this could create—the more you earned, the more you spent, the more you wanted: "But they say, you see there's something about that money, even though it is money, you get a little more, and you get a little more. You see, when you're broke, you're broke, but you get a little money then you want a little more money, and more, and so on."[38]

Expensive living and a beautiful Beverly Hills home could not stop Parker from becoming ill, however. In Denver she had developed a form of aggravated hay fever that often afflicted those from the East moving to a dry environment. "God's own torment," Parker wrote to Woollcott. Having decided she had tuberculosis, she "took to reclining on couches in profile and addressing the Wolf as Flush." It wasn't TB, of course ("End of profoundly unmoving autobiography," concluded Parker).[39] But what this attack of hay fever seemed to create was ongoing allergy complications that eventually resulted in her developing a case of hideous-sounding intestinal hives. She spent a week in Good Samaritan Hospital on Wilshire Boulevard, where she was subjected to a series of tests, yet the hives remained idiopathic. This explanation was met with scorn from Parker: "The doctor says something must be causing it; is it any wonder I have all the confidence in the world in him?"[40] She was equally unimpressed with the two Canadian nurses who tended to her. One day Parker was doing a crossword puzzle and put it aside to sleep. When she awoke from her nap, one nurse told her she'd finished the crossword. The other nurse never failed to enter the room without asking, "How are our little hivies?" Unsurprisingly, Parker declared, "My state is now such that I not only hate all trained nurses, but all Canadians."[41] Some ease was to be gained from various drug treatments, namely shots of adrenaline, which Parker claimed she'd had in such vast quantities that it left her feeling like Dr. Cornish's dog.[42]

Despite these health struggles, toward the end of 1934 and into 1935, Parker became increasingly involved in various political campaigns in Hollywood. Since her 1927 arrest in Boston at the Sacco-Vanzetti protest march, Parker had stayed committed to various left-wing causes, but in a rather muted fashion. Her move to Hollywood saw her begin to mix in circles with other writers and actors who were much more radical than she. Hemingway, whom she had met in Europe and admired immensely, appeared from time to time in Hollywood advocating for various causes. She also reacquainted herself with the detective fiction writer and self-proclaimed communist Dashiell Hammett, whom she had briefly met in Manhattan, as well as his partner, Lillian Hellman.[43] Although Hammett couldn't stand Parker, Hellman became a friendly foe. She and Parker jostled and jibed, but there seemed a connection underneath it all. Certainly, they remained close until Parker's death in 1967, when Hellman initially took control of Parker's estate. Other radicals in her orbit were her old Round Table friend Donald Ogden Stewart, Orson Welles, and the famed Hollywood star Fredric March and his actor-wife, Florence Eldridge. All these people would play a part in Parker's politicization that began to unfold seriously from 1934 on.

Various uncredited sources claim that in 1934 Parker declared herself a communist, but there is no record of her saying this, and in later years when she was questioned about it, formally and informally, she stated this was not true. There seems little reason for her to lie, given that she was open and fearless about most things, whether it made her popular or not. There was some speculation both from friends at the time and in later years by biographers that Parker's commitment to left-wing causes came from her own guilt about how much money she was making. The only way she could assuage her conscience was to fight on behalf of those less well-off. This seems to do a disservice to Parker's lifelong dedication to issues of social injustice. This began as a child, when she saw servants shoveling snow off the front steps of the family home, through to her campaigning on behalf of Sacco and Vanzetti during a not particularly wealthy period in her life. It is not difficult to imagine Parker being passionate about certain ideologies because she actually *believed* them, because she could feel empathy and concern for those outside her circle. What is difficult is when Parker's commitment was inconsistent. As in so many other areas, in this she was a paradox. She campaigned on behalf of those living in poverty or for civil rights, but she saw no problem having Black servants in her house. Just as she would be hugely sentimental about her dogs and animal abuse, she would step out wearing a fox stole (with the head still attached). It was almost as if Parker was so myopic about those issues that concerned her, she did not consider how they connected to a much bigger picture or, perhaps worse still, to her own behavior. The cultural context is important too. Parker was operating at a time when it was fairly uncomfortable, and dangerous, to be seen as "too" left-wing in Hollywood. She was also operating in an institutionally racist country. Although it may be said that her activism was more advanced than most people's, it was far from perfect. What is clear is that when Parker dedicated herself to a cause, she did so sincerely and wholeheartedly. Often, she almost bankrupted herself giving donations, and she lost work because of her outspoken political allegiances.

One of the first high-profile events that Parker and Campbell hosted in Hollywood was a fundraising party. In their second house move of 1935, they had bought a place at 914 North Roxbury Drive that was large enough for them to host a significant-size political affair. Built in 1923 just off Sunset Boulevard, the house was southern style, set on half an acre with a pool. They bought a Picasso gouache, *Pulcinella and Harlequin*, for one of the walls and parked a new Packard convertible phaeton in the driveway. It was in these surroundings that a fundraiser was held in support of the Scottsboro Boys, nine African American teenagers between the ages of thirteen and nineteen who had been accused of raping two white women in Alabama. Parker and Campbell threw a huge buffet dinner for some of their wealthiest friends to highlight the plight of the boys, who had been convicted of rape despite no medical evidence to support this (indeed, one of the women would later recant her accusations). Eight of the boys had been sentenced to death by an all-white jury and an appeal was being launched with the help of the NAACP and the Communist Party USA. Parker invited friends and colleagues including Donald Ogden Stewart, Fredric March and Florence Eldridge, and the actor Lionel Stander. With entertainment by the tap dancer and actor Bill "Bojangles" Robinson, the event raised several thousand dollars for the Scottsboro appeal fund.[44] Whatever her shortcomings could be, Dorothy Parker certainly had some understanding of her white privilege, and used it in the most helpful way she could think of—donating money and hosting fundraisers.

Oddly, despite her increasing engagement with political activism, the press seemed keen to preserve Parker as a fluffy wisecracker. In February 1935, despite everything else going on in her life, the Washington *Evening Star* ran an article titled "The 'WOLF' at Dorothy Parker's Door." Far from another piece about Parker's hatred of writing and mounting debts, this was a much more literal piece—the wolf at her door was her dog. Accompanied by a cute photograph of her two dogs Wolf and Cora, the article discussed how Parker had come to own the dogs. Wolf was a Bedlington terrier and chosen because the breed was trained to root up gardens and catch otters, "and my New York apartment was simply infested with otters."[45] Cora had come from overseas and demanded to be adopted. What is curious about this article is why it appeared at this time. Working in Hollywood on scripts and engaging in left-wing activism seemed not what the national press were after when it came to Dorothy Parker. It was almost as if the serious, thinking, political side of a woman was best quietly ignored. A search of the *New York Times* archives from 1935 shows there was not one article published about her that year aside from one with a passing reference to an introduction she wrote for Arthur Kober's *Thunder Over the Bronx* (a collection of witty sketches about the exploits of a husband-hunting character named Bella Gross). The review quotes Parker's appreciative introduction, but other than this brief mention, Parker's life and work do not feature in the paper at all. Part of this could well be that after working six days a week in the studio offices, Parker, who was naturally quite lazy anyway, had no intention of spending her Sundays working on verse or stories. In 1935 she published only one poem, "Autumn Valentine," about the fickle forgetfulness of a broken heart.

All her energy in 1935 seemed to be poured into film work. Along with Campbell she contributed to at least four films that year, despite all their work remaining uncredited. The scope of these is interesting because what becomes apparent when looking at Parker's work in Hollywood is that, as with everything else, she is the most unreliable narrator regarding her achievements there. She dismissed all her films as lighthearted fluff. The first two years she did indeed seem to be put to work on musical comedies and screwball romances. Yet tracking her film work and the reception it received, even if she didn't admit it, Parker really began to hone her screenwriting talent throughout 1935, and it would certainly come into its own the following year.

The films that we know she worked on in 1935 began with *Mary Burns, Fugitive*—in which Sylvia Sidney played a small-town coffee shop owner who haplessly falls for a gangster (Alan Baxter) and becomes engaged in a plot with the police to capture him. However improbable this melodrama sounds, it is significant that reviewers began to pick up that there was something different about this film. For starters, the gangster role was more nuanced. No snarling, aggressive uber-masculine criminals, but rather a cold, twitchy, icily detached villain with a real hatred for the world. Despite being a film about gangsters, Mary Burns is central to the plot, with the male characters circling around and reacting to her. Of course, when a writer goes uncredited, it is mere guesswork and speculation what role they may have played in the script and story development, but it is worth noting that in years to come Parker explained that one of her jobs was to make female roles more prominent. There is also much fun to be had trying to spot Parkerisms in the uncredited films for which she wrote. Is there perhaps a whiff of Parker wit when Mary Burns is told of the joy her soothing voice brings to an invalid, "You don't know what a relief it is to hear a woman that doesn't sound like morning in the barnyard!"

The next film, *Hands Across the Table*, was a screwball comedy starring Carole Lombard and Fred MacMurray. Lombard's character, a cynical gold digger named Regi Allen, wants to find a rich husband, setting the scene for the main theme of the film—should one marry for love or money? MacMurray plays an impoverished playboy, Theodore Drew, who, like Regi, wants to marry into a fortune. In many ways, this was the perfect escapist film for Depression-era America—the dream of prosperity just around the corner, the hope that life is about to change, that hardship is soon to be ended. However, plans go awry when, predictably, Regi and Theodore fall for each other and begin to consider that just maybe there is more to life than money. Once again certain features of this film caught the critics' eyes. To begin with, the charm and charisma of the two leads made it a delight to watch, but praise was heaped on the writing, which Andre Sennwald in the *New York Times* described as "uproariously funny," and a "brilliant screenplay" that contained "some of the best dialogue that has come out of Hollywood in many months."[46] Again, we cannot know for certain that Parker was responsible for this, but certainly a pattern was forming with the films she worked on, even while she remained uncredited.

The final two films that saw a Parker-Campbell contribution in 1935 were *The Big Broadcast of 1936* and *Paris in Spring*. Their involvement in the latter seemed much slighter, with Parker working on the treatment rather than on the screenplay or dialogue. Reviews for this musical comedy set in Paris were muted. But Parker's contribution to *The Big Broadcast of 1936* was much more significant. She wrote the lyrics to the song "I Wished on the Moon" (music by Ralph Rainger), which was performed by Bing Crosby. A beautifully gentle melancholy infuses the song, which contains a wistful chorus about wishing on the moon during long nights, with shadows in the air, stars, softening skies, and yearning for a loved one. The song ends with the hopeful words "I wished on the moon / Wished on the moon / For you." Over the years this song would be performed many times, by singers such as Ella Fitzgerald and Frank Sinatra. But perhaps its most poignant recording was made the same year as the film by Billie Holiday, whose voice seemed to perfectly suit the mournful beauty of Parker's lyrics.[47]

These years were a busy and fruitful time for Parker. Although she claimed to hate the work, her screenwriting was gaining attention, and outside of the studio she was partying with big Hollywood names, and she even took to playing golf in her spare time. But these years also marked a broadening of Parker's politics as she found herself being drawn not only into world politics but studio politics too. The previous year she had been appalled to see the Hollywood system turn its power against the

Democratic candidate running for governor of California. Over the years the novelist and socialist Upton Sinclair had sold two of his books to Hollywood but had been held at arm's length by the industry, regarded as way too Bolshevik for their liking. Deciding to run for governor, he based his campaign on the slogan "End Poverty in California" (EPIC). This doesn't seem especially radical, but some of his other proposals sent chills through Hollywood executives. His manifesto stated that his aims were to tax the film industry, subject studios to certain federal regulations, and rent out empty studios so unemployed actors could make films of their own. The whole situation was described as "state moviemaking—with a Communist screenwriter in control."[48] Studios set up fundraising stations in their offices for the Republican candidate, Frank Merriam. Employees were expected to donate with an unspoken threat that if they didn't, their contracts would not be renewed. Harry Cohn, who ran Columbia, set up a Stop Sinclair campaign, threatened staff with blacklisting if they didn't contribute, and even sacked those who refused. The William Hearst–owned press joined forces and launched a huge smear campaign against Sinclair.[49] Referring to him as "the Bolshevik Beast," they claimed, somewhat wildly, that he would dynamite churches and "Sovietize California."[50] MGM filmed a documentary aimed at discrediting Sinclair. They interviewed his supposed supporters, who invariably had Russian accents and bleary eyes. (In contrast, those supporting Merriam were all well-dressed, sensible, and sweet old ladies.)

A group of writers and the loosely formed, embryonic Screen Writers Guild (SWG) began to hit back. Appalled at the studio intimidation and believing Sinclair deserved the right to a fair campaign, they began raising funds for him. Dorothy Parker, who had slowly become more involved in the plight of Hollywood writers, was disgusted at the abuse of power shown by the studios. It was just another example of how tenuous employment could be in Hollywood and how open to exploitation and bullying writers were if they didn't do what the studios demanded. She soon realized that a more concerted effort was needed to unionize. And this became even more urgent when Sinclair suffered a resounding defeat in the election. The actor Fredric March was furious, saying, "But it was a dirty trick! It was the damnedest unfair thing I've ever heard of."[51]

Although Dorothy Parker described her part in establishing the SWG as small, she was once again underplaying her achievements. Trying to protect the rights of workers and bring about screen credits for everyone who worked on a film was no small feat. Much energy was taken up over the ensuing years fighting the studios, which tried to scupper the SWG at every opportunity, refused to accept its legitimacy, and even at one stage set up their own organization to steal members away. But in 1935, the Wagner Act was passed into law. This was a labor relations act that allowed private employees the right to form unions, to engage in bargaining, and to undertake collective actions, such as strikes. The main goal was to try to correct the inequality of bargaining power between employers and employees. Not every profession was eligible, though, and the act did not apply to certain workers, such as domestics or agricultural employees. But the SWG worked hard to make sure writers were eligible—

a campaign that was ultimately successful. This did not come about easily, though, and Parker recalled the conflict she encountered being on the executive board of the SWG and grappling with the studios: "It was dreadful for quite a while . . . But we got in through the union law, and we did it as an active working guild. But you don't know the bleeding bones that came from it."[52]

It is odd, despite all this activism, that many of Parker's male contemporaries failed to take her seriously. Ever keen to ascribe her political beliefs to other motivations, they had a tendency to present her as somehow inauthentic. Her biographer Arthur F. Kinney confidently declared, "We can agree with Harold Clurman that, 'Her radicalism was not insincere [but] it was sentimental . . .'"[53] Furthermore, apparently she suffered from "despairing idealism" and "[w]hen in 1934, Dorothy claimed she was a Communist [*she didn't*], 'All this really meant,' according to Harold Clurman, 'was that she was sorry for the poor and wanted to help them and was sore at the rich who wouldn't.'"[54] While it may be fair to refer to Parker's sentimentalism, for she certainly had plenty of that, this rather overlooks something much more passionate going on in Parker's belief system. She was full of anger and hate, two qualities that in a male-dominated industry were not seen as appropriately ladylike. Having witnessed the brutality of injustice and the behavior of so many rich people, Parker claimed, "They did much in my life to send me back to the masses, to make me proud of being a worker, too . . . I saw these silly, dull, stuffy people, and they sent me shunting. It is not noble that hatred sends you from one side to the other;

but I say again, it is not unique."[55] It is difficult to know what else Parker would have needed to do to be taken seriously by some of her contemporaries—over the years she had been arrested and fined, engaged in fundraising campaigns and protests, taken on the studios, formed committees and guilds, and unionized workers. But still she was "sentimental." Still newspapers were writing about her dogs rather than her activism. Perhaps if she had been a man it would have been different.

As changes began to take place in Hollywood, even bigger events were looming around the world. Europe entered a period of political turmoil that saw fascism rise in Germany and civil war break out in Spain between the left-wing Republicans and the Nationalists under General Franco. It was seen by many as a fight between communism and fascism. Dorothy Parker was soon to become involved in activism against both these events unfolding in Europe, and this involvement brought her to the attention of the FBI.

But back in Hollywood, as if in response to global unease, for the first time in her life the restless, chaotic Parker was keen to put down roots. Chatting with her colleague S. J. Perelman and his wife, Laura, she discovered that they hated Hollywood as much as she and Alan. The Perelmans had made it bearable by buying a place in Bucks County, Pennsylvania, and periodically escaping there, a tactic that greatly appealed to Parker and Campbell. "We haven't got any roots, Alan . . . you can't put down roots in Beverly Hills . . . Roots, roots . . ." soon became Parker's refrain.[56] In a scenario that could only have happened to Parker, Perelman introduced her to an unofficial Realtor, Jack

Boyle, who was tasked with finding Parker and Campbell a home in Bucks County. In his previous New York–based life, Boyle had specialized in stealing furs from large department stores by locking himself in the toilets overnight and then walking out the next morning wearing the pilfered coats. He gave any money he made away to the poor, regarding himself as a "philosophical anarchist."[57] In a move that surprised no one, he and Parker hit it off immediately. Boyle was employed to find a suitable home for her to put down roots.

In the meantime, reviews started to appear that summer of the first credited films Parker and Campbell had worked on that year. In April, *The Moon's Our Home* was greeted warmly by critics. Starring Henry Fonda as a novelist and Margaret Sullavan as an actress, the film follows the couple as they date and marry without knowing of each other's fame. The added edge here is that Fonda and Sullavan had previously been married but had divorced three years earlier. The film explores the quirks of marriage and various comedic episodes relating to it. As the newly married couple get to know each other on their honeymoon, the dialogue becomes sparky with insults and arguments, something that surely played to Parker's strengths. It was regarded as a light, charming comedy, and once again Parker's work was praised. The novelist Graham Greene, writing in the *Spectator*, singled out her written contribution and comedic talent.[58]

In July, reviews appeared of *Suzy*, a film that saw the only on-screen pairing of Jean Harlow and Cary Grant. Harlow plays Suzy Trent, a showgirl who believes that a German spy has killed her new husband, Terry Moore (Franchot Tone). Fleeing to Paris, she meets and marries a World War I pilot, Andre Charville (Grant), who introduces her to a more carefree way of life. Lo and behold, Suzy's first husband eventually turns up alive and well and happens to be Charville's best friend. Improbable, yes, but some of the dialogue is pure Parker:

TERRY MOORE: Do you like onions?

SUZY TRENT: Onions for two are delicious. For one they're a terrible hazard.

ANDRE CHARVILLE: Come on. We've got a lot to do. I've got to drink to you. You've got to drink to me. And we've both got to drink to each other. So what do you say? Shall we start?

SUZY TRENT: At your service, Monsieur.

Reviews for the film were a little sniffy. The *New York Times* found it somewhat lacking and felt that writers like Parker had backed away from the script rather than tackling it head-on. The reviewer Frank S. Nugent, however, was fully appreciative of the "shapely" Jean Harlow.[59] Sadly, Harlow's life and career would soon be over due to a misdiagnosed illness, and the following year she was dead, aged only twenty-six, from kidney failure.

On August 24, the *New York Times* ran a tongue-in-cheek headline, "Dorothy Parker, Farmer," reporting that Parker and Campbell had purchased a 111-acre homestead in Tinicum, near

Doylestown, Pennsylvania. Described as a colonial farmhouse of native fieldstone and featuring fourteen rooms and three fireplaces, it overlooked the Delaware River and mountains surrounding the borough of Netcong, New Jersey. Jack Boyle, stealer of fur coats, had finally found them a home, Fox House, an old farmstead with two lateral wings. Three enormous Norwegian maple trees shaded the house from the north side, and to its south lay an apple orchard. There was a stone barn and a long driveway ensuring privacy, and all for $4,500, which was less than a month's salary for Parker and Campbell. The downside, as Perelman reported, was that "the interior of the house was in an appalling state."[60] It had rotting floors, plaster falling off the ceilings, crumbling woodwork, and was inhabited by a Lithuanian couple raising chickens, who refused to move out until their latest batch of eggs had hatched from the indoor incubators. Since the couple had been living there rent-free, they were understandably reluctant to move out at all and pulled various stunts to deter the sale from going through, including laying the body of a moldering groundhog across the threshold of the front door. "In case the need ever comes up in your life, I present you with this, as a good system to keep out prospective buyers," wrote Parker in a piece for *House & Garden* called "Destructive Decoration."[61] Not to be deterred, Parker and Campbell employed an architect to renovate the house, though they soon fell out with him and would eventually take over restoring the house themselves. Staying in the nearby Water Wheel Tavern to oversee alterations, Alan Campbell was keen to tell anyone who would listen, "Don't they realize it's costing

Dottie and me seven hundred and fifty dollars a week to stay away from Hollywood?"[62]

As work continued to make the house habitable, more Parker-Campbell films were due to be released. In September, *Three Married Men* starring Lynne Overman and William Frawley met with strong reviews. Based on the story of two sparring families who meet at the wedding of their son and daughter, the film features dialogue laced with witty repartee and insults. *Variety* felt the film was lifted above the predictable run-of-the-mill comedy and much of that was down to the writing of Parker and Campbell, which was described as "elegant" and "sparkling."[63] That same month *Lady Be Careful* was released, featuring Lew Ayres and Mary Carlisle. The plot centered around the antics of American sailors, pre–World War II, during shore leave. Parker had been asked to rewrite this film to comply with the Hays Code. One scene had been written showing a sailor betting he would make it with a girl—this was seen as too dirty, and Parker was expected to take sex out of the film. Her mischievous solution to water down any raciness between sailors and their female conquests was to have the sailors hook up with each other, resulting in the studio reverting to the original story. "But would they accept our change, that triumph of ingenuity where the sailor just bets he will make [it with] another sailor? Oh, no. Sometimes I think they don't know <u>what</u> they want."[64] The lack of reviews in major newspapers suggests that this was a fairly low-key film, though in a short paragraph *Variety* referred to it as "amusing."[65]

On December 1, in New York, *Not So Deep as a Well* was published, a collection of Dorothy Parker's verse that, as always, was met with warmth. Henry Hazlitt reminded readers that "whatever her limitations, Dorothy Parker is still one of our foremost practitioners of light verse. Her wit is authentic, and some of her work is surprisingly viable."[66] Louis Kronenberger went even further and claimed, "After ten years, Mrs. Parker strikes me as having achieved—as one so often puts it in the case of 'weightier' writers—a kind of historical significance."[67] He predicted, correctly as it happens, that Parker was a writer whose work would survive.

As 1936 drew to a close, Parker had much to be content about. Her career was going well, she was happily married, she had just bought a refuge from Hollywood, and her latest book was garnering positive reviews. Yet one thing happened toward the end of the year that outshone all these achievements. One thing that made the forty-three-year-old Parker ecstatically happy. She discovered she was pregnant.

CHAPTER 4

The Dreary Ivory Tower

. . . I am hung with graveyard flowers.
Let me be tonight arrayed
In the silver of the showers.[1]
—Dorothy Parker, "Rainy Night"

At forty-three, Dorothy Parker was understandably nervous about her pregnancy. Although privately ecstatic, the Parker-Campbells decided to keep the news quiet until after the first trimester. It does seem, however, that some friends had already leaked the news to the press. After the *New York Times* ran the announcement in December, the Hollywood gossip columnist Louella Parsons contacted Parker with a request for an interview and photographs. Making the front page of the *Los Angeles Times*, Alan Campbell reported that his wife was "ecstatic" about her pregnancy, and the journalist E. V. Durling noted that although Parker was forty-three ("and made no secret of it"), she looked about ten years younger.[2] Confirming that her child was due sometime in June, Parker had already begun knitting tiny sweaters and boots and colorful crib blankets, and started work on her pregnancy wardrobe. Although knitting needles had made an appearance in Hollywood meeting rooms, friends were amazed at how beautiful her needlework was. "The idea of Dorothy Parker being good at this sort of thing had never occurred to anyone . . ."[3] The general mood toward this new, sweeter Parker was one of incredulity and, it would seem, a certain unpleasant sneering. Her biographer Marion Meade, who interviewed some of Parker's "friends," recorded their cynicism and judgmental scorn. The screenwriter Frances Goodrich, who had known Parker in New York but was now working in Hollywood, told Meade, "When she knew she was pregnant, she called up Hedda Hopper and Louella Parsons to give them the scoop. In God's name! Dottie Parker announcing she's going to have a baby when she's forty-five or something, nature's last attempt. And knitting for the cameras!"[4] Parker was never one for publicity, and it seems yet again as though those who knew her were ascribing the worst-possible motives to her. Others believed she would grow bored with motherhood because she had no staying power. Or would dislike her child because, unlike her dogs, it would one day answer back. An especially nasty comment doubted that Parker would have anything in common with children "because they don't drink."[5] Jokes circulated that when the child was born it would need a strong cup of coffee to sober up from its in-utero diet.[6] If Dorothy Parker as mother was not a role many could see her in, she did not care. In long conversations with her Bucks County housekeeper, Mrs. Beer, she spoke of her wish to have six redheaded boys and how desperately she had always wanted children. Wearing a peasant blouse, dirndl, sombrero, and rubber gloves, she pottered around in her new garden planting and trimming flowers. It was a serene time of nest-building. Photographs in the local paper show Parker standing at her garden gate looking radiant and settled with Jack, the relatively new addition of a spotty Dalmatian, at her feet. For once it really seemed as though Parker might just get her happy ending.

Work progressed on Fox House, making each room habitable with a unique Parker-Campbell style. Ignoring other New York literati who had moved to the county and fetishized country living with traditional décor, Parker decided to go for something a little more contemporary, a little more colorful (in every sense of the word). She declared that the locals "found us vandals."[7] In the dining room they lined the deeply recessed historical windows with sheets of mirrors to reflect the trees in the apple orchard. According to an unrepentant Parker this was regarded as desecration: "'Those old windows,' they cried. 'Oh, how could you?' Well, we could and we did. And we love it."[8] A black marble dining table contrasted with a red rug, a flowery Mexican candelabra, and dizzyingly patterned wallpaper. Photographs show that the room had *a lot* going on. They painted the outside shutters a Mediterranean pink, hung strawberry wallpaper in the front hall, and lined bookshelves in a Paris green. The living room alone had nine different shades of red and two crimson wingback chairs. Parker wanted a pretty room, a bright room. A room in which people could look and feel their best; "Nobody glints and glows when sitting on a Pennsylvania Dutch bench beneath a reprint of an Audubon wild turkey."[9] The upstairs hall was papered with blueprints of the house and shellacked to the wall with a rich sheen. Tables and mantelpieces were painted with a gray marble effect, something invented by Parker by dipping a feather in a paint pot. Large vases and copper bowls were filled with flowers from the garden. Electricity was installed, a swimming pool built, and a five-room apartment constructed over the barn for the housekeeper's husband, Hiram Beer, and his family. He farmed the land while his wife helped Parker about the house. There was also a cook and an errand boy. Stonemasons built walls in the garden, areas were landscaped with fountains and flower beds, and plumbers, carpenters, and electricians all worked away for months shaping the house to Parker's liking. Though they had paid $4,500 for the property, by the time they had finished, the renovations had cost them close to $100,000. Weird, eclectic, and totally unique, not unlike Parker herself—her description of a cabinet built by Campbell seemed to sum up their new home: "It is quite Swedish and yet at the same time Mexican with a pronounced touch of Chinese . . . it's for our own place and nobody else has anything like it."[10]

Two other important rooms began to take shape—the nursery and Parker's writing area adjoining the porch where she and Campbell set up desks facing each other beneath a large window that looked down the expanse of their lawn. The walls were painted bright blue, and two emerald-green upholstered chairs were installed to help the couple with their collaborative work. To get a clear view of the New Jersey mountains beyond the garden, they cut down the Norwegian maple trees, much to the horror of their neighbors, who, according to Parker, shuddered and swooned. This view can be seen in a photograph taken for a Condé Nast publication, with Parker sitting at a small desk, cigarette in hand, wearing an apron and looking like she's thinking about typing. Campbell is on the adjoining porch, sitting in an armchair reading what looks to be a script. Beyond them are huge picture windows with a sweeping lawn, flower beds, and way down at the bottom of the garden, a bank of trees. It looks light, airy, and peaceful. At the very edge of the shot appears to be one of Parker's marble-effect tables, which it is fair to say suggests she was much better placed as a writer than an interior designer. And a classic Parker touch of humor: on a shelf to the left is a jar of pulverized rhubarb powder, which was used to treat constipation.

Although Parker was distracted by building a home, she continued to work on scripts. The *Los Angeles Times* reported that the Parker-Campbell plan was to become "transcontinental commuters," shifting between the farm and Hollywood as their finances and fancy dictated. Parker had even lost focus on New York, claiming, "Something is the matter back there. It seems shabby and tired."[11] Her main focus was the excitement of readying their home for the arrival of their child the following summer. This makes what happened next even more harrowing.

At some stage between Christmas and New Year's, Parker suffered a miscarriage. She and Campbell had regarded her pregnancy as a miracle, so one can only imagine the horror and grief they felt about losing their child. Indeed, one *can* only imagine, because in many ways the worst part of this story is

Parker's reaction to what happened. Complete and utter silence. All the knitted sweaters and boots disappeared. The beautifully embroidered crib covers vanished. The nursery was quickly and quietly redecorated. The much-longed-for baby was never mentioned again.

In a moving article titled "The Moral Meanings of Miscarriage," Sarah Clark Miller explores just how confounding miscarriage can be, and how often it is "spoken about obliquely" or "shrouded in silence." And the silences are multiple: cultural, personal, historical, scholarly. Says Miller, "Women who miscarry can find themselves with few resources to help decipher the meaning of their loss."[12] They can feel shame, trauma, grief, and guilt, and often end up feeling morally responsible for something that was not their fault. Equally as difficult is the sense of self-betrayal, the idea of being undermined by one's own body, a feeling of having let themselves, their embryo, and their partner down. In essence, their guilt connects to a feeling of moral failure. In turn this can produce a sort of identity crisis where language fails to capture certain unrecognized categories. What is lost is a growing entity that is not quite human, yet not other. And the woman's identity now falls somewhere between mother and not.

Parker's age was always going to be against her. Coupled with her love for Alan and their joint delight in the pregnancy, it is easy to see how she could feel a sense of guilt and trauma. It is common for women who have previously had abortions to somehow feel they have brought this on themselves as a weird form of karmic punishment. Although there is no logic to this reasoning, often when women are made to feel shame and guilt for terminating a pregnancy, as Parker had been back in New York, that trauma does not simply go away. It festers and resurfaces to cause further damage. One horrific outcome of this is what Miller refers to as a void. An empty, vacuous space. And certainly, this seems an accurate description of the silence that surrounded Parker's miscarriage. A blank, silent vacuum where the horror of loss was more deafening than anything that could ever have been spoken.

Over eighty years later, there is something still disconcerting about that silence. Perhaps because it reveals how little has changed for women today. Perhaps because Parker so firmly shut the door on something, her trauma stays beyond, locked up, never to dissipate. We cannot know how shattered she felt, since she neither spoke nor wrote about it, but after her physical recovery she went to spend a few days alone in New York, staying at the Leonori Hotel near Central Park. According to her biographer Leslie Frewin, stories circulated, confirmed by Lillian Hellman, that while there, Parker locked herself in her room for two hours and recorded on tape an outpouring of all her unhappiness, going back to her birth, through disastrous love affairs, and the agony of her existence in general.[13] Many myths like this spring up about Parker, but if this is true, the recording has never been either found or made public.

The years 1936–37 were in many ways formative ones for Parker. It is difficult to deal with them in isolation or chronologically because the two merge into each other with consequences from the actions taken one year appearing the next. Zigzagging between the two on the one hand is messy and chaotic, but on the other hand so was Parker's life. Trying to pin her down is never an easy task with tidy results. By 1936, although it was clear she continued to detest the work in Hollywood, she had nevertheless centered her professional life there and begun to concern herself increasingly with politics both local and global. As she triangulated her time between Bucks County, New York, and the West Coast, two major things were happening. First, her political life took on new intent from 1936 as she became involved in establishing the Hollywood Anti-Nazi League as well as traveled to Spain to bear witness to the outbreak of its civil war. Her observations would later be published in the left-wing magazine *New Masses*. Second, throughout 1936 she began work on the script for *A Star Is Born*, a film that would result in an Oscar nomination for her for Best Writing (Screenplay) in 1938.

Throughout the 1930s Europe had been heading toward serious trouble, with disturbing reports emerging from Germany about the rise of the Third Reich and the treatment of Jews. Parker's relationship with her own Jewish connections had always been complicated. With a Jewish father and a Gentile mother, she referred to herself as a mongrel. But as is so often the case with Parker, trying to unpick fact from fiction is difficult. Friends claimed she married Edwin Pond Parker II partly to rid herself of her birth name, Rothschild, and that the reason she kept his name after the divorce was because she saw it as a "clean" name. It is hard not to see these observations as revealing more about the people who made them than anything they can tell us about Parker herself. There is no evidence whatsoever to suggest Parker regarded a Jewish surname as unclean. In fact, when asked why she kept Parker as her surname she replied,

"Because there was once a Mr. Parker."[14] All evidence suggests that although she was ambivalent about her own Jewishness ("just a little Jewish girl trying to be cute"),[15] when she saw the creeping fascism and treatment of Jews in Europe, she was both appalled and frightened. So she took action.

In the summer of 1936, during one of her visits back to the West Coast, she cohosted an evening with Donald Ogden Stewart, during which her wealthy Hollywood friends could hear a firsthand account of what was unfolding across the Atlantic. The speaker, Otto Katz, was a Czech agent who worked for the Soviet Union under Stalin and moved in intellectual and artistic circles. A former journalist, he had friends who had escaped the Nazis and realized early on that one of the most effective things he could do was persuade intellectuals to support the cause. While in Hollywood, for obvious reasons, he kept his communist allegiance low-key, but the Communist Party USA had instructed him to raise funds. So, at the dinner Katz spoke of the need for strong ties with the Soviet Union, primarily to defeat fascism. He called on the movie industry to join the fight. And this is exactly what Dorothy Parker did. "It is to my pride that I can say that Donald Stewart and I and five others were the organizers of the Hollywood Anti-Nazi League."[16] The founders of the HANL appear to have been Parker, Stewart, Campbell, Katz, Fredric March, Oscar Hammerstein II, and the actress Gloria Stuart. Within two years those seven founding members had grown to a membership of over four thousand. During an initial organizational event in June 1936 with a banquet lunch at the Wilshire Ebell Theatre, the four hundred attendees were encouraged to resist the threat of Nazi invasion. Parker spoke passionately to all her friends about the Nazi threat, but she was mostly dismissed as being overly dramatic, or drunk. The HANL established its headquarters at 6912 Hollywood Boulevard and attracted big names such as Fritz Lang, Eddie Cantor, and Sam Goldwyn. It was a mixed bag of political allegiances including both liberals and conservatives. The league did come into conflict with local Jewish groups, some of whom wanted the organization to be more overtly anti-communist. But it launched into existence in October 1936 with a huge party at the Shrine Auditorium, where Dorothy Parker gave a speech to over eight thousand people. The HANL was active from the beginning, publishing a weekly newspaper, the *Hollywood Anti-Nazi News*, and a journal, *Hollywood Now*. It organized rallies, speeches, lectures, dinners, and fundraising, and hosted two radio programs. It also carried out boycotts of German products and visits to Hollywood by prominent European fascists and those involved in that movement (perhaps most notably, Vittorio Mussolini, son of Benito, who traveled to Hollywood to study film, and the filmmaker Leni Riefenstahl, who had been invited to LA by Walt Disney). Parker believed that the league was doing "fine and brave work" and seemed somewhat surprised that out of everywhere, Hollywood was the place she found she could fight the things she loathed.[17] To mark the one-year anniversary of the HANL, a huge party was held on August 5, 1937 at the Ambassador Hotel (presumably in the Cocoanut Grove with the stuffed swinging monkeys), where the audience danced to a set of swing numbers sung by a soon-to-be extremely famous fifteen-year-old Judy Garland.[18]

It seems fair to say that Parker was not a woman who needed to compartmentalize her life. While engaging in all kinds of political activism and renovating an old farmhouse, she was working on a screenplay for a film that Hollywood had been trying to produce for some time, *A Star Is Born*. For whatever reason, this just hadn't worked out in the past. Certainly, there were concerns that the plot was far too similar to an earlier RKO production, *What Price Hollywood?* (1932), based on a story by Adela Rogers St. Johns. There was much speculation about who or what had inspired the plot. Was it the marriage of Barbara Stanwyck and Frank Fay? Was it the silent-film actor John Bowers? There were likely many people who saw themselves reflected in the plot of a kindly alcoholic actor treated badly by Hollywood and his up-and-coming wife who eclipsed him. Maybe this was an elaborate Hollywood in-joke. The subject matter must have been hugely cathartic for Parker. Here she was being offered the chance to expose everything she hated about the town and the industry. The result was a film that unpacked the ruthlessness of Hollywood with sensitivity and poignancy. The plot revolves around the figure of Norman Maine (played by Fredric March), a huge star whose career is in decline due to his alcoholism. He meets and falls in love with Esther Blodgett (Janet Gaynor), an aspiring actress from North Dakota. After a screen test, she is given a contract and a new name, Vicki Lester. When Norman arranges for Esther to be cast in his latest film, she becomes an overnight success. Norman proposes marriage and promises to give up drinking. But as Vicki's star rises, Norman's wanes, and the realization that his career is over, and his subsequent shabby treatment by Hollywood, send him back to drinking. One evening, Norman overhears Vicki announce that she intends to give up her career to take care of him. He walks out of the house and drowns himself in the Pacific.

Glib as ever, in later years Parker summed up her role in this story as, "He was an actor. It was Hollywood. There was a sunset. Now what you gonna do?"[19] It was standard for Parker to make light of her achievements, but some of the themes in *A Star Is Born* were serious and weighty. Alcoholism was something that Parker had experienced firsthand and would continue to live with for the rest of her life. She had also witnessed Hollywood at its worst, the brutal treatment of those who were no longer regarded as useful. She was horrified to see how one of her oldest friends, F. Scott Fitzgerald, had been spoken to by industry members when he outlived his purpose.

INTERVIEWER: Then what is it that's the evil in Hollywood?

PARKER: It's the people. Like the director who put his finger in Scott Fitzgerald's face and complained, "Pay *you*. Why, you ought to pay us." It was terrible about Scott; if you'd seen him you'd have been sick.[20]

A Star Is Born gave Parker, along with her fellow writers Alan Campbell and Robert Carson, the opportunity to highlight this seedier side of movies. One standout feature of the film is

Fredric March's performance as Norman Maine, a sad, nuanced figure bashed about by Hollywood as he gradually loses his power and his talent. With no surviving screenplay that specifically shows Parker's contributions, it is impossible to know for certain which lines she wrote, though there are surely echoes of her in an exchange between Norman and his producer, Oliver:

NORMAN: Do you think I'm slipping?

OLIVER: Can you take it?

NORMAN: Yeah, go ahead.

OLIVER: The tense is wrong. You're not slipping—you've slipped.

Or in the observation of Norman's behavior: "His work is beginning to interfere with his drinking." And during Norman's stay in a sanatorium: "Comfortable? It's positively luxurious! They even have iron bars in the windows to keep out the draft." These have all the features of Parkeresque quips with a more serious message underneath. As does a more poignant piece of advice given to Vicki Lester by her grandmother: "For every dream of yours you make come true, you'll pay the price in heartbreak." This could be Parker writing about her own life. The producer, David O. Selznick, claimed that "ninety-five percent of the dialogue in that picture was actually straight out of life and was straight 'reportage.'"[21] Parker's skill for listening and turning her skill to dialogue had finally been applied to a major Hollywood film.

The reason *A Star Is Born* is so pivotal in Dorothy Parker's life is because it brought about a shift in power. And this shift was so noticeable that it even made the national press. When the film premiered in April 1937 it received outstanding reviews and resulted in seven Academy Award nominations, including Best Writing (Screenplay) for Parker, Campbell, and Carson.[22] Much of the praise was centered on Parker's dialogue, with the *Evening Star* declaring that in this long-awaited adaptation Parker had paced the film fast enough to satisfy even the most urgent demand for action, and "at any rate, Technicolor has told a Dorothy Parker story that apparently everyone wants to hear."[23] A month later the same journalist, Jay Carmody, in the same newspaper noticed how the success of the film had altered Parker's status as a writer. Referring to writers' offices in the film studios as "the cell block," Carmody pointed out that traditionally studio publicity departments claimed nobody cared about the writers. Until, that is, *A Star Is Born*. For a film that everyone had tried to write for years unsuccessfully, Parker, Campbell, and Carson made it "superwow," and in the ultimate shock move, even the publicity department was saying wonderful things about them.[24]

One testament to the lasting power of this story is that the film has been remade three times: In 1954 with Judy Garland and James Mason. In 1976 with Barbra Streisand and Kris Kristofferson. And most recently in 2018 with Lady Gaga and Bradley Cooper.[25] Parker claimed she never watched the film, though this appears to be untrue, as without so much as drawing a breath after making this claim she immediately talked about going to see it alone at the movie house for a few minutes. Certainly she watched the 1954 version, as she felt Garland was wrong for the role. But this film changed how Parker was viewed by Hollywood and the type of films she subsequently worked on.

As her political and professional life picked up pace, her personal life remained as dramatic and chaotic as ever. Despite now having "roots" in Bucks County, she still ricocheted from place to place, a fact that was not lost on the Beer family, who looked after Fox House in her absence. Helen Beer, the daughter, grew to know Alan Campbell quite well as he tended to stay around much longer, but she observed that Parker was always "taking off."[26] When she was home, Helen would sometimes make breakfast and morning coffee and deliver it to Parker, who would be sitting in bed propped against a ton of pillows and surrounded by her dogs. When she was up and working, the children were told to stay away from her, as she needed peace and quiet to write. The Beers noticed the unconventional lifestyle led by the Parker-Campbells—dressing up for dinner parties, guests from New York, heavy drinking, staying up until dawn, then sleeping late. Helen was shocked to see a bunch of naked New York writers jumping into Parker's swimming pool at 2 a.m. One thrilling visit for the Beer family came in the form of Fredric March. When he touched the arm of Hiram Beer's mother, she refused to wash it for a month afterward. Glamour, celebrities, and Hollywood were brought to rural Pennsylvania. When Parker was away, Helen and her friend would sneak into her bedroom and dress up in all her fancy clothes and boas, pretending to be movie stars.

People who worked for Parker spoke about her warmly. Hiram Beer respected her as a hard worker and a kind person. If she forgot to pay them, she would give them blank checks. But if she was fastidious about her work, she was the opposite in her domestic life, taking no care of her exquisite clothes, leaving them strewn about her dressing room, and often mixing dirty underwear with clean. Mrs. Beer discovered it did no good to remonstrate with her. She was and always would be hopeless when it came to domestic issues. Hiram Beer found Parker to be much more approachable than Campbell, whom he described as having a quick temper. "One day Alan blew up at Hiram, whereupon the solid, square, tough-muscled and independent Pennsylvania Dutch farmer stared contemptuously at the handsome actor and told him where to go. 'After that,' Mr. Beer said, 'I had no more Alan Campbell trouble.'"[27]

Most accounts of Campbell do present him as an easygoing, understanding, slightly long-suffering husband, but here and there are glimpses of a more difficult character. Their errand boy, Louis Bohlman, speculated that Campbell married Parker, made a load of money, and became something of a spoiled brat. He was mostly good-natured, but when he snapped, he snapped. Perhaps the clearest evidence of this happened toward the end of 1937, an incident that resulted in Campbell's temper leading to him spending a night in jail. The story, as usual, is not without humor.

On December 3, Campbell was on his way from Fox House

to Baltimore to receive treatment for an eye ailment, driven in a farm truck by "chauffeur" Louis Bohlman. The pair were stopped in Kingsville, Maryland, for speeding at seventy miles per hour in a twenty-five-mile-per-hour zone. Slapped with a $101.45 fine both for speeding and for allowing his chauffeur to speed, a furious Campbell refused to pay. The Washington *Sunday Star* noted the following day that "Alan Campbell is in better humor today than yesterday when he went to jail rather than pay the fine against himself."[28] Described as the "actor-scenarist husband of Dorothy Parker," he made a court appearance on December 4 in a barbershop—the local magistrate doubled as a barber. Accompanying the article are two photographs. One is of Judge Harry D. Probert sitting with important papers looking suitably stern (in front of the barbershop window). The second is of Alan Campbell outside the court looking *extremely* pleased with himself, grinning and wearing a hat, dark glasses, and a long coat. When he was reprimanded for wearing a hat in court, he replied, "I thought this was a barber's shop." And the appearance went downhill from there. Campbell's lawyer argued that it would be a gross injustice for a man to be blamed for taking precautions to protect his eyesight. On the day of the offense, Campbell had put drops in his eyes and was wearing the abovementioned dark glasses. He had closed his eyes to avoid strain and was not able to read the speedometer. He'd never ridden in the light truck before, so he did not know the feel of it at high speed.

Campbell, however, was clearly not prepared for the cunning of the local sergeant, E. S. Haddaway, who told the court how he had tricked Campbell to catch him in his lies. When Campbell urged Haddaway to look up the number of his oculist in Baltimore, Haddaway deliberately looked under the *M*s in the phone directory. Campbell told him he'd have more luck searching under the *O*s. Haddaway had his Sherlock moment: "If he could see the Ms in the telephone book, I see no reason why he couldn't see the speedometer." If the judge reached a not-guilty verdict it would mean that "Campbell would be allowed to come through here at any speed when he wanted his eyes treated." At this point Campbell himself interjected with, "Not at 100 bucks a throw." Judge Probert sat in silence for a few minutes and rubbed his chin reflectively. "I find you guilty and charge you $100 plus costs." Campbell paid up.[29]

It's easy to see why Parker would be attracted to this mischievous charm. Mutual friends of the couple noted that Campbell was just as witty and sharp as Parker herself. They clearly seemed to make each other laugh, had much fun, and worked well together. We do not know what Parker thought about her husband's night in jail, or the barber-judge, making this another of many occasions when the lack of surviving Parker material is lamentable.

What we do have are existing accounts, and even the odd letter, describing other events in Parker's personal life throughout this two-year period. Late in 1936 she met a woman who would quickly become her archnemesis: her mother-in-law, Hortense Campbell. This was a woman who was deeply protective of her son, made a sport of directing sarcastic comments at her daughter-in-law, and had perfected the art of passive aggression to quite an impressive degree. Hortense, having firmly decided that Parker was too old and not good enough for her son, ironically took to calling her "my little daughter."[30] This infuriated Parker, who in turn ridiculed Hortense's strong southern accent ("the only woman alive who pronounced the word egg as if it had three syllables").[31] Though she lived in Virginia, which even then seemed nowhere near far away enough for Parker, Hortense decided she couldn't "help out" Alan and Dorothy from such a distance, so she suggested that she move to the farm and live with them. The prospect of this filled Parker with such abject horror that she told Alan plainly that he had a clear decision to make—his mother or his wife. A compromise was reached, and they bought Hortense a small place about five miles from Fox House in a community by the river called Point Pleasant. Gratitude, however, was in short supply. Hortense felt the house was not suitably grand like Fox House and referred to it as her "little shack."

In an undated letter to Alex Woollcott, Parker recounted some of her exchanges with her mother-in-law, whom she described ruefully as "so well, so active, so present!" Seemingly, turning up and passing judgment on Fox House and its décor was one of her favorite pastimes, and Parker noted that Hortense never held back her words or her observations: "Now yesterday, in typical instance, she came in, looked at my newly-made bouquets, and said, 'My, this room looks real pretty with all these flowers.'" It didn't end there, though, as Hortense finished with, "It certainly does look terrible without them."[32] When Parker and Campbell flew back to Hollywood for work purposes, Hortense would install herself in their home and make changes in their absence. Living out in the country in a house surrounded by acres of land, Parker never wanted drapes or blinds on the windows. But Hortense did not approve of this decision, so she waited until they were away on the West Coast and then arranged for drapes and shades to be fitted as her "present" to the "children." On her return to the farm, Parker had them all removed and thrown away. "'I don't know why Dottie hates me,' Hortense told Mrs. Beer."[33]

It wasn't just Parker who was challenged by Hortense's behavior. On a visit to see her friend in the country, Lillian Hellman witnessed a huge argument between Alan and his mother. One afternoon, she and Dottie were sitting in front of the fire, piling it high with logs as snow fell outside. As the afternoon darkened, angry shouting could be heard upstairs, and Parker occasionally sighed gently into the flames. Hellman recalled, "When the voices finally ceased, Alan appeared in the living room.

"He said, immediately angry, 'It's as hot as hell in here.'

"'Not for orphans,' Dottie said, and I laughed for so long that Alan went for a walk and Dottie patted my hand occasionally and said, 'There, there, dear, you'll choke if you're not careful.'"[34]

In some accounts there's almost a hint of secret pleasure in Parker sparring with her mother-in-law, but the more obvious intrusions into her married life appeared to cause genuine friction, particularly if Hortense meddled in affairs when work took the couple back to Hollywood.

It was over on the West Coast during 1936–37 that Parker

continued her involvement in political developments. With the Hollywood Anti-Nazi League established, other events in Europe were causing equal concern. In Spain, a left-leaning Republican government had no sooner formed following an election victory than it faced a coup mounted by a collection of right-wing nationalist groups—monarchists, conservatives, and traditionalists led by a military junta—presided over by General Franco. For many this was seen as the failure of democracy in Spain and a fight between dictatorship and a democratic republic. The Nazis were already supporting Franco, supplying him with arms and ammunition, and placing spies in cities and towns throughout Spain. In Hollywood, the usual suspects were watching this unfold with horror. Parker, Campbell, Stewart, March, Eldridge, Hellman, and perhaps most notably in the year to come, Ernest Hemingway. Some with hindsight regarded the Spanish Civil War as a dress rehearsal for what was about to erupt across the whole of Europe in just three years. But in 1936, the left-wing activists in Hollywood once again began to mobilize themselves and their wealthy friends into action. They organized fundraisers and awareness-raising evenings, wrote pamphlets, gave speeches, encouraged boycotts, and, rather than seeing what was happening in Spain as an isolated incident, believed that the erosion of democracy in one country was a danger to the entire world.

Over the next several years, a new, serious Parker emerged. No more asides or wisecracks. She began to scrutinize herself, those around her, and all the political failings in the world: "Well, you see, I don't feel funny anymore. I don't think these are funny times, and I don't think Franco is funny. I don't think I can fight fascism by being comical, nor do I think that anyone else can."[35] She felt ashamed that often she did the wrong thing. She felt angry to be surrounded by "silly people" who did not care. And she was infuriated by those intellectuals who just wanted to stay in their ivory tower. "Oh God, oh God, that dreary ivory tower, the only window of which looks out on the fascist side."[36] As she observed apathy around her, she reflected on her own political journey, which had begun when she was a child. The point at which she moved from silence into fighting fascism remained something of a mystery to her. "I cannot tell you on what day what did what to me. I must have read, I must have seen, I must have thought."[37] Her main problem was being able to find a practical outlet for these overwhelming feelings about social injustice. Hollywood appeared to be the one place, even more so than New York, where she found other radicals who shared her views.

But while finding solidarity among a few friends and colleagues seemed to happen easily, getting money out of the wealthy elites around her was hard. When she spoke to Richard Lamparski in a recorded interview thirty years later, she remembered that it was "extremely difficult" to raise funds in the US for the Spanish cause.[38] Those who were willing to act seemed well-meaning but often of less impressive means. One friend had discovered that his bank had given a large loan to Franco, so he wrote them a letter saying he was closing his account in protest. "This was perfectly great of him," Parker recalled, "except he was overdrawn at the time." (This anecdote is followed by a hearty Parker chuckle.)[39]

This was a time when Parker was absorbed in so many areas. She had thrown her lot in with Hollywood. She was writing *A Star Is Born*, fixing up her farmhouse, getting pregnant, suffering a miscarriage, moving once again from coast to coast. Then, as 1937 loomed, Parker would, by the following summer, end up doing something that terrified her. Something that scared her so much she declared death was preferable. Right in the middle of the civil war, she went to Spain.

CHAPTER 5

A Soldier of the Republic

When the day comes that you can accept
injustice, anywhere, you've got to kill yourself.[1]
—Dorothy Parker, *Dorothy Parker: In Her Own Words*

Dorothy Parker's visit to Spain was far from inevitable. If anything, she tried her hardest to avoid going because she was so afraid. From her position of privilege in Hollywood she felt much safer raising funds and awareness. "I still think that anybody who tells you that he is not scared when shells shake the ground, and iron rains from the skies, and children lie dismembered in the street, is—well, possibly he has an abnormal adrenalin secretion."[2] But this doesn't mean she shied away from the reality of what was happening there. In December 1936, along with Lillian Hellman, Ernest Hemingway, and other literary figures, she formed and funded a company called Contemporary Historians, Inc. Its main purpose was to back a film project by the Dutch filmmaker Joris Ivens exploring what life was like for ordinary people in embattled Spain. Aiming to support the

Republican cause, the film was to be a cry against fascism. Titled *The Spanish Earth*, it featured opening scenes showing villagers trying to grow crops from dry land to keep Madrid supplied with food so the city could be defended. The film explored the importance of irrigating fields, of keeping water flowing, and shifted between scenes of village life and city destruction. Hellman, Hemingway, and the writer Archibald MacLeish collaborated on the story, which was then narrated by Orson Welles.[3]

By July 1937, the film had been screened in the White House at the invitation of the Roosevelts, and following this, Hemingway headed to Hollywood to start agitating among the wealthy elites. A benefit screening was arranged at the home of Fredric March and Florence Eldridge at 1026 Ridgedale Drive in Beverly Hills. A more perfect setting for the Hollywood premiere is hard to imagine. In 1934, March and Eldridge had commissioned the architect Wallace Neff to design them a Tudor Revival/French Norman home set on 1.2 acres of garden. With a distinctive octagonal tower, twenty-two rooms, eleven bathrooms, and a swimming pool, there was plenty of space to invite all the Hollywood people who needed to be there. The vast timbered rooms and spacious courtyard made it one of the most expensive houses in Hollywood (in later years it would be more famous as the marital home of Brad Pitt and Jennifer Aniston). Hemingway was looking for a Hollywood studio to distribute the film, but he was also collecting funds for the Spanish Republicans. The night in Beverly Hills raised $35,000, with Parker contributing $1,000 to buy an ambulance for use on the front.[4] It was a hopeful atmosphere, with much affection between all in attendance, except perhaps for Errol Flynn, who disappeared to the bathroom at one point and was never seen again. In a moment of goodwill following the screening, Parker threw an impromptu party at her house for "nightcaps," which according to an unlikely story from Lillian Hellman, resulted in Hemingway smashing a highball glass against the stone fireplace, Scott Fitzgerald fleeing in terror, and Dorothy Parker wondering what on earth had happened to Errol Flynn.[5]

There was talk in Hollywood, and a certain amount of cynicism, about people of such vast wealth concerning themselves with left-wing causes. Accusations of phony compassion or activism to assuage guilt were rife. Parker had been subjected to this skepticism before, that somehow being wealthy was not compatible with a social conscience. It is of course possible some people *were* donating to such causes to make themselves feel better about the privilege they enjoyed. Perhaps there was even a certain prestige attached to being a rebel in the mainstream. But all evidence suggests that Parker's concern with injustice went back much further and had existed long before she was lucky enough to be one of Hollywood's highest-paid writers. She dated her socialist awakening to the age of five during a blizzard in New York when her rich aunt ("a horrible woman then and now") pointed out men shoveling snow in the street.[6] They were lucky, claimed the aunt, to have work. Parker, though, saw freezing men, desperately working for their lives in terrible conditions. Men who when the weather cleared up would have no work at all. "That was when I became anti-fascist, at the silky tones of my rich and comfortable aunt." It's interesting to see

Parker associating such wealth with social disregard. Yet having witnessed this firsthand appears to have made Parker aware that financial security breeds indifference, a callous condescension. It was a position that Parker never wanted to inhabit, however rich she became. The main difficulty for her was knowing what to do. "But there I was, then, wild with the knowledge of injustice and brutality and misrepresentation. I knew it need not be so; I think I knew even then that it would eventually not be so. But I did not know where to go and whom to ask."[7] There had been moments in her life when this political activism flared into being, but never in a sustained way until Hollywood. To observers, Parker's activism was interpreted as the comfortable route of a wealthy woman throwing crumbs to the poor. To Parker it was because she finally found an equally committed group of comrades, her own people, who could use their positions and power in a number of political ways. In her piece for *New Masses*, she namechecked Donald Ogden Stewart as the one person she admired above all others. A man who had dedicated his whole life to fighting fascism, "he keeps on, and he will keep on. I know a great man."[8] The reality was that despite their Hollywood platforms, studios would not really allow writers or actors to politicize their films, and mainstream magazine editors were wary of publishing anything that appeared too revolutionary. If the activists wanted to raise awareness and inform people, they were going to have to produce and fund their efforts themselves.

The previous year of 1936 had been an exhausting one for Parker. Although she had enjoyed professional triumphs, there had been great personal heartbreak, and persistent, ongoing activism required so much time and energy. Sometime around June 1937, the Parker-Campbells moved again, from North Roxbury Drive two blocks over to 710 North Linden Drive, into a house they both found hideous. Another move so soon after the last, such a short distance, to a house they didn't even like seems inexplicable yet in keeping with their transient lifestyle. So, two months after their most recent move, Campbell suggested they take a trip to Europe, primarily Paris, for a proper vacation. Given the care he showed toward Parker, this was likely his way of trying to ease the lingering pain she was feeling about her miscarriage the previous year and the realization that they were unlikely to be able to have children. But Parker's biographer Marion Meade also noted that all was not well in Hollywood. Sam Goldwyn was not planning to extend the option on their contract, and so their projected joint income of $1.3 million over a five-year period suddenly dropped, without warning, to $52,000.[9] No explanation was given for this decision, which seems extraordinary in light of Parker being nominated for an Oscar and the glittering reviews for *A Star Is Born*. Could it be that Parker's deepening left-wing politics were making studio bosses nervous? It is impossible to know, but Robert Benchley wrote to his wife that "[t]heir jobs blew up."[10]

There were absolutely no plans during the European vacation for Parker to visit Spain. In mid-August, sailing aboard the SS *Normandie* for France, Parker and Campbell's fellow passengers included Lillian Hellman and the writer-journalist Martha Gellhorn, who at that time was having an affair with Hemingway (she would marry him three years later). Parker was immediately taken with Gellhorn, admiring her style, sass, and bravery. She was also impressed by how Gellhorn managed Hemingway, for as much as Parker liked him, she felt his treatment of women was not always what it should be.

In Paris, Parker reunited with her old friends Gerald and Sara Murphy. There were parties and sightseeing (Campbell had never been to Europe) and nights full of heavy drinking. Gellhorn and Hemingway had gone to Spain. But a month later, a chance meeting one night with the Pulitzer Prize–winning journalist Leland Stowe, who had arrived in Paris from Spain, lent Parker's vacation an unexpected turn. He asked her, didn't she want to *do* something? Defensive and frightened, Parker later realized her arguments for not going to Spain were unconvincing. She didn't want to use their food when they had so little. Fine, take your own, said Stowe, and donate what you take to the cause and eat their terrible food. "So I was licked," said a shamed Parker, "and I went, and I did."[11]

There is debate about what Parker produced during her time in Spain. Some critics describe her writing as sentimental; others argue it was some of her most powerful work. Friends noticed that she seemed changed by what she had witnessed. Whatever the position, Parker deserves some credit. It was 1937. She was operating in a male-dominated world of writing and journalism. The death toll in Spain was alarming. She lived a privileged and safe life moving between Hollywood and Bucks County. Had she wanted to avoid visiting Spain to report on events there, she could have easily done this. For anyone doubting Parker's sincerity or authenticity, the fact that she decided to bear witness deserves respect. In a piece called "The Siege of Madrid," written for *New Masses* in November 1937, Parker dissected her own privilege and presented what was happening in Spain for an American audience. She situated herself firmly as someone who did not have an axe to grind. "I am not a member of any political party."[12] In fact, she wrote that the only party she ever seemed to belong to (an oblique reference to the Algonquin Round Table) was one that used out-of-date humor and ridicule as an effective weapon. "Well, now I know. I know that there are things that never have been funny, and never will be. And I know that ridicule may be a shield, but it is not a weapon."[13] This sentence has never really attracted the scrutiny it deserves. Parker, a woman known primarily for her wit, her quips, and her willingness to dismiss even her own traumas with a glib, defensive joke, openly rejected humor as a powerful force for change. Though it can be a form of armor, ultimately, she believed, it could never be used as ammunition for transformation.[14]

There is no humor in Parker's reports from Spain. There is admiration, astonishment, fear, respect, trauma. But she does not try to wisecrack her way through the experience. There appear to be no extant letters from her time there, but we do have journalistic pieces and a short story. What she aimed to capture was the ordinariness of a country trying to exist, trying to keep going, in an extraordinary time. Madrid, a city that had been under siege for almost a year when Parker arrived, was described as "as big and as beautiful and as modern as Washington, D.C."[15] It was clear that Parker was writing to engage an American audience. Although she was told she had arrived during a lull in the fighting, she could not help but notice in the background "the dull boom of the big guns and the irritable cackle of machine guns."[16] She knew that this noise equated to blood and death. Nevertheless, she was surprised to find people going about their daily business in crowded streets with shops open. Despite some families evacuating, Parker wrote that there were still over a million people in the city refusing to leave their homes and possessions. She lauded the education system there, which was ensuring children from all backgrounds had a chance to thrive in whatever career they chose, and although food was scarce, the Republican government had set up feeding stations where mothers could collect milk, eggs, and cereal for their babies. Children played in the street; refugee youths were taken into homes or put into colonies and educated. Parker visited one colony by the sea in Valencia and was surprised to see that far from being a grim institution, it was a happy place of play and learning. Trauma, though, was not far beneath the surface. Children drew pictures of planes, exploding bombs, houses on fire, and body fragments blown into the air. After one raid in Valencia, Parker witnessed two little girls who saw their father killed trying to get back into the rubble of their house to find their mother. She saw collapsed homes, piles of bricks, people wandering trying to find lost loved ones, the broken body of a dead kitten, and strewn children's toys. Parker wrote about her experiences of the air raids. During the night, she found them "almost beautiful, it is like a ballet with the scurrying figures and the great white shafts of the searchlights."[17] But daytime raids were different. "You see the terrible resignation on the faces of old women, and you see the little children wild with terror."[18] As if echoing scenes from *The Spanish*

Earth, she contrasts the farming life in Valencia with the chaos of city living. Speaking directly to her American readers, she asserts, "They want the same thing that you have—they want to live in a democracy. And they will fight for it, and they will win."[19]

Parker wrote only one short story based on her time in Spain, "Soldiers of the Republic," set in a café in Valencia on a dark Sunday afternoon. Care must be taken not to read the story as straight autobiography, though the description of the main protagonist sounds an awful lot like Parker—a well-dressed, hat-wearing American. She encounters a group of six soldiers in the café on forty-eight-hour leave from the front. They had pooled their money to buy cigarettes, but something had gone wrong, and the cigarettes never got to them. The American woman pulls out a packet of fourteen cigarettes and hands them to the soldiers. Here the story takes an odd shift. The narrator turns on herself with disgust: "Darling of me to share my cigarettes with the men on their way back to the trenches. Little Lady Bountiful. The prize sow."[20] It was almost as if Parker had absorbed some of the criticism thrown at the left-wing radicals in Hollywood. After talking for a while, the soldiers leave the café and head back to the front. When the narrator and her companions ask the waiter for their drinks bill, they are told it has been paid by the soldiers.

One reason Parker wrote so little about her time in Spain is explained in a piece called "I Went to Spain." In this article she states, "I feel that it is my duty and my function as a writer to get my pieces into papers the readers of which do not yet know [what was happening in Spain], and if one of them or two of them are made to think, then I have done my work."[21] However, getting editors to accept her work was a whole other thing. Magazines dismissed her articles and referred to them as unpleasant. One editor ("who may as well be nameless because he has all the other qualities of a bastard") told her he would only publish her piece if she changed focus and made it in support of Franco. As a final insult, he threw at her, "God damn it, why can't you be funny again?"[22] The *Los Angeles Times* even devoted a whole article, titled "Can Laughter Die?," to criticizing Parker for "giving up" humor in the face of the atrocities she had seen in Spain. The journalist Ed Ainsworth argued that American people were able to bear their troubles because they were free to grin, laugh, and chortle. Only laughter can save us, he insisted, demanding that Parker recant and make herself and others laugh. "Dorothy Parker will return to the fold even though she may feel that she cannot ever be gay again. She belongs to the apostles of laughter, the genii of humor, the scribes of wit."[23]

Arriving back in Hollywood, Parker appeared in the press with Alan Campbell, looking like royalty, waving regally in a glamorous white coat and black hat with a clutch bag under her arm. The accompanying text noted that from then on Parker would be writing in a more "sympathetic vein."[24] But the media and critics were increasing their skepticism toward the left-wing radicals. *Newsweek* sneered at "the startling conversion to the Loyalist cause of hitherto class-unconscious intellectuals" and singled out Parker as someone whose flippancy had been unhinged by her visit to Valencia. She had "heard the call of the proletariat" and lost all her humor.[25] Others thought the wealthy elite were supporting revolution to save their own skins in case there really was one. In later years, Parker would stress how difficult it had been to raise funds for the Spanish cause, yet this is exactly what she did for the next two years. She became national chair of the North American Committee to Aid Spanish Democracy and felt frustration when her effort to raise funds for milk for Spanish children was met with "What are you doing for the children of America?" Trying to explain how it was all connected sometimes seemed beyond hope. As did some of the people who asked that sort of question. Parker lamented, "How can you answer dopes?"[26]

Even up to the end of the conflict she remained convinced that fascism would be defeated. Having visited Spain, she found the Republicans some of the finest people she had ever met. In 1939, when it became clear that the fascists were going to win (she preferred the Spanish word for *invasion*, rather than *war*, to describe what was taking place), Parker still maintained that solidarity was the only way forward. "But do you think people like that can fail for long, do you think that they, banded together in their simple demand for decency, can long go down?"[27] Her outspokenness may have received attention, but not always the type she would have wanted. Campbell became increasingly uncomfortable that Parker was drawing attention to herself in a dangerous way, not least by organizations like the FBI, which had started closely monitoring what they deemed pro-communist behavior.

There is a sense that by the time Parker returned to Hollywood toward the end of 1937, her political life had taken precedence over anything else. She had to keep on working to earn money, but after what she had witnessed, the settled, idyllic country life seemed well and truly over. As a new year began, even her marriage to Campbell came under increasing strain as he tried to rein in her perceived radicalism, worried that this would impact their careers in Hollywood. She began to drink more and started to lash out both publicly and privately at her husband. For almost twenty years Parker had turned to alcohol at difficult moments in her life, and 1937 had seen her subjected to significant trauma. In an article exploring Parker's alcoholism, Ellen Lansky argues that one reason an alcoholic woman is subversive is because she disrupts the paradigm in alcohol culture of the man as alcoholic and the woman as his accomplice. When a woman occupies the male-marked alcoholic position, she becomes subversive, partly because she is occupying a traditional space she is not supposed to inhabit. In Parker's case, because she was a writer, she was already subverting gender expectations by commanding a salary and an audience. Throw being a wife into the bargain and Lansky argues that for such women, "their relationships with the men in their lives were a bewildering mix of writing talent, alcohol, and power struggles."[28] Parker was eleven years older than Campbell. She had the economic earning power and he enjoyed taking care of her, yet in so many ways he took on the role of drinking accomplice and enabler. Lansky concludes that often women who internalize the writer/alcoholic masculine identity assert their femininity in their outward appearance—jewelry, furs, hats, little dogs. This described Parker perfectly: men usually commented on her "feminine" appearance while equally treating her as some sort of honorary man. When drunk, Parker turned nasty, though, making homophobic comments about Campbell's sexuality and generally implying he was useless. Friends felt awkward and upset to see her turn on him like this and they never saw him retaliate. He appeared to believe that she needed to let her anger out and showed remarkable restraint about it all. Given Parker's behavior in the past, there was no doubt much shameful remorse following these drunken outbursts. But words cannot be unsaid. And Parker had a self-destructive history of pushing away her only sources of support at times when she needed them the most. It is to Campbell's credit that he understood this and stayed with her.

There is no doubt that Parker and Campbell were seen as a duo. Toward the end of 1938, Sheilah Graham ran a snide, gossipy piece titled "Feminine Writer Discovers Gold in the Scenario Hills." Printed on the first page of the amusement section in the Washington *Sunday Star*, the piece contended that there were only two ways for a woman to make big money in Hollywood—either to act or to write. Claiming that Parker was earning $2,500 per week, Graham wrote, "Dorothy, in spite of the acknowledged excellence of her writings, was always short of cash until she married Alan Campbell—her second mate—and came to the Hollywood gold mine." Graham explained that it was down to Campbell's organization that they found themselves "in the top bracket of the in-demand scenarists" and that despite Parker constantly panning Hollywood and saying she would never return, she always did. Graham concluded that this was because it had put Parker on "easy street" and given her a house in Beverly Hills, a farm in Pennsylvania, and an apartment in New York.[29] The house in Beverly Hills was once again a different one, as in October 1938 yet another Hollywood move saw the couple buy a new home at 9560 Cedarbrook Drive out in Coldwater Canyon, a place that initially delighted them but ultimately oppressed them. This was their fourth Hollywood house within four years. The constant moving about, often to places they didn't even like, sometimes buying, sometimes renting, sometimes even staying in Hollywood hotels despite owning a house, just seemed to add unnecessary chaos and disruption.

Despite the tone of the piece, what Graham said was true. Parker *did* continue working in movies because she was so well paid ("It's all right. No art but you can make a little money and clear up that national debt . . . We're up to 1912 now."). But Graham overlooked the important sense of political solidarity Parker found there. And despite everything, they did have genuine moments of fun and farce.

Since their return from Spain, Parker and Campbell had completed work on two films, *Sweethearts* (1938) and *Trade Winds* (1938). The first was a musical comedy starring Jeanette MacDonald and Nelson Eddy playing married Broadway stars who are tempted by the lure of Hollywood. Drawing on the play-within-a-play device, the plot centers around a Broadway producer desperate to keep the stars on the stage in New York, and a Hollywood talent scout keen to tempt them out west. Various dastardly plots are unveiled by each side, but in the end the happy couple stay on Broadway. This was MGM's first three-strip Technicolor film, which explains the dazzling visual assault of color (something MGM would get under control before releasing *The Wizard of Oz* the following year). Other collaborators on the film were S. J. Perelman and his wife, Laura, along with the producer Hunt Stromberg. In one production meeting, Parker was knitting with her glasses on the edge of her nose. Stromberg was striding about lighting his pipe. Alan Campbell noticed a strange nimbus around Parker's head. "Dottie! You're on fire!" he shrieked.[30] The stuffing in her armchair had caught some of the pipe ash and started smoldering, so Campbell and Perelman yanked her out of the chair and began rolling her across the floor. Other people rushed in and started throwing unnecessary cups of water on the chair cushions. Sadly, we do not have Parker's response to this unfortunate accident.

Sweethearts was released in time for New Year's and with its elaborate song-and-dance numbers was perfect festive fodder. With singing, dancing, and color everywhere, the movie allowed Jeanette MacDonald to model the latest fashions for 1938. Frank S. Nugent of the *New York Times* described it as a "sumptuous Christmas package . . . a dream of ribbons, tinsel, Technicolor and sweet theatrical sentiments . . ."[31]

But the contrast with Parker's other writing material was stark. While scenes in *Sweethearts* showed Jeanette MacDonald sitting onstage in pink frothy dresses of tulle, a short story Parker wrote that same year tackled a very different topic. "Clothe the Naked" was an unsettling look at the life of a character named Big Lannie, a hardworking Black woman who made her living by washing clothes for rich white women. Big Lannie had been left to bring up her blind grandson, Raymond, after his mother died in childbirth. Life was hard and there was never enough money. When Big Lannie went to work, Raymond would sometimes sit outside the apartment listening to the bustle of talking and laughing neighbors. Guiding himself by touch, he would walk to the end of the street and then back again. As Raymond grew quickly, Big Lannie struggled to keep him clothed, and one winter his rags were so thin he had to stay inside. When spring came around again he longed to sit out in the sun, so Big Lannie did what she had never done before: she begged one of her rich employers, Mrs. Ewing, for help. After making a fuss ("She said that if she found she could spare anything, Big Lannie was kindly to remember it was just to be for this once.")[32] Mrs. Ewing condescended to hand over a package with a large suit and a pair of shoes, all of which were far too big for Raymond. Excited with his new clothes and unable to wait until they were altered to fit him, he went out the next day to enjoy the sun and spend time with the neighbors. But suddenly the laughter he had known was not the same—"It was coming at him to kill him."[33] And Raymond found himself under attack for his appearance. As he tried to escape he fell over, and when Big Lannie came home from work she found him curled up in the corner of the apartment covered in blood and dust. The story ends with "She did not try to make him explain. She took him in her arms and rocked him, and told him, over and over, never mind, don't care, everything's all right. Neither he nor she believed her words."[34]

Parker's political concerns were spreading as she became

increasingly concerned with union work, fighting fascism and racism, and speaking to women's groups about social issues. Hedda Hopper mocked Parker's support on the picket line for struggling newspaper writers, pointing out how Parker loved that sort of thing so much that she would picket for a dog that had the wrong puppies. But as much as the media sneered and wanted her to return to her quipping, Parker saved any light-hearted work for her film scripts. She and Campbell, along with the writer Frank R. Adams, had worked that year on *Trade Winds*, a movie starring Fredric March and Joan Bennett. Directed by Tay Garnett, this was a film that had been constructed in a curious way. While Garnett was on a world cruise, he had an idea for a story that involved travel, so he shot scenes of doorways in Japan, a pier in Bombay, a racetrack in Singapore, and various other locations around the globe, then Hollywood filled in the gaps, as March and Bennett were filmed in front of a green screen. The plot involved the socialite Kay Kerrigan (Bennett) avenging her sister's suicide by shooting Thomas Bruhme, the man she held responsible. Although she shoots Bruhme in the stomach, when the body is discovered it is revealed that he was killed by a gunshot to the head. Changing her appearance and going on the run, Kerrigan manages to avoid the police until they employ Detective Sam Wye (March) to take on the case. The two meet on a ship sailing to Singapore and fall in love, whereupon Wye reveals that the fatal shot was fired not by Kerrigan, but by a jealous husband whose wife was having an affair with Bruhme. Thus, Kerrigan is cleared of murder and the two are free to marry.

The film met with a positive reception upon release in December 1938, with Frank S. Nugent singling out the dialogue and praising the "frequently humorous frequency of Dorothy Parker and Alan Campbell."[35] But there seemed nothing much to laugh about for Parker. With the success of *Trade Winds*, the Hollywood press agents turned up at the couple's home to whip up public personalities for the screenwriters. The journalists were completely unprepared for the lack of cooperation they received.[36] How had she enjoyed working on the film? they inquired. She hated it, she replied. She hated working at all, for anything. How long had she been writing for films? "Almost since they learned to talk." Who was her favorite collaborator? Alan Campbell because they could just snarl at each other and finish a script. What was her life like? "Terrible." What did she like? "Flowers, French fried potatoes, and a good cry." After being offered drinks, the visitors left without daring to ask Parker for a photograph. She was, it would seem, the despair of Hollywood press agents.

In January 1939, Parker once again found herself at the center of a political press scandal when she agreed to give a talk to raise funds for the Spanish loyalists. Held at the Beverly Hills home of the economist Leon Henderson, the reception in Parker's honor was sponsored by the American Congress for Peace and Democracy. It perhaps got off to a bad start when Parker turned up an hour late, and Henderson demanded that all the photographers leave the room. This was an odd decision given that it was an event to raise awareness and funds, but Henderson was adamant that no pictures be taken. Parker then perched herself on top of a piano and with arms outstretched described the desolation, bravery, poverty, and starvation she had witnessed. In tears, she begged the audience to help the loyalists, and dollar bills poured into her lap. But just at that moment mayhem broke out when a flashbulb went off. Henderson ran full-tilt and grabbed the photographer, Joseph S. McCoy, by the back of the neck and bundled him into the next room. At this point Parker stopped speaking and the silence was broken by the thud of flying furniture. Henderson had smashed McCoy's camera to pieces and was proceeding to bang the photographer's head against the wall. The other photographers who had been hanging around the house piled into the room and pinned Henderson to the wall to give McCoy time to escape. Henderson's two young daughters (dressed in Chinese outfits to honor a guest) were sobbing in their mother's arms. As McCoy left the house there was the sound of smashing glass as someone put their fist through the plate-glass door. At the end of the night, Parker told a reporter, "I don't see how you can help being unhappy now. The humorist has never been happy, anyhow. Today he's whistling past worse graveyards to worse tunes."[37]

Parker's propensity for getting involved in scrapes like this worried Alan Campbell, and he was probably right to be worried. Nineteen thirty-nine would see no film work come their way as scrutiny in Hollywood increased. People—studio spies— were attending these political talks and building dossiers of activists who were speaking at them. The information was passed on to the FBI and the House Un-American Activities Committee (HUAC). From the radicals' point of view, this showed just how effective their campaigning was. Parker didn't care and she was not afraid. She refused to tone down her activism or her visibility as a left-wing spokesperson. Newspaper reports from both Hollywood and New York show a dizzying number of receptions, dinners, rallies, and talks, often with Parker as guest speaker. Her name was guaranteed to attract sponsors, though she hated public speaking. "It is difficult for me to speak before an audience and sometimes I think that if I have to hear my voice uttering the syllables of 'fascism' once again, I shall vomit."[38]

When Madrid fell on March 28, 1939, and the fascists won, Parker relied even more heavily on those who shared her belief that in the end social justice would prevail. Hanging on to that belief was her life and strength. But she was also compelled to keep going, to stay close to her comrades and not stop because "when I am not with them, I think I have no waking moment through the day or in the night when I am not guilty . . ."[39] This guilt was not about her privilege, but her feeling that however much she did, it just never seemed enough.

According to Marion Meade, 1939 was also the year Dorothy Parker fell pregnant again and suffered another miscarriage. As before, Campbell's response was to suggest a relaxing vacation in Paris. It is perhaps telling that one person Parker did confide in was her sister, Helen, who was mother to two children but had experienced the sadness of a marriage breakdown. In a telegram to Helen, Parker anticipated escaping to Europe, writing, "Things have been pretty bad as I think you guess and this may be a life saver."[40] Yet despite these hopeful words, Meade's observations suggest a much more run-down, depressed Parker. She had gained weight, which upset her, and subsequently she wanted to shut herself away in her room and never leave. It was Campbell's pushing that convinced her a vacation would be a good idea. They crossed the Atlantic in June on a Dutch ship and during the journey encountered a group of students from Amherst and Princeton. Meade managed to track down some of this group and interviewed them about their impressions of Parker. What they had to say revealed the desperately sexist scrutiny that women writers had to endure. As she was a famous author, they were disappointed with Parker's appearance. One student found her "the sloppiest woman I ever met" and spoke with disapproval of her "broad derriere," shapeless dress, cracked nail polish, and stringy hair. The other thought Parker wore too much makeup and didn't approve of the way she applied her rouge.[41] There is something depressing about the amount of attention given then—and now—to a woman's appearance. Little wonder Parker wanted to lock herself away when she gained weight. Though one student was able to appreciate Parker's humor, she also found her unpredictable and moody, switching between being hilarious and being angry and bitter about Spain. It was noticeable how well Campbell handled her. Although the students claimed to be aware of her recent miscarriage, it is not clear if they knew anything about the last three years that Parker had spent tirelessly campaigning only to see fascism triumph.

In Paris, Parker and Campbell stayed in a borrowed apartment. They met with Sara Murphy and drank cocktails, and Parker shopped for hats. In the weeks before they sailed, Parker's latest collection of stories had been published by Viking Press, *Here Lies: The Collected Stories of Dorothy Parker*—dedicated to Lillian Hellman—which included some of her more political pieces, such as "Soldiers of the Republic" and "Clothe the Naked." But Paris seemed to be a time to forget work. They relaxed, they drank, they attended a reception at the American embassy. These weeks would be good for them, for had they known what was on the horizon, it would have been a very different story. Following Parker's miscarriage, all did not seem to be well with her physically. Her marriage, though enduring, grew increasingly tense. As the fascists seized power in Spain, Nazi Germany was just months away from invading Poland. As Parker and Campbell left Paris and headed back to Hollywood, everything was about to fall apart.

CHAPTER 6

Smash-Up

Fascism isn't coming here—it is here.[1]
—Dorothy Parker, *Evening Star*, Washington, DC, 1947

One of the first things Parker and Campbell did in Hollywood after their vacation in Paris was sell their home on Cedarbrook Drive along with everything in it. This was now their fifth move in just over four years. In an advert for the *Los Angeles Times*, surely written by Parker, an auction of the house's contents was due to take place over three evenings, from December 11 through the 13, hosted by the Beverly Wilshire Art Galleries. It was listed as "An Auction Event of Supreme Importance."[2] All furniture, furnishings, and bric-a-brac of the "world renowned authoress, Dorothy Parker, and the equally famous Alan Campbell" would be available to buy.[3] Included in the advertisement is a list of what they were selling: an English Chippendale dining room suite, a sleigh bed, a baby grand, a pair of Sheraton commodes, an eight-piece Louis XVI bedroom suite, a rosewood whatnot, cocktail tables, French Sèvres lamps, bronzes, drapes, paintings, and broadloom and Persian carpets. This list offers a fascinating insight into Parker's style and taste and what the inside of the couple's home must have looked like, even down to their flowered faille fireside chairs. It's not entirely clear why they decided to offload all their possessions, but Parker's biographer Leslie Frewin mistakenly reports that the lease was sold to Laurence Olivier and Vivien Leigh. In fact, the house was bought by a couple named Siegfried and Betty Herzig, who gave a clear description to Marion Meade of some of the quirkier aspects of the property. Parker had found the house increasingly oppressive: "There descends on the house in the late afternoon what I would call a suicide light."[4]

Parker's mood generally seemed low as her political life continued to get her into hot water. She had been faced with a difficult situation in August when Soviet Russia signed a non-aggression pact with Nazi Germany, the two countries agreeing not to take military action against each other for the next ten years. Parker, who had established the Hollywood Anti-Nazi League with support from the Communist Party of America, suddenly felt that her political allies had sold out. A clause included in the agreement mapped out how the Soviet Union and Germany would divide up eastern Europe between them.[5] After seeing the death and destruction fascists had caused in Spain aided by the Nazis, Parker must have been horrified. Although she did not publicly speak out against the agreement, in 1940 the HANL quietly changed its name to the Hollywood League for Democratic Action and focused its campaigning against anything that seemed to be leading America into war.

But there is no doubt that for many left-wing supporters, this was a tricky time.

Despite this, in her personal life Parker still seemed able to play pranks on her Hollywood friends. In his gossip column Jimmie Fidler reported that Parker and Campbell had been invited by James Cagney for a day out on his yacht. Cagney, who suffered from chronic seasickness, insisted that rather than head out to sea they spend the day moored to the pier. In return, Parker invited him for a picnic, got him in her car, reversed halfway out of the garage, and spread their lunch out in the backyard.[6]

At some stage, going back and forth between Bucks County and Hollywood, Parker and Campbell rented a house at 602 North Bedford Drive. Unlike their Coldwater Canyon home, this was a hacienda-style house off Santa Monica Boulevard and just eight blocks from their old home on North Canon Drive. Parker did not like the house and sent Alan out on a new home–finding mission. She appeared to be doing little work, and her restlessness grew as she drifted between Hollywood, Pennsylvania, New York, and a visit to Sun Valley to stay with Ernest Hemingway and Martha Gellhorn. This inability to settle anywhere or to work seemed to manifest itself in heavier-than-usual drinking and irritation toward Campbell, who, despite remaining patient, took the brunt of Parker's seething dissatisfaction. The drunker she got the worse the abuse got, and friends had to listen to her referring to Campbell as "that shit" or "that pansy" or "my homo husband" and sighing, "What am I doing in Hollywood at my age married to a fairy?" Campbell was, she insisted, "as queer as a goat."[7] There seems to be no evidence as to when or why Parker came to this conclusion. Friends began to speculate that he would surely leave her. They felt he had a rough time putting up with her.

What seems odd about Parker's behavior is the blatant homophobia. As she was always a champion of the oppressed and the bullied, it is curious that she would fall back on such hostile insults. We do not know whether Campbell had ever had same-sex relationships or whether he was having homosexual affairs. Even so, given Parker's politics, one might expect she would be more upset by the betrayal itself than by Campbell's sexuality. Parker did not demonstrate any wider cultural homophobia; she happily partied with gay men and lesbians. Certainly, she operated in an environment that nurtured homophobia (even their friend S. J. Perelman took to calling Campbell "the fag").[8] Perhaps it was what psychologists call "interpersonal homophobia"—homophobia that occurs when a personal bias affects relations among individuals, often resulting in name-calling.[9] There can be any number of causes, such as religious beliefs or repressed desires. But certain theories suggest that this type of prejudice can come from anxiety, or a desire to create a power imbalance in a relationship. It is always dangerous to attempt any posthumous diagnosis, but what we do have are witnesses who knew the couple and testified to Parker's public belittling of her husband. From these testimonies there is no doubt Parker was exercising her power, but inadvertently demonstrating her anxiety, too, about abandonment and loss. There was the age difference between them, she was experiencing undiagnosed health issues following her latest miscarriage, and she was on the receiving end of Campbell's disapproval about her very public political activity. Implying that she was the sole breadwinner, when a friend asked Parker what she was complaining about—after all, Campbell was handsome, charming, and adoring, what more did she want?—Parker sniped back, "Presents."[10] Whatever the explanation for what was going on in their marriage, for a woman so committed to issues of social justice, this side of her was shocking, and her behavior, in this context, undeniably abhorrent.

In 1940, film work finally came Parker's way. She collaborated on the screenplay, adding mainly additional scenes and dialogue, for Lillian Hellman's *The Little Foxes* (1941). Based on Hellman's 1939 play, this was a film set in the Deep South about the scheming, malignant Hubbards, a family fighting over an inheritance. Bette Davis played Regina Hubbard Giddens, battling her brothers for her share of their father's wealth in an era when only sons were regarded as rightful heirs. Desperate for independence and wealth away from her ailing husband, Regina poisons the family with her toxic manipulation and control. A subplot concerns the way the wealthy southern family treat their Black servants (as treasured members of the family only when it suits them). Running parallel to the unpleasant family dynamics is an innocent budding romance between Regina's daughter, Alexandra, and her childhood friend David, who share some of the most delightful dialogue in the film.

DAVID: Do you like me?

ALEXANDRA: Not today.

DAVID: Why, I'll come back tomorrow.

In later years, Parker would single out this film above all others: "Once I worked on a picture that I was proud of, only because it was a good picture. That was '*The Little Foxes*.'"[11] But by the end of the 1930s, she did seem increasingly capable of appreciating other movies being made. Having been invited to an advance screening of *The Grapes of Wrath* (1940) at 20th Century Fox, Alan Campbell noted that Parker claimed it was the best film she had ever seen. She was intending to write a fan letter to the producer, Darryl F. Zanuck ("If that doesn't kill him, then nothing will").[12]

The Parker-Campbells were also hired to work on a film, *Week-End for Three* (1941), that was intended for Cary Grant and Irene Dunne but ended up starring Dennis O'Keefe (Jim) and Jane Wyatt (Ellen). The plot centers around a young married couple whose weekend is ruined by the arrival of an old friend, Randy (played by Phillip Reed), who knew Ellen before her marriage. Boisterous and overbearing, Randy causes havoc during his stay and the couple try desperately hard, but very politely, to get him to leave. Much disruption and farce ensue, with Ellen being asked a rather Parkeresque-sounding question: "Well, how you gonna get rid of him? Burn the house down?" Once again, this dialogue-heavy plot played to Parker's strengths, but equally she must have been writing it under great strain.

At some point toward the end of 1940, she was finally diagnosed with benign, but enlarged, uterine fibroid tumors, a condition that almost certainly had an impact on her pregnancies. She entered Cedars of Lebanon Hospital to undergo a hysterectomy on November 16 and would remain there for almost three weeks.[13] One of her rare letters survives from this time, handwritten to Alexander Woollcott on pale blue paper in pencil ("the dirtiest of all impositions").[14] She was recuperating in the much-hated North Bedford Drive house, "the most hideous, ill-equipped, uncomfortable, and depressing house ever assembled." To cheer her up, Alan had sent for one of her favorite dogs from Fox House, Six, a Sealyham terrier, to greet her when she was released from the hospital. The letter to Woollcott is open, honest, and touching, as Parker describes the "peaceful, negative joy" she felt now that the operation was over. She was not without some regret and horror about it all, though, mentioning how unattractive she felt walking about knowing all the time she was carrying these fibroid tumors inside. And even worse, although she knew about pain, "I didn't know about a life in which there is nothing but pain." She found the whole thing a very strange experience. With her usual wry eye, though, she couldn't resist describing the one thing she really remembered from the hospital. While being given a fancy enema by an enthusiastic young nurse, she lay on the bed with her eyes closed trying to pretend nothing was happening. The young nurse suddenly piped up, "'That's an awfully cute bed-jacket you've got. If you'll pardon me for being personal.'" For Parker, this event stood out with a slightly horrifying and mortifying "eternal clearness."

The rest of the letter is wonderfully gossipy—excessively praising Martha Gellhorn and taking great delight in tales of Alan's house-hunting exploits, in particular regarding a house he found in North Hollywood that was nice but horribly furnished ("but you expect that"). Parker tells the story, though she got many of the details wrong. Her version goes: the house had belonged to the singer Ruth Etting and was the location of a shooting when her gangster ex-husband, Martin Synder, caught her in "an embrace" with her new husband, Myrl Alderman. But the story was much more convoluted than that, and Parker described it gleefully to the last detail. Etting's stepdaughter, Edith Synder, who was also present, had pulled up a chair to watch "the embrace." She ran to the kitchen to get a gun when her gangster father showed up. He wrestled the gun from her, fired two shots, and the lights went out. Alderman took a bullet in the abdomen but survived.[15] What amused Parker most was that she and Alan were barred from taking the house because they were writers. And not just any writers, but writers connected to the movie industry. "'We can't have that kind of people in this house,'" said the agent.

During Parker's convalescence a sad but not entirely unexpected event occurred—F. Scott Fitzgerald died. His ongoing battle with alcoholism, his debts, and his difficulties writing for the studios (they repeatedly dismissed him from films, believing he did not have the knack for producing dialogue) had left him in a low place. When MGM canceled his $1,250 a week contract, he was in terrible financial trouble. Throughout 1938 he had sold only ninety-six copies of his books; in 1939 his royalties amounted to thirty-three dollars. Going freelance was risky, but Fitzgerald tried and he wrote to Zelda, "I don't know what the next three months will bring further, but if I get a credit on either of these last two efforts things will never again seem so black as they did a year ago when I felt that Hollywood had me down in its books as a ruined man—a label which I had done nothing to deserve."[16] His final assignment from Hollywood was to adapt an Emlyn Williams play, *The Light of Heart*, for $700 a week for ten weeks. The story was about a former celebrity actor ruined by alcohol, which surely must have felt a bit close to home for Fitzgerald, despite having gotten his drinking under control the last year of his life. As usual, he poured himself into the writing and once again was taken off the picture. In November he had a cardiac episode in Schwab's that left him temporarily unconscious. On the night of December 20, as he was leaving the theater with Sheilah Graham, he experienced a dizzy spell and struggled to walk to his car. He was worried that everyone would think he was drunk. At home the following day he collapsed and died of a heart attack at forty-four. Dorothy Parker said, "It was terrible about Scott; if you'd seen him you'd have been sick."[17] She had known him for decades, both in New York and Hollywood. There was even gossip that they had once been lovers. She was concerned with how the studios had been treating him and had encouraged him to come along to political meetings and get-togethers. But in the end, she felt everyone had turned their backs on him. She was disgusted that no one attended his funeral or even sent flowers. At the service, Parker said, "'Poor son of a bitch,' a quote right out of *The Great Gatsby*, and everyone thought it was another wisecrack. But it was said in dead seriousness."[18] Fitzgerald's death would be the start of a series of losses for Parker over the coming years that would cause her to reflect seriously, and with some anxiety, on the aging process and death.

Some of this anxiety was expressed in heavier-than-ever drinking. Throughout 1941, Parker took to having her first drink as soon as she woke up and continued steadily through the day and into the night. The previous year had seen her undergo major surgery, and despite any relief she may have felt from pain, it also signaled the end of any possibility of her having children. By now she was forty-eight, so the likelihood of that was already slim, but the emotional impact of undergoing a hysterectomy should not be overlooked. Today there is more understanding that some women grieve the loss of their fertility. Research is ongoing (and inconclusive), exploring whether the operation leads to increased depression and anxiety or even whether it interferes with sexual function. Some women report that it alters how they view themselves. We do know that Parker was relieved to no longer be in pain, but we do not know anything beyond this. As with her miscarriages, she remained silent.

Film work throughout 1941 was sparse. Parker and Campbell started work on a baseball movie intended as a tribute to Lou Gehrig, the New York Yankees first baseman, called *The Pride of the Yankees*, but Parker got herself kicked off the production. The studio retained Alan but replaced her with a younger writer, Helen Deutsch, though all three would remain uncredited for the work they did. Parker's biographer Marion Meade interviewed Deutsch years later about how it felt to step into Parker's shoes: "I was too green to know the score, although somebody told me that Dorothy Parker had got stinking drunk and had been taken off the picture."[19] Deutsch found Campbell pleasant but a little creepy. She noticed he spent hours leaning out of the window, which sounds like unusual behavior for him, given that he was the driving force when he worked with Parker. Deutsch observed him watching the story editor and decided he might be homosexual.

One outcome of this for Parker was that, for the first time in a while, she returned to writing short stories. In between fuming about being replaced by a younger, inexperienced writer whom she suspected Campbell was having an affair with (clearly she was not privy to Deutsch's real view of Alan), she produced two strong pieces of fiction. The first was "The Standard of Living," about two young girls, Annabel and Midge, who work for the same company for very little money and still live at home. One of their favorite hobbies is playing a game imagining what they would do if they were to suddenly inherit a million dollars. The only stipulation in the will is that they must spend every nickel on themselves. The story has a dreamy quality as the two girls indulge in escapism and fantasize about what they think are lavish demands. One day they catch sight of a double row of pearls in a fancy jewelry store. They enter and ask the price. They are told the pearls cost a quarter of a million dollars. Quietly, and somewhat shaken, they leave the store and walk down the avenue, stooped and defeated. Then suddenly Midge pipes up with a new game: imagine what you would do if you were suddenly left ten million dollars . . .

The second story, "Song of the Shirt, 1941," opens with a beautiful sentence that shows Parker's ability to perfectly capture a moment, a description: "It was one of those extraordinarily bright days that make things look somehow bigger."[20] Featuring

Mrs. Martindale, a well-to-do woman who is working for the war effort, volunteering five afternoons a week stitching coats for soldiers, the story gently lampoons the good intentions of society women who somehow end up missing the point. The war-effort headquarters is due to close for the summer when suddenly there is a call for hospital garments, and Mrs. Martindale decides to give up her time to stitch more of these items at home, though she is slow and clumsy. When her wealthy friend calls asking her if she has any work for a destitute woman who is trying to survive and take care of her sick daughter, Mrs. Martindale goes back to her sewing, racking her brains to think what work she could possibly find for the poor woman. Although this is a story that describes stitching and sewing in painstaking detail, Parker does allow her narrator an aside to discuss knitting. It is hard when reading it not to think about Parker herself sitting in the film studios and movie meetings, clacking away: "Knitting once you have caught the hang of it, is agreeable work, a relaxation from what strains life might be putting upon you. When you knit, save when you are at those bits where you must count stitches, there is enough of your mind left over for you to take part in conversations, and for you to be receptive of news and generous with it."[21]

The rest of the year saw Parker take off to New York for two months, leaving Campbell behind to work on films. This seemed successful, with RKO offering him a weekly salary of $1,250.

By the end of that year, when the journalist Hubbard Keavy turned up to interview Parker at 602 North Bedford Drive in December, he was a little surprised by what he found. She answered the door and all in one breath said, "'Come right in and have a drink and what do you drink?'"[22] Keavy noted, "Miss Parker is smallish and early fortyish, who does up her hair in a tight bun at the back and bang-y in front. She was wearing a peasant blouse, a full candy-striped skirt and low-heeled cloth sandals." Throughout the interview Parker returned to familiar gripes: how awful Hollywood is, how everyone earns so much money but is always broke, how she is not witty, how she is serious about her writing. As if to acknowledge this, Keavy stresses in the piece that Parker's strength in movies lies in enlivening dull scenes with sparkling dialogue. And what Parker reveals is that she is at that moment working with Alfred Hitchcock on his spy thriller *Saboteur* (1942). In particular, she sees her role as "giving the girl more to do."

The day this article was published, December 7, Japan attacked Pearl Harbor, heralding America's entry into World War II, and within days Dorothy Parker entered rehab to try to get her drinking under control. By this stage, her marriage was in serious trouble and Alan's patience was wearing thin. S. J. Perelman and his wife, Laura, functioned as go-betweens while Dorothy was in the hospital. They noted that she had gotten to the point where she was completely loaded on brandy by eleven in the morning, was fed up with Hollywood and everyone working in it, resented Alan collaborating with Helen Deutsch, and got into such a state that she took herself off to a sanatorium. Alan complained that she was completely unreasonable.[23] When the Perelmans informed Alan that Parker had decided to end the marriage and return to New York, he dashed to the hospital and smoothed things over. She returned home with him, but things were far from okay.

In January 1942, Parker published another volume, *The Collected Stories of Dorothy Parker*, featuring most of her well-known pieces: "Arrangement in Black and White," "Mr. Durant," "Horsie," and "Just a Little One." She also included her more political stories, "Soldiers of the Republic" and "Clothe the Naked." Franklin P. Adams, her old friend from the days of the Round Table, wrote the foreword. Published by the Modern Library in New York, the book had a handsome blue cover and a tagline that read, "Twenty-four short stories by one of the greatest writers of our time." However excruciating Parker found praise, this was quite the acclaim, and being acknowledged in this way seemed fair after years of working hard at her craft.

Back between Hollywood and Fox House, Parker decided to stop taunting Campbell about his sexuality. Instead, she switched to calling him a coward for not signing up to fight fascism. But Campbell had already experienced a taste of military school in his younger years, and he did not like it.

It was surprising, then, that in the spring of 1942, despite being in his late thirties, Campbell decided to enlist. In July back at Fox House waiting to hear about his application, Parker wrote to Woollcott about how proud she felt. Referring to it as "a time of inescapable guilt and unease," she described how Campbell was keeping himself busy with a whirlwind of activities.[24] They appeared to temporarily be without any help in the house (possibly because Hortense kept firing the staff, much to Parker's outrage), so the couple were fending for themselves. Alan was cooking; her tasks were to clean, make the beds, and wash the dishes. She was swiftly so "undone" by her own incompetence that she employed a matron to help her scrub the floors. The real delight of this letter is Parker's description of the cleaning woman's son, Horse, who "has four years in time; in depravity he resembles a boulevardier of eighty." Horse spent his time peering in windows and making faces at Parker. "I do not know what to do about this," she admitted. Thankfully, Hortense's interfering seemed temporary, as the Beers reappeared at some point and imposed some sort of order.

Alan Campbell did not have to wait long to hear that his application had been successful. At thirty-eight he was older than the average age, and upon Parker's "urging" he did not apply for a commission but was accepted as a private. This made her doubly proud of him. In some ways, despite the circumstances, this enforced separation was what they both needed. Friends noticed that Alan's drinking had increased, and the more the couple drank the more they sniped and argued. They were no longer amusing or pleasant to be around, and some acquaintances began deliberately avoiding them, tired of sitting up late each night watching them get drunk, then having to drive them and their car home when they were incapable.

But not everyone was pleased about Campbell heading off to war. To Parker's disgust, Hortense threw herself into some high-drama moments, first crying and wailing and making a scene, calling her son selfish and heartless. She followed this with a brokenhearted performance, visiting her friends and talking about the sacrifice *she* was making (this didn't work, as all her friends' sons had already enlisted). Finally, she tried heart attacks ("We brought our doctor who pronounced her in perfect shape").[25] Parker's loathing for her mother-in-law drips from a letter she wrote to Alexander Woollcott. She claimed she was not really a vengeful person because "if you just sit back and wait the bastards will get what's theirs, without you doing anything about it, and it will be fancier than anything you could ever have thought up." But Hortense challenged to the hilt Parker's belief that waiting for someone's downfall was the best tactic. For the sake of immediate action, she would "give quite a large bit of my soul if something horrible would happen to that woman for poisoning Alan's last days here."

On September 2, Parker accompanied her husband to the enlistment office in Philadelphia to say goodbye as he was sent to camp. Her letter to Woollcott is remarkable in its length, detail, and emotion. She described with much pride (and a hint of patriotic sentimentality) the scene that awaited them when they arrived. A large hall with benches down the side was filled with men—from all social groups—signing up to join the army. She noted that this truly was a democratic war; the men were young, old, poor, wealthy, Black, and white. Although she seemed most moved by the sight of poor men in stained shirts with no coats, she reined in any condescension or pity, saying there was nothing heartbreaking or pitiful about them. They all signed forms, gave their fingerprints, and were lined up in blocks to take the oath of induction. Private Alan Campbell was assigned to Fort Cumberland in Maryland for a couple of days to be assessed, tested, and fitted with a uniform. To Parker's pride, her husband was chosen to take charge of the new recruits. Then off to the station they went for final goodbyes. Parker heard Alan giving orders, followed by a very polite "if that's ok with you," and in her letter to Woollcott she declared, "I love Alan. Don't you, Alec?"

The goodbyes were emotional. Most families did not know when they would be reunited; some must have thought that maybe they never would be. Parker seemed to have a rush of regret, admitting that she had acted like a shit toward Alan. For the first time she realized just how much he was giving up—his career, his house, and a new, lucrative six-month contract from Hollywood. He had enlisted without telling anyone and although Parker understood he had done the right thing, she made the rather outrageous claim that "no one told him what was right, except himself." One suspects that Alan Campbell might well have had a different take on this.

What happened next at the station seems inexplicable and inexcusable. Perhaps it was Parker's heightened emotions, her feelings of guilt and regret, or the fact that she was about to say goodbye to Alan. Either way, none of these factors excuse what she did. As the new recruits were boarding the train, a woman recognized and approached Parker ("a fat, ill-favored, dark little woman"). She started haranguing Parker to give a talk at her local Better Living Club and blathered on about how Parker should never have written what she did about women in glasses.[26] Parker politely told her she was terribly sorry, but she was rather busy just at that moment. The woman looked at the lines of new soldiers and called them poor suckers. Parker described how an "almighty wrath" descended upon her as she turned on the woman and spat out a racist insult: "Those are American patriots who have volunteered to fight for your liberty, you Sheeny bitch!"[27]

Already horrified with herself as she walked away, she admitted to Woollcott that she had never used that expression in her life, but also knew that if the woman had been Black, she would, in the moment, have used an equally offensive term. "Dear God. The things that I have fought against all my life. And that's what I did." Parker's self-reflection is worth thinking about in detail because what it unpacks is the deep-seated racism that lurks at the heart of white privilege. Parker believed that she somehow understood her privilege. Unusually for her time, she did not try to speak on behalf of others, but rather created a platform for people to speak for themselves. When she did not have the lived experience to fall back on, she campaigned where she could be most effective—raising funds. She was anti-fascist, anti-racist, and staunchly left-wing. Yet despite all her years of activism, somewhere inside, when under pressure, that's where her mind went. She did not make excuses for this comment. She lived both with the horror of having said it and the horror of the ease with which she said it.

Alan had gone. And now it fell to Parker to hold things together. She felt as though the world was on fire and it was her responsibility to keep campaigning, to keep working on films and short stories, to make enough money to support Fox House and her mother-in-law, to make sure there was something for Alan to return to. In the coming months she would even try to engage in war work, traveling to Europe as a journalist, but her request was refused due to her political activities in Hollywood. The country had entered the world war, but there was another type of domestic war brewing that would make life very difficult for people like Dorothy Parker.

And still, in the middle of this, people just wanted Dorothy Parker to be funny. Three weeks after saying goodbye to Alan she appeared at a Russian War Relief concert near Fox House. Asked, yet again, why she wasn't writing anything witty anymore, Parker replied, "Time enough for humor when there's something to laugh about."[28] It was all a myth anyway, she claimed, about her being a bad girl and a "conversational hellion." Really, she was just very nice.

The next three years for Dorothy Parker are badly documented. We know as usual she was restless, moving between a two-room apartment in the New Weston Hotel in New York, Fox House, and Hollywood. Sometimes she stayed at hotels in Beverly Hills; sometimes she returned to the Garden of Allah. We know that sometime in 1942 she was in the hospital in New York for an operation on her elbow to try to alleviate the symptoms of bursitis, which left her high on codeine with her arm in a sling.[29] We know from newspaper reports that she continued in her war efforts, speaking at rallies and meetings. We know that she completed her work in Hollywood with Hitchcock on *Saboteur*. The film starred Priscilla Lane (Patricia Martin) as the female lead and Robert Cummings (Barry Kane) as the hero who is wrongly accused of sabotage. He goes on the run to find the real culprit and prove his innocence. Parker expanded the role for Lane but mainly wrote Kane's patriotic speeches. Hitchcock revealed that he and Parker shot a cameo playing a clueless married couple driving in a car. When they pass Patricia on the side of the road struggling with Kane, the wife remarks, "They must be very much in love!" Sadly, Hitchcock decided not to use this in the final cut. The cameo he replaced it with was also removed, this time by the censors. It showed Hitchcock and his secretary playing deaf pedestrians. Hitchcock's character makes an indecent proposal in sign language and the woman slaps his face. (In the end, Hitchcock's cameo was more prosaic—him in front of a drugstore.)

One person who is not silent during these three years is Alan Campbell. Almost all his letters written to Parker from the military camp and then Europe survive in the archive at the University of Michigan.[30] It is not clear how they ended up there. Obviously, Parker saved them. There are a few possibilities. Perhaps at some point Parker gave them to his family and they were donated by a Campbell relative. Or it is equally possible that these are the letters Lillian Hellman found in Parker's apartment after her death and, given their personal nature, passed on to his family. What we do have is, in some cases, an almost daily account of Campbell's movements, his thoughts, feelings, and, most poignantly, his longing for his wife. The great tragedy here is that the correspondence is one-sided. The letters themselves are fascinating documents. Some are written on tiny scraps of paper; some have cramped handwriting squeezed onto official War and Army Departments V-mail stationery (Campbell refers to writing on such tiny paper as like writing on the head of a pin), each with a black censor's stamp. When he managed to get hold of a typewriter, the letters were more legible, some on standard paper in airmail envelopes. He addresses them almost exclusively to "Darling," but sometimes he uses "Honey" or "Dottie" or "Baby." In between minute detail about his days, getting his uniform (the pants are too long!), and the chaos of where they will be shipped to, there are truly tender moments. The first letter he writes to her is on the train just after they have said goodbye. It is postmarked 10:30 p.m. that night. The rest of the letters unfold day after day after day. He is upset about their first New Year's Eve apart, pointing out it is the first time they have not been together on that day since they met in 1933. He remembers the nicest one they had was at Fox House when they tried to get the dogs to sing along to "Auld Lang Syne" (but they wouldn't cooperate). Sometimes his letters are rushed as he moves between places, but he wants to say hello and send his love. Once he arrives in Europe he is concerned about Dorothy. Where is she? What is she doing? Is she okay? Has she returned to Hollywood? Will she be okay there on her own? He gets mutual friends to check if she needs anything. He writes letter after letter, enclosing little ink drawings of bunches of lilacs or clothes he has seen in Paris. He sends her a poem referring to her as his "little knitting sweetheart." Occasionally, Parker makes phantom appearances as he thanks her for her letters and comments on things she has said (we don't know what they are; we must guess). He repeatedly tells her how much he misses and loves her. He is witty, teasing, flirtatious, thoughtful, romantic. There are newspaper clippings, postcards, and sometimes photographs—one taken of a wrapped-up

Campbell on the Champs-Élysées in Paris with the snow so thick that the Arc de Triomphe is not even visible. We live Alan Campbell's war as Dorothy Parker knew it. There is no doubt these are moving and touching documents.

But letters can be deceiving, because before Alan Campbell left for Europe, he and Parker went on a vacation to Miami, where something terrible happened. Observed by the writer-director Joshua Logan, who had met the Parker-Campbells in New York, their relationship, he believed, was desperately unhappy. This was confirmed by Logan's girlfriend, the actress Nedda Harrigan, who was also present. Parker was grumpy, Campbell was tense. Logan thought Parker would be tough, with an acid voice, but instead he found she sweetly delivered devastating barbs "as though it killed her to say them."[31] Everyone was partying and heavily drinking. One night there was an almighty fight and when Parker appeared for lunch the next day, she had a black eye. She said, sadly, to Nedda, "That's not very pretty is it? Not very pretty at all." She felt that Alan was distancing himself, using the army to escape her. He pointed out that she was the one who urged him to enlist. Their arguments were exhausting and circular, each accusing the other, both bitterly resentful. It was out of character for Campbell to be physically violent, yet shockingly he had turned on her in the worst way possible. He made clear that since enlisting he had loved military life, in fact he thrived on it, a theme that would emerge from his letters repeatedly over the next three years. Parker miserably told Nedda that Alan didn't need her anymore now that he had his war.

The hotel sign that remains today at the site of the Ambassador Hotel, Wilshire Boulevard, Los Angeles. © Kevin Cummins

The parking sign that remains today at the site of the Ambassador Hotel, Wilshire Boulevard, Los Angeles. © Kevin Cummins

Inside the Cocoanut Grove, the nightclub in the Ambassador Hotel, now demolished. © Michael Ochs Archives/Getty Images

Dorothy Parker reviewing a manuscript, January 1948.
© New York Times Co./Getty Images

Parker's closest friend, Robert Benchley, reading the *New Yorker*, 1936.
© Granger Historical Picture Archive/Alamy Stock Photo

First edition book jacket of *Not So Deep as a Well*, Viking Press, 1936. © Gail Crowther

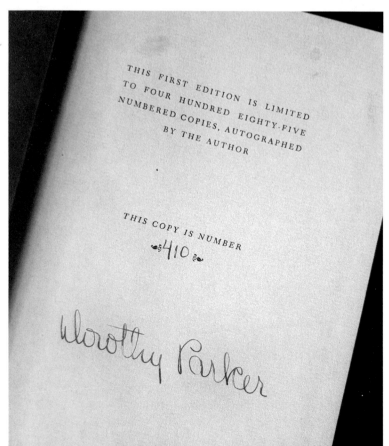

THIS FIRST EDITION IS LIMITED
TO FOUR HUNDRED EIGHTY-FIVE
NUMBERED COPIES, AUTOGRAPHED
BY THE AUTHOR

THIS COPY IS NUMBER
410

Dorothy Parker

Rare surviving example of Parker's handwriting, 1936. © Gail Crowther

In the foreground, the location of the long-demolished Garden of Allah, with
Chateau Marmont across the road, Sunset Boulevard, West Hollywood.
© Kevin Cummins

Dorothy Parker and Alan Campbell, Hollywood, late summer 1936. © Masheter Movie Archive/Alamy Stock Photo

One of Parker and Campbell's first rented Beverly Hills homes, at 520 North Canon Drive. © Kevin Cummins

One of Parker and Campbell's many Beverly Hills homes, at 914 North Roxbury Drive. Their neighbor was James Stewart. © Kevin Cummins

Paramount Studios, Hollywood.
© Kevin Cummins

Dorothy Parker and
Alan Campbell arriving in
Hollywood, September 1936.
© Bettmann/Getty Images

Fredric March and Janet Gaynor,
A Star Is Born, 1937. © Everett
Collection, Inc./Alamy Stock Photo

Dorothy Parker weeping
on the piano at a Spanish Civil
War fundraiser in Los Angeles
just before a fight broke out
between the event's host, Leon
Henderson, and photographer
Joseph S. McCoy, January 1939.
© Bettmann/Getty Images

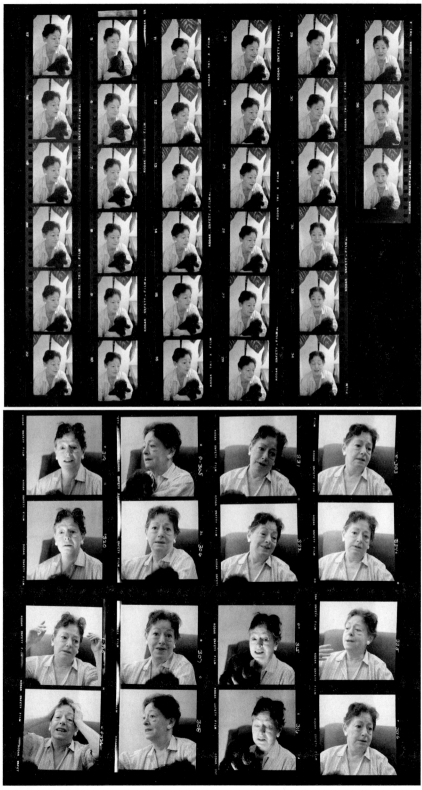

Dorothy Parker contact sheets by Norman Parkinson, 1959. © Courtesy the Norman Parkinson Estate and Iconic Images, London

Parker and Campbell's final home together, at 8983 Norma Place, West Hollywood.
© Kevin Cummins

Dorothy Parker's grave in
Woodlawn Cemetery,
the Bronx, New York.
© Kevin Cummins

Nineteen forty-three did not show any promise of being a better year. It began in January with the death of Alexander Woollcott, who suffered a heart attack, quickly followed by a cerebral hemorrhage. Parker was shocked and saddened to lose one of her oldest friends, and one of the few people she often confided in. It sparked in her a reflection about mortality and age that she would eventually write down and publish the following year. "The Middle or Blue Period" is an uncomfortable read musing upon the horrors of encroaching age and how to resist sinking into despair. There is no answer. "Years are only garments, and you either wear them with style all your life, or else you go dowdy to the grave."[32] The problem is not so much living or dying, but the middle bit in between. "People ought to be one of two things, young or old. No; what's the good of fooling? People ought to be one of two things, young or dead."[33] Joshua Logan noticed how Parker seemed to be struggling both physically and emotionally. She appeared both needy and in need of care, and her hangovers left her "a pale grey-green. Her cheeks throbbed slightly and her eyes were more rheumily tearful than usual."[34] His description suggests someone battling depression and addiction. As she felt Campbell slipping farther away, alcohol got the better of her. She was twitchy and unable to function without a drink in the morning.

As 1943 progressed, Parker invited her sister, Helen, to visit her in Hollywood. In her biography, Marion Meade includes a photograph taken during this visit. Far from the frumpy wreck described by Joshua Logan, Parker looks glamorous and polished in a fur coat, heels, and a splendid hat. She took Helen around the studios and film sets and introduced her to Joan Crawford and Marlene Dietrich. They ate at the legendary Romanoff's on North Rodeo Drive, where all the stars, including Cary Grant, Frank Sinatra, and Clark Gable, dined. (Romanoff himself was typically reclusive and ignored his clientele, preferring to lunch with his dogs.) Helen was dazzled but exhausted by her visit. In a letter sent back home, she wrote that she felt as though she was continually drinking (to be fair, she probably was), but was impressed by how everyone seemed to know and like Dorothy. It made it even more inexplicable, then, why she had to listen to her sister complaining all the time about Hollywood and everyone in it. "I can't understand why she hates it so."[35]

This time spent with her sister would be their last. The following January Helen had a stroke, followed by pneumonia, and died. She was only in her midfifties. Alan Campbell, feeling helpless, wrote to his wife wishing he could be with her, trying to offer platitudes that at least it was not a long, slow death. It was not to be the only sibling death that year, either. In October, Parker's brother Bertram, also still young, died at age sixty. Although they had not stayed especially close, the loss of her brother and sister, along with the unknown whereabouts of her eldest sibling, Harold, left Parker feeling as though her entire family were gone. It is little wonder that she wrote in "The Middle or Blue Period," *"Oh, come in, Middle Age, come in, come in! Come close to me, give me your hand, let me look in your face . . . Oh . . . Is that what you are really like? . . . Oh, God help me . . . help me . . ."*[36]

Throughout this year, it is only possible to track Parker's

movements through secondary sources. In May, Viking Press published *The Portable Dorothy Parker*, a collection of poems, stories, and articles selected by Parker herself, which outsold any of her previous collections and was still bringing in substantial royalties over twenty years later when she died. This book, still in print today in a slightly expanded version, received much coverage on publication. Even Marilyn Monroe had a copy on her shelves.

Parker often appears as a ghostly presence in Campbell's letters, which he seemed to write every couple of days. Things may have been tense between them, but despite the war and being apart, he indulged her in presents all year. He organized a fur coat to be sent from Wanamaker's. He sent her favorite powder puffs from France and ordered Edward Molyneux in Paris to make Parker a fine hat. He commented every time she published a piece and sent congratulations when her photograph appeared in *Vogue*. He had been corresponding with Joan Crawford and urged Dorothy to meet her for drinks in Hollywood. He complimented his wife on her full and newsy letters telling him everything he wanted to know and seemed relieved that she was getting out with friends. But the postal service was irregular and unreliable. Both complained to the other that they were not writing enough, then a flurry of letters would arrive, followed by apologies. At one stage in Paris, Campbell showed Joshua Logan a letter he had received from Parker that he declared should be in the Smithsonian. Neatly typed and full of seemingly random gossip, the letter ended with "P.S. If you will read the first letter of each sentence in this epistle you will find my real message."[37] The letters spelled out FUCK YOU. It is difficult to know whether this was serious or Parker's savage playfulness.

Campbell's war in 1944 by his own description was exciting, sometimes thrilling. He spent months in England enjoying dinners in fancy houses with well-off residents (but those British teeth!). He sent minute, detailed descriptions of house interiors, food, and people's clothes. This gives an insight into their mutual interests, showing how they must have worked together constructing stories from observing their surroundings in detail. Some of his letters read like scene directions for a film. He had nights out in London. His picture appeared in the *Tatler*, causing a stir in his squadron. By August he was in France and had been made a captain. By November he was touring air force bases with the actor David Niven, whom he initially found charming but two weeks later referred to as a shit. His adventures with Niven saw them staying in a Belgian château with a Dutch family who owned a tame wild boar (it followed them on walks and nuzzled them in the drawing room at night). Later that month he was drinking champagne with Noël Coward in Paris. In so many of these letters he expressed his longing for Parker, his wish to share everything with her, and saying that he got to brooding when he didn't hear from her. In September something had clearly happened, as he wrote a letter to Parker telling her not to let other people upset her. From what can be gleaned, it appeared that Nedda Harrigan had boasted about receiving long, romantic letters from Joshua Logan, didn't it upset Parker that Alan didn't do the same for her? Campbell was furious, accusing Harrigan of causing trouble, and annoyed with Parker for listening to her. He implored her not to let other people cloud their relationship. He explained that he tried his best with the letters he wrote and that there was much that he wanted to say but felt as though the paper came between them. Anyway, he said, what Harrigan didn't know was that Logan was having an affair with a married woman in London. Campbell tried hard to appease Parker and even mentioned that he had heard from a mutual friend that Dorothy was looking marvelous, thin, and in good shape.

In an era of texting, it is difficult to imagine the frustration of trying to hold a marriage together by letters—and letters written during a war, when everything was in chaos. Often Campbell would receive mail that had been posted six months earlier. The fragmented and out-of-order correspondence can only have exacerbated their problems. As Parker read about Campbell's dashing exploits in Europe, she dutifully sent him boxes full of socks, cigarettes, pencils, and gloves to help him deal with the bitterly cold winters. In one letter, as he was shivering with his feet stuffed close to a pathetic electric heater, he told her to keep cool in California. Their lives could not have been more different.

In 1945 they began the year arguing whether Campbell sent Parker some perfume. Despite this, he expressed his wishes that they be together for the next New Year's Eve. But clearly all was not well. In February, the gossip columnist Dorothy Kilgallen ran a report that the Parker-Campbells were divorcing, and this left Parker deeply upset. Campbell told her to ignore it, but he was tired of "too fucking many people" causing trouble between them. For most of the year they discussed back and forth the *Portable F. Scott Fitzgerald* that Parker was compiling, deciding which stories worked best and which to exclude. But until May, Campbell continued to enjoy quite a lovely war, attending a soiree at the home of the Vicomtesse Marie-Laure de Noailles in Paris, admiring walls filled with art by Picasso, Matisse, Rubens, Dalí, and Degas.[38] His dining companion was Gertrude Stein. In the spring, Parker sent him a photograph that he declared the best he had ever seen and called her his "favorite pin-up girl."[39]

It is difficult to know what Parker was up to; undoubtedly she was moving around as much as ever, and some of her letters made Campbell laugh out loud, which he likely needed because on VE Day he was in Dachau helping to liberate the camp. In June he had a jeep accident and was in the hospital for months with a smashed-up leg that he could not bend (but was cheered by visits from Mickey Rooney and Gertrude Stein). Longing to get home, he asked Parker to find a place for them to live, somewhere they wouldn't be bothered and could enjoy a life of their own. His mother, Hortense, continued to cause trouble, and by August had seemingly moved herself into Fox House, grumbling that her own home had no proper well for water or a washing machine. Campbell complained that he was already sending half his salary to his mother, but it never seemed enough. One consequence of this was that Parker had to cover all the costs for the farm, for the apartment in New York, and for wherever she stayed in Hollywood. In Europe, Campbell was trying to live on $165 a month, but even then he would receive bills that his mother had run up in various stores. With obvious frustration, he wrote to Parker, "I get no mail at all now, except an occasional querulous note from my mother saying how her spirits droop when she doesn't hear from me. And how mine do, when I hear from her."[40] With financial pressure once again an issue, Parker accepted a job in Hollywood working with the screenwriter Frank Cavett, along with a salary that Campbell described as "whacking." Although the movie is not named, it was almost certainly the start of building a story for *Smash-Up: The Story of a Woman*, which would be filmed in 1946. Back in Hollywood, for the first time in a decade Parker found herself afflicted once again with hives, again with no known cause. Campbell suggested it had to be nerves. This would hardly be surprising given their prolonged separation and sniping in transatlantic letters. He wrote to her that he felt like an incompetent husband, and he worried about where she would stay in Hollywood. (As it happened, initially she was at the Beverly Hills Hotel, then moved in with Frank Cavett on Monteel Road while trying to secure Benchley's apartment in the Garden of Allah.)

From October 1945 onward, Campbell's letters are full of longing and homesickness. He repeatedly tells Parker how much he misses and loves her and desperately wants to get home. Often this desire is firmly underlined in black ink for emphasis. Parker seemed to be more restless than ever, and Campbell struggled to keep track of her movements as she ricocheted between New York and Hollywood. The one-sided correspondence and Parker's silence creates a unique sense of confusion, and it is not difficult to share Campbell's bewilderment at where she is and what she is doing.

In November, however, this silence becomes particularly powerful because a life-changing event occurred. Robert Benchley died. Although he and Parker had drifted slightly, mainly because he did not share her commitment to left-wing politics, they nevertheless had enjoyed a vital, unique, and long-standing friendship. The writer Adela Rogers St. Johns, who had observed them both together, believed Benchley had been the most important man in Parker's life. She felt that Benchley provided Parker with her inspiration and that theirs was the rare nonsexual love-friendship. She noticed that they were deeply protective toward each other and recounted a Hollywood party where a boring studio executive attempted to read, and subsequently butchered, a sketch written by Benchley. During the reading Parker stood up from the table, picked up a magnum of champagne (which was almost bigger than her), clunked the reader over the head with it, and calmly poured the contents over his prostrate body. Her excuse was the insult to Benchley's work. "'It was a desecration,' she said."[41] His death must have been a blow to Parker. Across the Atlantic, Campbell understood this, and there is a sense of panic in his letters as he shared how "incredulous" he felt that Benchley had died. "I wish to God I could be with you now, because I know what you're feeling and thinking."[42] Whatever it was, we do not know, and Parker stayed silent about Benchley's death until the late 1950s.

By 1946, Campbell had been promoted to major and was able to send some money to Parker. In January, they both helped to get a young, Jewish, half-Polish, half-Irish boy who had survived Dachau into America (this was not the first time they had offered someone aid of this nature). They each wrote an affidavit saying they would take full responsibility for him when he entered the country. His story was so horrible, Campbell refused to tell Parker what had happened. Though one gets an idea what Campbell was witnessing from an earlier letter in which he describes visiting an anti-Nazi family in Berlin. One family member was a half-Jewish woman who had been sent to Buchenwald, where she lost seventy-eight pounds. Campbell noted that although she was only forty-three, she looked seventy.

By the end of January, Hiram Beer had offered to buy all the machinery and farm the land for himself at Fox House, paying Campbell and Parker a quarter of his profits for rent. This meant Hiram would cover all the bills for the farm, remain responsible for the upkeep, and would no longer take a salary; he was even willing to buy their truck. Campbell thought it the perfect solution and accepted immediately without even consulting Parker, happy to shed at least some of their financial burden.

Yet Campbell was not living like a man suffering from money troubles. From late 1945 and into 1946, he seemed to increasingly visit London from his base in Paris. He attended plays and parties, and even went to watch a Christmas pantomime. Parker wondered if her husband would ever come home, and she presumably wrote this, seeing as Campbell assured her that he missed her dreadfully, "whatever you say."[43] She was suspicious and felt he was dragging his feet, that he did not want to return to her or to their life in Hollywood. Given her failing health, her grief over her friend, and her increased restlessness, it must have been hard to receive letters from Campbell containing sentences such as "I feel wonderful and am definitely not bored, for a number of reasons."[44] He may have felt homesick, but he remained in Europe. They appeared to have reached an impasse in their relationship.

But of course, nothing ever stays the same. There are missing letters at this point in their correspondence, either lost, destroyed, or deliberately withheld. The silences can be filled with gossip from friends or people who were not present; we do not really know. But events took an unexpected and shocking turn. Parker knew that *something* was not right, but she did not know what it was. Eventually she found out but could never have anticipated what she was about to be told. Alan Campbell was not returning to Hollywood. He had fallen in love with another woman in London and their marriage was over.

CHAPTER 7

No Happy Endings

I want to overthrow prejudice and injustice.
—Dorothy Parker[1]

The end of the Parker-Campbell marriage appeared to create an explosion of gossip among their friends and in the media. Was Campbell's London affair really with a woman or was it secretly a man? (It was a woman.) Did Parker become so depressed in the period afterward that she subjected herself to electroconvulsive therapy? (Completely unsubstantiated.) What was Alan Campbell's breaking point that made him walk away? There were so many theories and much speculation. In May 1947, finally back in America, he settled in Las Vegas and sued Parker for divorce on the grounds of mental cruelty, claiming a wartime separation had turned them into strangers.[2] Parker immediately lodged a cross-complaint, which she won, and was granted a divorce by Judge Frank McNamee on the grounds of Campbell's mental cruelty. A property agreement was to be drawn up in New York, but effectively the marriage was dissolved.[3] Gossip columnists took sides. Hedda Hopper was firmly with Parker and happy to imply that Campbell would be finished without his more famous, talented wife. While he was in Vegas, she reported, Campbell had decided to combine business with pleasure and write a book about divorcées but could find no spicy yarns and didn't meet anyone interesting, "so he left without his story. But I dare say Dorothy will write it for him one of these days."[4] While the gossip raged, Fox House was quietly sold at a loss. Everything they had built together over almost thirteen years of marriage was gone.

Yet while her relationship with Campbell had been disintegrating, Parker had been unusually productive. She had spent much of the previous year in Hollywood working on the script for *Smash-Up: The Story of a Woman*, which was released in March 1947. Little attention has been given to this movie, both as a piece of social commentary and as to what it must have meant to Parker to work on it. Though she was always quick to dismiss her achievements, this is a film that deserves revisiting for several reasons.

Most significantly, it was one of the first films to deal seriously with female alcoholism. In 1945 *The Lost Weekend*, about the demise of Don Birnam, an alcoholic writer played by Ray Milland, had been released. This movie had sailed close to the winds of breaking all production code ethics given that excessive drinking was not allowed to be depicted on film. When Walter Wanger, the producer of *Smash-Up*, approached the Production Code Administration, they tried to dissuade him from making the film. He successfully argued that showing excessive drinking in this case was necessary for the plot and characterization, and surprisingly, they gave him the go-ahead. With echoes of *A Star Is Born*, the story centers around Angie Evans (Susan Hayward), a successful nightclub singer, who meets and falls in love with another singer, Ken Conway (Lee Bowman). His career has stalled, so Angie uses her contacts to get him work, and before long his fame eclipses hers. Now married and staying at home with their daughter, Angie watches her success fade as Ken's work takes him away for longer periods of time on tour. The separation breeds suspicion, and Angie begins to suspect her husband is having an affair. Then she begins to drink. As her alcoholism grows increasingly worse, her behavior at parties becomes aggressive and embarrassing—there is an impressive hair-pulling fight that takes place in a bathroom—and Ken eventually demands a divorce. Without giving away too much of the plot, Angie sinks further into her addiction, and it is only a shocking and dangerous incident that offers a shred of hope at the end of the film.

There are some notable parallels between Angie and Dorothy Parker, who was working on the original story with Frank Cavett. After a long time away from Campbell, she was suspicious that he was involved with someone else in Europe, and her suspicion turned out to be correct. But she was also drinking heavily and had been for years. Yet given Parker's notorious self-loathing, the message of the film is remarkably contemporary. There is none of the woman-shaming you might expect from such a story, but rather a sensitive handling of alcoholism not as a weakness but as a collective problem. Rather than treating

Angie as an individual who has no self-control over the demon drink, it offers a much fuller picture of addiction. Writing about alcoholism in 2022, Dr. Carl Erik Fisher claimed that viewing addiction through a disease paradigm is insufficient. It is a complex problem that requires community support and needs placing in a historical, philosophical, sociological, and economic context. What people need is hope and a picture of addiction that allows them to see it not as pessimistic but as contiguous with all human suffering.[5]

This bears similarities to the message in *Smash-Up: The Story of a Woman*. Although the disease paradigm is used from time to time, it is placed in a wider context to show why Angie becomes an addict, how support from many places offers her hope, and the type of issues she needs to think about to overcome her addiction. Key to this is learning to love herself again after no longer caring about her life (at one point she cries, "It's my business what I do. I don't hurt anybody but myself!").

Although the film was initially a loss at the box office, it was nominated for two Academy Awards, and brought Dorothy Parker a nomination for Best Writing (Original Story).[6] If *A Star Is Born* gave Parker the opportunity to vent her dislike of Hollywood, *Smash-Up* allowed her to creatively engage with and represent what it felt like to be a female alcoholic.

And this alcoholism undoubtedly contributed to the next thirteen years of Parker's life, which have a hallucinatory, confusing, and chaotic feel to them. They are badly documented, difficult to trace; she pops up from time to time only to disappear again. Key moments leap out, then fade. While her divorce was being finalized, she appeared to be based in New York, becoming increasingly involved in political movements and activism. Most notably, in 1947 she helped to establish, and became chair of, the Voice of Freedom Committee. This was a left-wing collective attempting to fight the increasing anti-communist hysteria present in American media and to democratize "the disfiguring mirror of our press and radio."[7] Parker did not mess about and immediately called in favors from her Hollywood friends. An exchange of telegrams between Parker and Orson Welles is held in the Lilly Library, Indiana University, revealing not only a warm friendship but also political solidarity. Upon meeting Welles for the first time, Parker had said, "It's like meeting God without dying," and she was keen to get him involved in the committee's activities.[8] Welles was someone Parker described as the number one person displaced by radio's iron curtain, and she asked him to appear at a "dramatic" rally the committee was planning in New York.[9] Even the mention of his name made their stock go through the roof, claimed Parker. Welles was eager to help, but when his latest film was brought forward and he could no longer fly to New York, he offered to record a broadcast instead. Addressing his telegrams to "Dottie" and signing them "Much love Orson," Welles assured Parker that she could always count on him.

This was just as well, since later in the year Parker witnessed a spectacle she described as "shocking, dreadful, terrifying."[10] Nineteen left-wing Hollywood writers and directors had been cited for contempt of Congress for refusing to answer questions put to them by the House Un-American Activities Committee.

As establishment paranoia grew about left-wing activism, the Civil Rights Congress held a reception in honor of the Hollywood Nineteen at the Park Central Hotel. In front of four hundred people, Parker gave a speech about the HUAC session she had viewed, declaring, "It was incredibly hideous, as though the Gestapo was there and fascism was there."[11] Ominously, she concluded, "Fascism isn't coming here—it is here."[12]

While her political world appeared full and productive, she tried to resurrect other areas of her life by replacing Alan Campbell both personally and professionally with a young lover named Ross Evans. It seems she had first met him in Miami just after Campbell's application had been accepted and before he was sent to Europe. He partied with the couple while he and Campbell waited to be assigned. Evans was young, good-looking, and an aspiring writer. But, most dangerous for Dorothy Parker, he was known by his friends to be a chronic alcoholic. During conscription, when he was taking exams, he was so drunk that his friends claimed they helped him cheat. While Alan Campbell was in Europe he occasionally saw Evans and reported back to Parker that Evans was being typically Evans. The implication was that Evans was nice but in some ways clueless, not too bright, a bit chaotic, a bit of a mess. Why Parker chose him is a mystery, but they immediately moved to Hollywood and started collaborating on *The Fan*, a movie version of Oscar Wilde's play *Lady Windermere's Fan*. It must have been an unimaginably painful time for Parker. Her marriage had ended, the care and support Alan had offered were gone, Robert Benchley was dead, and the Garden of Allah, the site of so many happy memories, was already in so much of a decline that it was not an especially desirable location in which to stay. Immediately across the road, however, was a much more alluring location, and Parker and Evans moved into the Chateau Marmont.

Opened in 1929 on Sunset Boulevard, the Chateau was a jumble of gables, turrets, and slate roofs based on a Gothic castle in the Loire Valley, France, called Château d'Amboise. While the original castle looked across vineyards and orchards and shared a celebrity history (Leonardo da Vinci was buried on the grounds), the hotel version was designed to look across Los Angeles and its growing community. Although in its early years it was initially known as a quiet place for out-of-towners who wanted to avoid Hollywood's glitz, things changed just after World War II. When Parker moved in, both the hotel and Sunset Boulevard were "opening its doors to all—straight, gay, sober, addled, black, white, from all walks of life, at reasonable prices, making up with discretion and tolerance what it might have lacked in luxurious touches."[13] It seems likely there were political reasons why Parker chose to stay and felt comfortable there. The owner, Erwin Brettauer, had had the good fortune and means to flee Germany in the early 1930s and was openly anti-Nazi. Having witnessed increasing hatred and anti-Semitism in his home country, he was determined that the Chateau Marmont be not only discreet but, more importantly, *accepting*; "Chateau Marmont was more than a hideaway, it was a sanctuary."[14] In 1947 a pool was built, and it was as convenient for Schwab's Pharmacy as the Garden of Allah had been. Bungalows were built on the grounds, and Garbo now stayed there during her visits from New York, but more radically, Brettauer introduced a policy that no one would be refused a room based on race, religion, or sexuality. According to Shaun Levy, who wrote a history of Chateau Marmont, throughout the forties and fifties, hotels such as the Beverly Hills, the Beverly Wilshire, and the Hollywood Roosevelt refused to book Black guests, but the Chateau Marmont had no color barrier.[15] It's easy to see why Dorothy Parker, with her social and political allegiances, felt happy staying there.

But it is hard to know how she filled her days. *The Fan* was released to mixed reviews. Most critics did not really like the film but appreciated that Parker was at least the right person to try to Americanize the wit of Oscar Wilde. The *Los Angeles Times* claimed, "Dorothy Parker has the icy glitter of sheer wit and the sparkling perfection of phrase to match Wilde." The paper even went as far as to claim that some of the lines she rewrote would have Wilde wishing they were his from beyond the grave—"Nothing looks so much like innocence as an indiscretion."[16] But there was a feeling of a falling-off, of Parker's power not quite hitting the mark. Sadly, this is the last film that she ever worked on in Hollywood that made it to production.

The rest of her time seemed to be taken up with Evans, collaborating on an ill-fated play, *The Coast of Illyria*, based on the lives of brother-sister duo Charles and Mary Lamb. It was staged in Dallas in April 1949 but only lasted for three weeks, then disappeared. The press noted that Parker seemed to spend most of her time in the Players, a bar-restaurant in the shadow of Chateau Marmont, so close by that there was reportedly a secret tryst tunnel running between the two. With no Alan to curb her drinking, and given that she was living with another alcoholic who would get even drunker than she did, her life seemed an uneasy cycle of drinking, hangovers, debts, and undirected work.

But her political activism, as Alan Campbell had feared it would for years, was gaining attention. Parker was both fearless and irritated in response to this. In 1949 the espionage trial of a young woman named Judith Coplon got underway. Coplon worked for the Department of Justice but was accused of having become a Russian spy (code name Sima) in 1945. Although she was convicted in 1949 for espionage and in 1950 for conspiracy, both convictions were subsequently overturned on appeal. It was during her first trial, however, that an FBI report read in court listed the names of noted Hollywood celebrities who were regarded as communists. Dorothy Parker was one of the celebrities, along with others such as Fredric March, Edward G. Robinson, Frank Sinatra, Orson Welles, Danny Kaye, and Gene Kelly. The Washington *Evening Star* ran an article with ten photographs of the named and shamed looking like mug shots. But the press did give the accused a right of reply. Fredric March called the FBI accusations "[a]n unmitigated lie. My record and conscience as an American and as a man are clear."[17] Frank Sinatra was more bullish: "If they don't cut it out I'll show them how much an American can fight back, even against the State, if the American happens to be right. And I'm right—not left."[18] Interviewed in her Hollywood apartment, Parker ridiculed the claims and took the opportunity to assert her political stance even further. "This makes me very sick. I'm damned glad to be an

American and always have been. I regret to say I know no Russians, but I wish I did. Maybe it would help understanding if we all knew some Russians."[19] With a glimmer of Parker acerbity and ambiguity she further declared, "I have no desire to sell any secrets, because I don't know any. Overthrow our government? I want to overthrow prejudice and injustice."[20] These were very clever answers. Some readers must have been left wondering.

With not much work coming their way in Hollywood, Ross Evans suggested he and Parker move somewhere quieter where they could work and live cheaply. At the top of his list was Cuernavaca, a town south of Mexico City, so in March 1950 they drove across the border and rented a cheap house on the edge of town. Apart from managing to meet up with Martha Gellhorn, who was living nearby with her son, Parker was profoundly unimpressed. For a woman used to Manhattan and Hollywood, small-town living without reliable electricity was far from ideal. In the wake of the Coplon trial and the fallout of being publicly named a communist, it is not clear how aware Parker was of the level of surveillance she was under. But under surveillance she was, even in Mexico. In May 1950, the director of the FBI requested an information-gathering exercise on Parker to establish whether a full investigation was warranted. She had been named by the informant Louis Budenz as a "concealed communist" (the term referred to members of the Communist Party who were so high profile, their membership was kept under the radar, away from scrutiny).[21] Budenz claimed he could name around four hundred concealed communists, but when the FBI requested a list of names, he said he had only composed a *mental* list. Parker, though, he was sure, was one of them, despite his never having met her. He had been repeatedly *told* she was an active member. As the FBI got to work tracking down every organization Parker had supported, and even more challenging, every address she had lived at, it became clear that the FBI regarded even the most benign group as a front for the Communist Party—including the League of Women Shoppers. Parker's involvement in establishing the Screen Writers Guild was unearthed, as were her role in forming the Hollywood Anti-Nazi League, all her work for Spanish aid during the civil war, and her more recent role as chair of the Voice of Freedom Committee. Page after page listed every rally she had attended, every dinner she spoke at, any letter or article she published in a magazine or paper. A female informant said she had attended a party at Parker's house, and a guest, Eli Jacobs, spoke about Marxism. From the way he spoke, claimed the informant, "he was not just trying to entertain them."[22] Newspaper clippings were included, one citing Parker's public scorn for the FBI. Another page noted that Parker resided in a boardinghouse in Cuernavaca and that when the proprietor, Constancia de la Mora (a well-known communist), died, Parker took over running the boardinghouse. If anything stretched credulity, the thought of Parker running a boardinghouse, when she could barely take care of herself, is possibly the most unlikely claim in the whole report. Though the fact that de la Mora had died two months before Parker even arrived also highlights the unreliable and somewhat fanciful nature of these claims.

Perhaps if Parker had known she was under surveillance during her time in Mexico she might have had more fun. As it was, Ross Evans began an affair with a woman who ran a clothing shop, and a furious Parker took a flight to New York and booked herself into the Plaza. Declaring that she now planned to live alone forever, it came as something of a surprise to her friends to hear that three months later she was married again. To Alan Campbell.

According to the story they told the press, Campbell, who was in Hollywood, called up Parker, who was in New York, and asked her to marry him. He claimed, somewhat curiously, "She said yes. You never know why you do these things."[23] Parker told the press they had no plans for a honeymoon because they had already been everywhere. If romance seemed low on the list of reasons, despite the arguments and conflict there was nevertheless a deep connection between the two. Wyatt Cooper, who would get to know the couple over the coming years, noticed their unusually close relationship, the type of bond that comes when you know another person's habits, good and bad, and still love them. He wrote movingly, "It is often said of married couples, 'They couldn't be happy together and they couldn't be happy apart,' and this certainly applied to Dottie and Alan. They were two of the most engaging people in the world, and absolutely right for each other. Probably they were *too* right for each other. Their relationship was an extraordinary one, incredibly close, each strongly identifying with the other, but also mutually antagonistic and somehow fearful and bitter toward the other."[24] So on August 17, they remarried in Campbell's rented Bel Air home at 240 Bentley Avenue, with various writers, actors, and industry luminaries in attendance. Parker wore a dark dress with a sweetheart neckline and ruched sleeves. Her jewelry was simple, a slim pearl necklace, and her hair was swept up at the back with her customary bangs in the front. Campbell, as immaculate as ever, wore a dark double-breasted suit and tie and a matching boutonniere from Parker's bouquet. Of course, both looked older because they were. Sixteen years had passed since their first marriage. Yet in photographs taken on the day, they both retain a certain youthful charm. Parker, who would turn fifty-seven five days later, looked at least a decade younger. Campbell, still in his forties, was strikingly handsome, but had an older air about him. He had witnessed things in Europe during the war, the liberation of concentration camps, survivors of the Nazi regime, and, more recently back in America, the death of an actor-friend and roommate through an overdose. But without Parker his Hollywood career had somewhat stalled. An executive at Fox told him to hook up with his ex-wife and they would employ him, and that's exactly what happened after their remarriage. But in the meantime, the wedding ceremony itself was celebratory, a huge Hollywood bash with wild games afterward, sumptuous food and drink, and, according to Parker, people mingling who had not spoken to each other in years, "including the bride and groom."[25]

Yet all was not well. The Parker-Campbells may have reunited but there was a tenuous air about it. More forebodingly, on the front page of the *Los Angeles Times* announcing their remarriage was an article about the "Communist Hand" at play in California. In December, the FBI were hot on Parker's trail, listing her address as 8221 Sunset Boulevard (which was the

Chateau Marmont) and still investigating the claim by Budenz that she was a concealed member of the Communist Party and active on several communist fronts. The report also lists where she stayed when in New York (the Plaza) and that her publisher was Viking Press.[26] One informant named in the file also claimed that Parker had admitted to him she was a member of the Communist Party, "but probably on being confronted with this, she would deny having ever made that statement."[27] Which really left Parker in something of a bind—if questioned, any denial she made couldn't possibly be believed. And this is what happened the following April when two FBI agents turned up at her house to conduct an interview. Her address was listed now as 216 South Westgate Avenue, where they proceeded to ask her about her political affiliations, organizations she had funded, and whether her friends were communists. She stated that she had never been affiliated with, donated to, or been contacted by a representative of the Communist Party. The agents noted that Parker was about five four, weighed approximately 125 pounds, had brown-black hair and a fair complexion, and appeared to be a very nervous type of person. The report did not note that during the interview Parker's dog barked, jumped up at the men, and misbehaved the entire time. When they asked if she had conspired to overthrow the government, she replied, "Listen, I can't even get my dog to stay down. Do I look to you like someone who could overthrow the government?"[28] Based on the interview, the agents concluded that no Security Index card "is being recommended at this time."[29]

But what did become a real problem was the number of times Alan Campbell's name appeared in the reports. He had always been nervous about Parker's political activities and felt any radical associations threatened their livelihood in Hollywood. He was right to think this because it did. Parker was blacklisted and never worked on another film that went into production. Although their remarriage had been a celebratory event, if it *was* partially based on regaining a working relationship, this failed, and so within a year the second marriage failed too. After an explosive row, Campbell walked out and left for New York. Parker remained alone in their Hollywood home, and a few days later moving vans arrived to strip the (presumably) rented furniture from the place.

This moment marked the beginning of a ten-year descent for Parker. And ten years is a long time. Living alone in an empty house, she welcomed two lodgers: the screenwriter and former film critic for *Time* James Agee, and his companion, a young woman named Pat Scallon. Agee was in terrible shape: recovering from an alcohol-induced heart attack, he remained firmly addicted to drinking and badly neglected his personal hygiene. He wore the same filthy clothes each day and could easily consume three bottles of scotch in an evening. Both he and Parker seemed to drink themselves senseless, often until they were falling over or crashing into things. Who knows how long this would have continued if within a couple of months Agee had not suffered a second heart attack and been taken away to recover. With her house now a fetid mess, in fact so disgusting that friends no longer wanted to visit her, she decided to leave Hollywood and return to New York.

Between 1951 and 1961 it is hard to imagine what life was like for Dorothy Parker. The days appeared to drift in her small apartment in the Volney Hotel, which soon became as dirty as her Hollywood home. Drinking to excess, living among piles of dog waste, smoking, falling asleep, waking up to start drinking all over again. On the one hand, she just simply seemed to disappear. On the other, her legacy began to cement itself as though she were already dead. She began to receive awards; she spent time at the prestigious Yaddo writers colony in Saratoga Springs; and in a final burst of regular income, *Esquire* magazine invited her to be their book reviewer (and generously overlooked the sporadic nature of her submissions, loyally paying her whether she turned in copy or not). In 1952 she collaborated on a play with Arnaud d'Usseau called *The Ladies of the Corridor*, a powerful exploration of ladies of a certain age living in a certain kind of establishment that bore more than a slight resemblance to the Volney. The characters, too, were familiar, echoes from earlier short stories and even film scripts. It was as though Parker was weaving a tapestry of her own work, her own life, her own experiences. The play was, she later claimed, the only piece of work she was truly proud of, despite it only receiving a six-week run on its debut in October 1953. She remained disappointed for the rest of her life that it was never adapted into a movie.

In 1955 she was finally called to appear in front of the HUAC in New York, where in an exquisitely polite manner she answered all questions, until she was directly asked if she had ever been a member of the Communist Party. On this, she invoked the Fifth Amendment. Nevertheless, the FBI decided that she was not dangerous enough to appear on the index and closed their investigation into her activities. At this stage it hardly mattered. She was already blacklisted, and the damage had been done. And blacklisting existed in Hollywood, claimed Parker, primarily because "several gentlemen felt it best to drop names like marbles."[30] Whether there was any substance to the accusations made no difference: once you were tainted you were tainted, and there was no sympathy or support to be had. Parker wryly noted that "Sam Goldwyn said, 'How'm I gonna do decent pictures when all my good writers are in jail?' Then he added, the infallible Goldwyn, 'Don't misunderstand me, they all ought to be hung.' Mr Goldwyn didn't know about 'hanged.'"[31] And that, said Parker, is all there is to say about it.

Yet toward the end of the 1950s, Parker seemed to increasingly spend time looking back on her Hollywood career. Although she assumed it was over at this point, her overall take was that it *could* be destructive for writers, but that it didn't have to be. She admitted that she never just turned in any old writing but rather always worked hard, even on projects she didn't necessarily care about. That, for her, was one of the tragedies of screenwriting— using time and energy and skill on something one didn't necessarily choose or value. The hook, of course, was always money, and lots of it, but then this tension between creative freedom and earning a living is one that writers have always faced, and still do. Parker also knew it was not Hollywood that stopped her from writing fiction, it was herself. In the ten years away from movies, she wrote only three short stories, "I Live on Your Visits" (1955), "Lolita" (1955), and her last, "The Bolt Behind the Blue" (1958).

Yet even if her output was as slow as ever, in 1959 she was elected a member of the National Institute of Arts and Letters (where she was so drunk at the ceremony that she gave her speech twice). The same year she made an appearance on *Open End* with Norman Mailer ("that awful man who stabbed his wife")[32] and Truman Capote. But there is no doubt that Parker looked like an anachronism. The truth is she *was* from another century, and she felt it too. As poets like Anne Sexton and Sylvia Plath were receiving first reading contracts from the *New Yorker*, Parker's stories were being rejected. And as the Beat poets took over New York, Parker saved some particularly acidic words for them in several interviews—namely wishing they would beat off somewhere else (though one suspects this is not the word she used in private).

Yet there was something about Parker being so difficult to please that made people want to be liked by her even more. This was the woman who in 1934 was asked by the University of Michigan to judge a poetry competition, which she enthusiastically accepted. Things turned sour when upon receiving the shortlisted poems, she replied that none were worthy of any award or indeed of any consideration whatsoever. (Cue: an outraged organizer demanded she return the poems immediately, which she did, saying there was no need to pay her, it wasn't worth it.)[33] In a 1956 interview for the *Paris Review*, whose title, "Writers at Work," probably amused Parker greatly, she dismissed several contemporaries but saved the greatest praise for E. M. Forster as probably the greatest living novelist. Unknown to Parker—unknown because his letter remained unposted—

Forster read this interview and was unable to contain his delight. King's College Library, Cambridge, holds the unmailed letter from Forster, in which he gushes about her interview and her words, and declares that he must control himself. He does, however, manage to suggest that she may enjoy reading Mrs. Gaskell's *Wives and Daughters* if she has not done so already.[34] Even if she felt irrelevant or that she had outlived her time, her opinion mattered, and people desperately wanted her approval. Those who did gain it—Arthur Miller, Eudora Welty, John Osborne, J. D. Salinger, Katherine Anne Porter—gained it because Parker felt they had something to say, and because they had something to say, she believed that they would last. Unlike the Beat poets, who mystified Parker: "I don't know why they are so pleased with themselves . . . I don't think they are saying anything on earth other than look at us, aren't we great? . . . I don't think the beat generation is worth much worrying about, I should say oh very soon, the near future [they] will be forgotten . . ."[35] Yet when it was put to Parker that her own writing had something to say and would be lastingly great, she admitted that the thought made her embarrassed and frightened.[36] This seems a peculiar choice of words for a writer to use. Parker did seem embarrassed when she was praised, but being frightened that her work might last is more puzzling. The obvious question is what did she fear? The responsibility of a literary legacy? Not being able to slip into some sort of cultural oblivion? She did not expand and so we do not know.

For many of Parker's ten years in New York, Alan Campbell had been based in Hollywood or acted as somewhat of a professional, but charming, guest at various friends' houses when times became tough. It does seem as though they were sporadically in contact, and that Campbell sometimes visited her at the Volney, though these visits were awkward and forced. Their mutual friend Wyatt Cooper was present at one of them and found the strained atmosphere both uncomfortable and sad for a couple who had once meant everything to each other. Significantly, though, during those years they never divorced.

In 1961 many were surprised when Parker announced that she was moving back out to Hollywood to stay with Campbell on a purely professional basis so they could work together for Fox on a film called *The Good Soup*. Touted as a vehicle for Marilyn Monroe (whom Parker described as just as frightened as the rest of us but prettier), she believed that with a title like that and written by the Campbells, nothing could possibly go wrong. The producer Charles Brackett told the *Los Angeles Times* that Parker and Campbell had renamed the film *Love Is for Other People* and that they were writing it with "sad wisdom, comprehension, and wit."[37]

A few years earlier Alan had invested in a small one-story house at 8983 Norma Place in West Hollywood on a street that formed part of what was known as the Norma Triangle. Bordered by Doheny Drive on the west, Sunset Boulevard on the north, and Santa Monica Boulevard on the south, the area between these roads made the shape of a right triangle. The origins of the name are disputed. Some claim it is after the silent-film star Norma Talmadge, others that the streets are named after executives of the Los Angeles Pacific Railroad Company, which built the homes for its workers. A large portion of the triangle contains part of Boys' Town, a popular gay district, and many friends whom Parker and Campbell made were gay. Given Parker's earlier slurs toward her husband, she seemed remarkably quiet about the area in which he chose to settle. Norma Place and surrounding streets had moved out of the hands of railroad workers after World War II, and creative types as well as people connected to the movie industry began to move in. Estelle Winwood lived farther down the road, along with Tuesday Weld and Dorothy Dandridge. Hedy Lamarr and Judy Garland would pay visits to friends and attend parties in the neighborhood.

At first, given that their reunion was a professional one, Parker was unsure whether to move in with Campbell and for a while considered living in a hotel. But the small house had two bedrooms and she finally decided to take up residence in the front room with twin beds and a desk. She did, however, keep the lease on her apartment in the Volney for all of the following year. Life at Norma Place had a chaotic air about it. In interview transcripts held in the Marion Meade Papers at Columbia University Library, friends who visited recalled dirty and squalid living conditions: dog mess dotting the floors, rotting food in the refrigerator, endless renovations that Campbell would begin and never finish, piles of rubble, and overflowing ashtrays. This seemed to be borne out in 1962 by an interview Parker gave to Dorothy Townsend of the *Los Angeles Times*, who noted that their conversation was punctured by hammering and sawing from another part of the house.[38] When Townsend inquired if all the building work meant Norma Place would be their permanent home, Parker replied firmly, "I'm a hobo and mean to be forever."[39] At sixty-nine, she had no intention of settling down. A series of photographs that accompany the article show a radiant Parker, sometimes with a cigarette, always with a dog in her lap, and in front a table loaded with books and a pot of pens. Parker's hair is in its customary style with bangs, and she is immaculately groomed, with dark lipstick and an engaging smile. Even in the still images she looks as though she has absolutely no control over her poodle, Cliché.

But photographs are not always reliable storytellers. The reality of life on Norma Place was much grimmer. Alan's drinking had become even heavier over the years, and Noel Pugh, a friend of the couple and a resident of Norma Place, noted that Campbell was drunk all the time and Parker half of it. But more disturbingly, Campbell was also heavily reliant on barbiturates, in particular Seconal. Although this drug was used in the 1960s as a sleeping aid, recreational abuse was common, which may explain why Campbell often looked drugged or stoned to observers. Although the couple mostly got along well, their vicious cycle of drinking and fighting seemed to pick up where it had left off, and one or the other would frequently be staggering about or falling over. Gossip at the time reported Parker being so drunk late one night that she fell into a hedge in the adjoining road and had to be pulled out. Although this was told with a humorous edge, in fact the thought of a sixty-nine-year-old woman wandering around alone and so drunk that she cannot stand does not seem so funny on reflection.

Most neighbors seemed puzzled by the relationship between

Parker and Campbell, wondering what was in it for each of them. They observed that Campbell acted like a social secretary with plenty of time on his hands, organizing dinners and outings, shopping each day at the local grocery store wearing his pink sailor's hat, and walking the dogs. He had a sort of dishevelled elegance about him. If Parker was being interviewed by the media, he would take on the role of a butler, wearing a silk tie and ironed trousers, delivering pots of tea and being overly polite. Friends spoke more warmly about him than they did of Parker, who appeared to confuse them with her mix of helplessness and viciousness. Nina Foch, an actress and neighbor who lived directly across the road, drew parallels between Parker and Judy Garland. There was always a back-and-forth between sweet helplessness and "also I will kill you."[40] Foch felt Parker had a desperately sad ruthlessness about her, presenting herself as a broken bird, but if anyone went near, she'd squash them dead, despising the help she so clearly needed. Understandably, neighbors were wary, especially given that she was not above making rude comments about them within earshot. Occasionally she would get into direct confrontations, usually over trivial domestic issues. The screenwriter Hagar Wilde recalled yelling at Parker for letting Cliché use her front lawn as a toilet, insisting that Parker clean up the mess, which Parker flatly refused to do. Wilde threatened to call the police while shouting, "Who do you think you are? If that animal shits on my property one more time—," to which Parker calmly interjected, "There's no need to be tasteless, my dear," and tottered off home with Cliché in tow, leaving a pile on the lawn for someone else to clean up.

While Alan was seen as part of the neighborhood, many regarded Parker as much more aloof. Most people were undoubtedly fascinated and wanted her at their parties because she could be fun. But many noticed that her conversation was quality over quantity, and she often sat in a corner not really saying too much. Sometimes sitting in the corner was also her attempt at going under the radar if someone was present whom she had eviscerated in print.

Between the years of 1961 and 1962, the Parker-Campbells worked on the script for *The Good Soup*, often taking a ride to the studio with Wyatt Cooper, who was now living a few doors away on Norma Place. Eventually Campbell would splurge on a fancy green Jaguar, but until then the young writer was happy to act as chauffeur and spend time with Parker, of whom he remained completely in awe. The three of them would take long lunch breaks and spend hours eavesdropping on studio secretaries to keep up to date with any gossip. One of Parker's favorite activities was lurking in the studio restrooms so she could listen to conversations and discover the scandal of the day. She would immediately seek out Campbell and Cooper to report back. Often the three would drive for a lazy afternoon to Santa Monica, where on one trip Parker bought a set of model Napoleonic soldiers. She could not explain why she was so drawn to them, but for someone with scant personal possessions, she found this set of soldiers important. She made Alan build a special shelf for them in their home, with a spotlight, and they were one of the few possessions she kept until her death.

At some point in early 1962 the script for *The Good Soup* was finished, but in a letter dated "Ground Hog Day" Parker com-plained bitterly to the playwright John Patrick that the studio, "20th-Century Fucks," had hacked and ruined their work, which she described as a "darling, bawdy farce."[41] Although the letter is undated, it must have been written during the filming of Mari-lyn Monroe's final, unfinished film *Something's Got to Give*. Monroe, experiencing health problems, was frequently failing to show up on set, and it would be in June that Fox fired her. Parker, always on top of studio gossip, makes references to these ten-sions in her letter, writing, "The studio is beginning to view her as Marat must have regarded the lethally-poised Charlotte Cor-day."[42] As for Parker, who rightly predicted *The Good Soup* would never be made, she acknowledged that if it had gone ahead, Monroe would have been a "terrible problem, though I am crazy about her." Noel Pugh also noticed that whenever Parker spoke about Marilyn it was with affection; she clearly believed her to be both a beautiful and sensitive creature. Showing real compas-sion, Parker understood that Monroe could not help her behavior. She felt it came from Monroe being in a perpetual state of ter-ror. And Parker was not wrong, for in August of that year, Marilyn Monroe died. Alan Campbell told Hedda Hopper that Monroe's death had deeply upset Parker, though the two only knew each other slightly. What a loss to movie history that we never got to see Parker's bawdy dialogue delivered in Monroe's inimitable style.

There seemed little prospect of further film work, so Parker pretended to focus on book reviewing for *Esquire*, a pretense that often failed since Campbell would place a hair over her typewriter to see if she had been working. Invariably she had not. The hair remained in place. Nevertheless, she assured *Esquire* that she had indeed written and posted her reviews and could never understand why they did not arrive. Her New York–based agent, Leah Salisbury, sent various offers of work, but nothing seemed to be quite right. Doubleday requested Parker write her autobiography. Wyatt Cooper, who was present when the crumpled letter was presented to him, knew that it would never happen as he watched "her eyes sweep the room in hopeless supplication of those invisible but omnipresent forces that so capriciously shape our destinies."[43] If she *could* write it, she would call it *Mongrel*, she declared.

What Parker seemed to really enjoy with relish was the gossipy life of Norma Place, a one-block street so small that secrets were impossible, and everyone telephoned or visited each other constantly. Parker called it Peyton Place, West. According to Wyatt Cooper, nothing was beneath Parker's notice, no gossip too big or small. Who was starring in which film (when Cooper told her Estelle Winwood had won a part in *Camelot*, Parker retorted, "Playing a battlement, no doubt"), who had gone to the beach, who was having drinks with whom, and who'd gotten drunk and fallen off a porch. "Now and then," wrote Cooper, "we had a little extra excitement, like when a character lady's canary got out and all the fellows joined (unsuccessfully) in trying to recapture it, while the tearful owner jogged along, calling out to the fugitive bird, and Dottie tried to keep up, offering comfort as best she could."[44]

Though Parker was no longer producing new fiction, her

earlier short stories still captured readers. *The Portable Dorothy Parker* continued to bring in fresh royalties every year, and in May 1962 three of her stories were adapted for television.[45] Although Parker had always been dismissive of TV as a medium, in an interview that month she went a bit easier on it, even admitting there were certain programs she enjoyed watching (Hitchcock's weekly forays into amusing murders, and Dick Powell). She had no time, however, for *Thriller*, a series of macabre tales hosted by Boris Karloff, who came in for some classic Parker treatment. The show was obnoxious, she told her interviewer, as was the host: "And there is Boris Karloff up there saying, 'As sure as my name is Boris Karloff.' Actually his name is not Boris Karloff."[46] In a surprising admission, Parker claimed she would love to write for television, but nobody seemed interested in employing her. In many ways, the intimacy and colloquial nature of some of Parker's best work seems much better suited for TV than the movies, and with her skill for dialogue and love of ludicrous gossip, she would surely have made a perfect soap opera writer.

Instead, it seemed to be her own life that had turned into a soap opera, with various characters coming and going, drunken dramas, and neighborhood happenings to keep up with. When local forest fires were destroying acres of land and homes, Wyatt Cooper offered to take her to witness the inferno from a nearby hilltop. It was too unbearable, she said, and she couldn't possibly watch, as she pulled on a sweater and headed for the door. Looking across the conflagration, she cried with some distress of how frightened all the poor little animals must be before asking, "Do you think we could get any closer?"[47]

From time to time Parker gave public talks and lectures. One in late 1962 apparently left the audience of librarians "breathless," though one wonders whether this was for good or bad reasons. Always nervous, and often drunk, Parker could be an unpredictable speaker. During an evening in the ballroom of the Hotel del Coronado in San Diego, over a thousand people packed into the seats and aisles to hear Parker talk about her work, her life, and, in this case, how dreadful young writers were.[48] The journalist Dorothea McCall recalled how raptly everyone listened as Parker responded in an "outgoing" manner to her interviewer. "In agony," she urged librarians to get emerging writers to read, to stop them being so stuffy, because to date their contributions to literature amounted to nothing.[49] They came nowhere near one of her literary idols, F. Scott Fitzgerald, and his finest novel, *The Great Gatsby*. Yet despite being able to sell out a public lecture, McCall wrote that Parker was "from another day . . ."[50]

Royalties and occasional public lectures, though, were not enough to support Parker and Campbell, or to keep them supplied with the necessary amounts of alcohol and cigarettes. From her habitual place on the couch with a dog on her lap, refusing to move even to answer the door, Parker liked to welcome guests and hold court, but increasingly the scotch was of poorer quality. Neighbors noted that when Parker's glass was empty, she would hold it in the air and Campbell would quickly leap up and fetch her a refill. But despite this social veneer, there was an undeniable sense of disintegration occurring. Campbell, who seemed to become less steady on his feet by the day, would still attempt to do home renovations and all the cooking, though this became noticeably more erratic. One evening he served strips of aluminum foil in the salad to his guests. Loyal in the face of possible criticism, Parker complimented him on his cooking. Visitors noticed that the renovations were becoming stranger and that the bungalow appeared to be increasingly divided into what they described as smaller and smaller cubicles, none finished, none tidy. Open cans of dog food littered the space and exuded a pungent smell.

Clearly financial support was needed, so under the guidance of Wyatt Cooper, the three of them went to the unemployment office to apply for benefits. In the 1960s this was common in Hollywood, given the tenuous nature of the movie industry, and it was not unusual to see actors such as Marlon Brando turning up to sign for their weekly checks. Parker and Campbell acted as though they were about to commit major fraud, and Cooper had to assure them that it was perfectly fine, and that they had paid more than enough taxes over the years to be entitled to a hand-out now and again. Campbell was barely competent to complete the forms and it was pointless asking Parker, so Cooper did it for them, but he was not able to be present when either was interviewed. Watching Parker approach a clerk's desk, he felt a sinking feeling of dread, but Campbell, watching alongside him, noticed that the female clerk was wearing glasses, and he sat back smiling, saying how everything would now be okay. Sure enough, when the clerk read the name on the form, she looked up, removed her glasses, and excitedly got all her colleagues to gather around the desk, where they proceeded to pile praise on

Parker, who smiled sweetly and generally had a lovely time. Then they kindly arranged her weekly signing appointments to coincide with Cooper's so he could chauffeur her there.

Though the benefits, which amounted to about $75 each per week, eased things, it was still a significant comedown for a couple who had previously been earning up to ten times that amount. An acquaintance, Parker Ladd, who worked for the publisher Charles Scribner's Sons, noted with some concern Parker's precarious financial situation. He contacted his friend Frederick Shroyer, an English professor at California State College, to see if anything could be done. Shroyer, eager to help, decided it was possible that Parker could occupy the role of visiting professor that was just about to be vacated by Christopher Isherwood. Ladd, suspecting that Parker would immediately turn down the role, over the summer of 1962 enlisted the support of Campbell, and they plotted to make Parker an offer that she would find difficult to refuse. With a salary of $20,000 and the title of distinguished visiting professor of English, Parker would be expected to teach two courses over the coming year: one on twentieth-century American literature and one on English literature. She accepted.

With the luxury of hindsight, it is easy to see why this was not the ideal job for Parker. She was hopeless at timekeeping, she rarely met a deadline, and most of her interviews had suggested she was deeply disappointed with the younger generation. Cal State tried to make it as easy as possible: they provided a driver for her, and Shroyer took on all her grading. She essentially had to turn up and speak to the students, who were by all accounts excited to have such a grand name lecturing them. It was of course something of a disaster. It wasn't that Parker was a poor teacher, but it was almost certainly connected to her inability to be organized. She claimed she ran out of things to say after ten minutes. Sometimes she wouldn't show up at all. Then, in April 1963, she gave an interview to the *Los Angeles Times* that ran with the headline "Students Appalling to Dorothy Parker."[51] Criticizing students whom she was still teaching seemed inexplicable, particularly subjecting them to her Parkerish observations. In fairness to her, for every negative thing she said about them, she also said something negative about herself, but comments such as "They're sweet but not very young—most of them over 25 and a few grandmothers" and "No, I don't think any great writing can come from them" were perhaps insensitive, given she was still having to see them every week. Her main complaint was that they were not well-read enough and that they were too compliant with society. They all wanted happy endings, like with TV plots. She appeared to feel sad that education was not for education's sake but for career purposes or financial gain: "I guess I'm a romanticist. Not every step or brainwave or heartbeat should be for a practical purpose." Yet she took plenty of responsibility herself, openly stating that she was a terrible teacher because she was mostly terrified, and that she never finished high school. But most tellingly, she realized she felt too old, too out of time. "I feel like their grandmother's grandmother and that isn't great-great! I'm just not from their school—in fact, no school at all." The only thing she heaped praise on was Cal State's integration policies. Having just moments earlier complained about the age of her students, she thought the mix of races, ages, and especially foreign students was inspiring and "beautiful."

Amazingly, Parker lasted for her full year's contract, though one suspects mostly due to the patience of the college. It was characteristic that people wanted to help her, but then when they did she often seemed ungracious or uncooperative. It was as though she knew she needed their help but resented needing it. There seemed no malice on her part, yet somehow accepting help increased her self-loathing. Perhaps she felt if she were going to fail that she'd rather do it on her own terms. She was certainly fearful of *something*, not just of the idea of leaving a literary legacy, but almost of making any mark at all. It's an odd place to inhabit for a writer, who usually at least wants people to read their work, or indeed for their work to have longevity. It is hard to know without asking her whether Parker didn't want it or felt she didn't deserve it. Certainly, she believed other writers, such as Fitzgerald and Hemingway, should be read by everyone forever. But not her own work. Never her.

Life at Norma Place continued as Parker's teaching finally ended in spring 1963. Once she was again dependent on her own writing, the usual pattern commenced. *Esquire* book reviews were neither started nor finished. More house renovations were underway, increasing the chaos and mess. Frederick Shroyer, who had arranged Parker's job at the college, described the kitchen at Norma Place as "an absolute disaster," with things rotting and bubbling and "all kinds of spontaneous life in the ice box."[52] Parker's poodle, Cliché, had three puppies (named Première, Deuxième, and Troisième), adding to the general disorganization. One job Campbell did complete was adapting a door into his bedroom into a concealed bookcase with a secret catch on either side to open it. If he wanted to escape marital bickering, he would retreat to his room and close the bookcase door, making it difficult to reach him.

Although there were occasional outings, most of Parker and Campbell's time was spent in and around Norma Place. Over the years neighborly antics had kept Parker entertained and fascinated, not least the shocking rape of a woman who lived across the street. Known for lying naked on her bed in full view from the driveway (a fact that Campbell and Wyatt Cooper both knew because they often went to take a look—Parker always chickened out), she was raped at knifepoint in the early hours one night by an eighteen-year-old who broke in. In public, Parker expressed horror. In private, she expressed some skepticism toward this story, partly because she felt some of the details were suspect. The young man appeared to be blond by the texture of his skin, though he kept a shirt over his head the entire time. Following the rape, the woman and the boy apparently shared drinks and a cigarette. (How did he negotiate the shirt and the drink? speculated Parker. She concluded that in desperate situations such things can be managed.) She also heard rumors that the woman was to be arrested for giving alcohol to a minor. Far from displaying any female solidarity, Parker raked over every detail of the rape, refusing to believe it happened, and going so far as to scoff at the use of a jar of Vaseline, "because he was so large, or she was so small . . . in either case, a fantasy."[53] So taken was she with the goings-on on the street that often she did not want to go to work for fear of missing something while she was away.

However, something terrible did happen on June 14, 1963, while she went to buy dresses and get her hair styled. Campbell, who had started the day with Bloody Marys, was "drunk as a skunk" when their cleaning lady arrived sometime in the morning.[54] Despite being unsteady on his feet, and looking and feeling dreadful, he insisted on going to collect his dry cleaning, though he had to stop once or twice on the way there and back to gain his equilibrium. He usually had to walk for groceries, alcohol, or dry cleaning because, whatever the time of day, he was too drunk to drive. He had taken to afternoon naps, and Parker had told friends that he even took Seconal to help him sleep in the afternoon. There is no doubt that Campbell was heavily reliant on, probably addicted to, both alcohol and prescription drugs. He had appeared increasingly unhappy and downbeat to friends, who could see with some distress his physical and emotional decline. Neighbor Nina Foch had noticed the previous day that Campbell had wandered into her courtyard with the dogs, looking sad and lost. Although he retained his charm, many around him worried that there was an element of uncharacteristic depression creeping into his life. On this afternoon he either deliberately or accidentally took too many pills with too much alcohol. Whether intended or not, by the time Parker returned home a little after four, she found him dead on his bed, with a cigarette stub between his fingers, and the plastic bag from his dry cleaning draped around his neck and shoulders. Sixteen Seconal capsules were scattered at the side of the bed, and another sixteen were found in his dresser drawer. The coroner ruled the death probable suicide. Friends were divided about this verdict. Some felt it had to be an accident, that the Alan Campbell they knew would never kill himself, but his increasing addictions had left him vulnerable, an accident waiting to happen. Parker believed it was a horrific mishap. Others were convinced he meant to do it, or at best, as in a terrible game of Russian roulette, he didn't care if he lost.

There is something especially tragic about how his death was reported. Having lived all his life in the shadow of his more famous wife, and not always having been credited with being the person who enabled Parker to work when she needed support through difficult times, he was similarly neglected in death. The front page of the *Los Angeles Times* read, "Husband of Writer Dorothy Parker Dies." The *New York Times* reported, "Husband of Dorothy Parker Is Found Dead on the Coast." Neither headline included his actual name.

Parker was in deep shock. Her life companion since 1933 was now gone. His family was informed and insisted his body be returned for burial in the family plot in Virginia. Parker was in no state to disagree and was told by her doctor not to attempt to travel to the funeral. When family members received Campbell's body, they could hardly believe it was him, such was the deterioration in his appearance since they'd last seen him. Years of drinking and drugs had altered him beyond recognition.

To some, Parker appeared callous, refusing to talk about Alan or making wisecracks about his death. When a concerned neighbor asked if she could do or get anything, Parker quipped, "A new husband." Appalled, the neighbor said that was the worst thing she had ever heard, so Parker replied, "Ok then, get me a ham and cheese on rye and hold the mayo." If Parker was using her default setting of humor to deflect grief and shock, it only disgusted others and hurt her. The reality was that without Alan, Parker, by her own admission, was not able to do "a damn thing."[55] But, as at so many other moments in her life, it seems as though Parker was never really given the consideration needed for what she had been through. Certainly, friends were sympathetic to her loss, but no one really seemed to consider the trauma she must have experienced as the one who found Alan dead. When she entered his bedroom and could not wake him, she realized that rigor mortis had already set in. Her life partner of thirty years was gone. Today there is a greater understanding of what that sort of discovery can do to people—numbness, guilt, horror, even fear. It is perfectly possible that what neighbors were interpreting as callousness was shock.

What soon became obvious was that Parker seemed to be completely incapable of looking after herself. The best she could manage was to make tea and toast in the morning, but if neighbors failed to bring her food during the day, she simply went without eating. The actor John Carlyle, who lived across the street on Norma Place, claimed that when he visited with food, "I had to cut her lamb chops for her."[56] As if unable to face what had happened, Parker found herself unable to touch Alan's things and could not enter his bedroom for months after his death, behavior that seems to support the notion she was experiencing some sort of trauma. She quickly became noticeably frailer and fragile, increasing her smoking to three packs a day and opening bottles of scotch earlier each morning to maintain her numbed state. A neighbor, Sally Foster, tried to persuade Parker to hold off drinking until 5 p.m. and even took to hiding bottles of liquor in places Parker could not reach. But if she couldn't find a supply, she would simply stagger out of the house to the store a couple of blocks away. This was never a good idea or safe, and in the nine months after Alan's death, Parker suffered four nasty falls. One fall saw her crack the back of her head open, and after refusing to go to the hospital, she proceeded to bleed all night. Another resulted in a broken shoulder, which then gave her pain for the rest of her life. The injuries increased her physical helplessness, and sometimes when Sally Foster turned up in the morning to visit, she would find Parker had slept in her clothes because she had been unable to unzip her dress the night before.

If Parker had found Hollywood an empty existence before, it was even worse without Alan. If previously she had felt old and out of time, she now believed she should be dead. Almost all her family was gone, plus all her friends—Benchley, Woollcott—her writing career appeared to be over, she could get no more work in Hollywood, and now she had lost Alan. Even her beloved dog Cliché died. All that seemed left to do was sell the house and its contents and move back to New York. Which is what she did.

In early 1964, the house was sold to the actress Peggy Sears. After rifling around in drawers and desks, friends discovered that Alan's small insurance policy, which could have helped the move back east, named his mother as beneficiary. Parker received no help toward the costs. A yard sale of the house's contents was arranged by friends. Since she'd hardly been able to bring herself to touch Alan's possessions, they thought the sight of people pawing and buying them might break her spirit. But they vastly underestimated her. She pulled up a chair, lit a cigarette, and watched the whole proceedings with a steely gaze. If someone asked her how much something cost, she told them they could just take it. One of the few things she kept for herself was the set of Napoleonic soldiers she had bought on that happy day out in Santa Monica with Wyatt Cooper and Alan. As if to shed almost everything from her Hollywood life, she even gave away two of her poodle puppies, keeping only the smallest one, Troisième, known as Troy, for herself.

At the end of March 1964, wearing a blue and white polka-dot dress and red shoes, she traveled to the airport and left Hollywood forever. Years earlier she had said to Sam Goldwyn, obviously referring to death but perhaps also something more, "I know this will come as a shock to you, Mr. Goldwyn, but in all history, which has held billions and billions of human beings, not a single one ever had a happy ending."[57]

Dorothy Parker was no exception.

EPILOGUE

Yet, as only New Yorkers know, if you can get
through the twilight, you'll live through the night.
—Dorothy Parker[1]

After she left Hollywood, Dorothy Parker lived for another three years. She spent this time in a small apartment back at the Volney with Troy and a collection of friends who would drop by to take care of her. Her old friend Sara Murphy from the days in Antibes and Paris lived in the same building. They truly were ladies of the corridor. In keeping with her ever-transient life, Parker managed to move apartments during this time, from 8E to 6F. Her health declined sharply, as did her mobility, and she began to lose her vision. Still drinking, still hopeless with money, and still unable to write, she spent her days smoking, reading gossip magazines, and watching soap operas. Worse still, she found herself needing a nurse. The pianist and composer Oscar Levant always recalled Parker telling him, if you don't want a nurse, just call one.

Ensconced in the Volney, she seemed to revel in the impersonal surroundings, making no effort to make her rooms feel like home, a feature that just about everyone who visited noticed.

Aside from her set of Napoleonic soldiers, which once again took prominence on a shelf in the living room, nothing else reflected the personality of the woman living there. Perhaps the only clue was the perpetual pile of books and magazines on the table.

In so many ways these three years were difficult for Parker. Having finally lost the anchor of Alan Campbell, who made at least her domestic existence possible, she experienced a sort of drifting toward death. She even told a friend not to be sorry when she died, because she felt as though she were already dead. Yet to present her as a hopeless case with a disintegrating mind would be far from the mark. Parker was made of much steelier stuff than that, and if her body was starting to give up here and there, her mind certainly was not. This was never more apparent than in two interviews she gave after her return from Hollywood, one in the winter of 1964–65, the second in March 1966. Both were conducted in her Volney apartment, and both covered similar topics—her career, her hatred of the Algonquin legacy, contemporary writers, and her desire to get back to work.

The first of these interviews was by Gloria Steinem, which she turned into an essay, "Dorothy Parker Comes Home," for the *Ladies' Home Journal*.[2] What a meeting of minds that must have been, seemingly witnessed only by Troy, Parker's small poodle. Steinem paints a vivid picture of the sheer physicality of Parker, small and neat, wearing a red plaid skirt, a red embroidered Mexican blouse, and red slippers on dainty feet. Everything about Parker, in contrast to her Norma Place days, was tidy and contained, yet she seemed to hum with energy. Steinem felt as though she was dealing with a thirty-year-old woman trapped in the body of a seventy-year-old. And she was somewhat in awe, calling the apartment with trepidation and politely asking if she could carry out an interview. Steinem recalled Parker's response: "'All right, dear,' she said briskly, 'we can talk. But not about that damned Algonquin; I'm fed to the teeth with Algonquin.'"

When Steinem arrived at the Volney, she immediately noticed that Parker's apartment was "pure hotel," no personal touches apart from books and a white plastic lace tablecloth that Parker explained had been bought by the nurse: "Isn't it horrible? . . . I try to think of it as pop art, but I can't . . ." Although Parker complained of various health issues, lingering pain from her broken shoulder, bursitis in the other, and "a heart thing," she nevertheless appeared engaged and up-to-date with writers, plays, and television. Her one regret was that she did not get out more to visit off-Broadway, her favorite restaurants, and, more surprisingly, discotheques. The thought of Parker sitting in a corner of the emerging New York club scene of the mid-1960s, passing comment, is a truly wonderful image.

But even more intriguing is Parker's claim that she had a couple of short stories she really wanted to write but was too scared to begin. She gave no indication what the subject matter might be, and if she ever did write them, they have not survived. Most likely they never materialized at all, since she admitted that her fear of starting a story got worse, not better, with age. This did not stop her appreciating what other writers were producing, as she openly praised Edward Albee, James Baldwin, and Louis

Auchincloss. Books that dealt with sex, however, came in for some Parker treatment: "Must they describe the sex act *all* the time?"

Steinem leaves us with an image of Parker physically caged in her small, impersonal rooms, yet mentally as free as ever, inhabiting books, reading plays, and so happy to be back in New York, the only place to be in the whole country—"It *smells* different." Yet despite all this energy, Steinem detected a wistful loneliness in Parker. So many of her friends from the old days had died, leaving "gaps in the circle." Parker, walking Steinem slowly to the door to say goodbye, noted that when she read something funny or sad, there suddenly seemed no one to share it with anymore.

A year later, Parker gave a second interview, captured in a rare recording that runs to just over an hour and eleven minutes. The fact that this exists at all is testament to the persistence of the interviewer and writer, Richard Lamparski. It took him six months of phone calls, flattery, and negotiation to persuade Parker to record a conversation with him. Finally, in March 1966, in her apartment, and with the help of a sound engineer, they sat down to chat about her career, Hollywood, contemporary writers, and politics. Parker sounds spirited and sprightly, Lamparski putting her at ease with his relaxed manner. What is most fascinating about this recording is that it offers an insight into Parker's legendary habit of delivering barbs in a seemingly sweet and innocent voice. Lamparski engages her in gossip about people she once worked with in Hollywood, asking if she felt some of the people there were really as committed to political causes as they appeared. When she came to mention her old nemesis Anita Loos, in the loveliest voice Parker assured Lamparski that Loos almost certainly thought she was committed, "if she thinks at all"—the aside delivered with such subtle charm that it almost escapes attention.

But like the Steinem interview, it equally shows that Parker had not given up on life or writing. There is a longing in her voice when she vehemently talks about desperately wanting to write short stories again or, failing that, book reviews for *Esquire*, "if they'll have me back." (When Lamparski asks whether she was gotten rid of by the magazine, she replies, "Well sure, I wasn't doing anything.") But often when Parker speaks, moments of great significance are given such a quick, light touch that they hardly register. She admits very quietly and briefly that she has been unable to write because she has been so sick since Alan died.

But if one topic would get her writing again, purely out of anger, it would surely be what Lamparksi called the jet set, and what Parker referred to as the "Beautiful People." She admitted, "I love to read about them. . . . It does make me want to write—Idiots!" This suggests that a year earlier when she told Gloria Steinem she had a couple of short stories in mind, they may well have been lampooning the jet set of the day.[3] What a loss to literature that they do not exist. Parker found the increasing obsession with wealthy celebrities unhealthy, seemingly overlooking that by purchasing the magazines and reading every word she was buying into the whole scene herself. She even admitted that when she couldn't sleep at night she would invent wonderful futures awaiting these Beautiful People. But even more curious is that despite her dislike of the jet set, over the years Parker herself had spent time with celebrities, both in Hollywood and New York. The difference, she claimed, is that years ago people had more socialistic leanings, and that the nonpolitical Beautiful People back in the early days "were just a nuisance and a drag." But even more telling, it doesn't even appear to occur to Parker that she herself may have been one of the Beautiful People once, living between Hollywood and New York, earning vast amounts of money, and having her every move reported in the national press.

The Lamparski interview is possibly the closest we can get to Dorothy Parker, a woman who otherwise remains elusive, today. We hear her chatting to and about her dog, who is present on the sofa. We can listen to the noises outside her apartment and sense the intimacy of her living room. In this aural moment of time travel, Parker's voice occasionally sounds frail but never weak, and she has the hearty, chesty chuckle of a heavy smoker. She slightly overplays her modesty, but it is amusing to hear her unreliable narration and sweet insincerity in places. After a little more than an hour of her audio presence, it becomes more understandable why people were too scared to leave parties before her. Even Lamparski realized she likely tore him to shreds behind his back, and although there is no evidence of this, he is probably not wrong.

Shortly after he had recorded his interview, he moved apartments and deliberately withheld his new contact information from Parker. In the last memory he has of her, she is standing in her doorway saying goodbye, stirring her drink with her index finger. The draft from her open door wafted the odor of her apartment into the hallway. All Lamparski could smell was cigarettes, white lilac toilet water, and J&B whiskey.

Parker's days passed, one much like the other. There were the occasional parties and outings to the theater or cinema, but they were rare, nowhere near as frequent as she would have liked. One highlight, in March 1967, was a dinner thrown in her honor by her Hollywood friend Wyatt Cooper and his wife, Gloria Vanderbilt, in their New York apartment. These two people held the unusual position of being *liked* by Parker, and she rarely said anything scathing about them. Despite her reservations, she seemed quietly delighted about the evening and turned up at their apartment wearing a gold brocade kaftan encrusted with tiny pearls, which was a gift from Gloria specially for that night. Although it was six inches too long, she refused to have it shortened, claiming the extra length made her feel like an empress. Her sharp eye noticed the exquisite flowers, tablecloths, and silver. When one guest waxed lyrical about the beautiful glassware and how good the wine tasted out of it, Parker, with some of her old fire, replied, "Oh yes, paper cups aren't right."[4] Wyatt Cooper found himself suffering from a fit of nervous coughing.

But despite these social moments, Parker was mostly alone. Her old friend from Hollywood, Adela Rogers St. Johns, observed, "No woman ever showed more *guts* than Dorothy Parker did in the last years."[5] It was not a happy or easy time. Yet the odd pieces of writing that she did manage were truly beautiful—gentle and poignant, and certainly with the air of a person at the end of their life looking back. Reviewing an exhibition of the artist John Koch, Parker wrote, "I am always a little sad when I see a John Koch painting. It is nothing more than a bit of nostalgia that makes my heart beat slower—nostalgia for those rooms of lovely lights and lovelier shadows and loveliest people. And I really have no room for the sweet, soft feeling . . . it is the sort of nostalgia that is only a dreamy longing for some places where you never were."[6]

One can only hope that, as she lay in bed on June 7, 1967, she was dreaming of such soft, lovely places when she died of a heart attack, her dog, Troy, by her side.

For some it seemed incredible that Parker had lived so long. Her seventy-three years were a kaleidoscopic swirl. From the young, motherless, troublemaking girl who terrorized the nuns at school to the Manhattan girl-about-town wheedling her way into jobs and causing chaos in the offices of *Vogue* and *Vanity Fair*. From nights in the dark speakeasies with Robert Benchley and Alex Woollcott to becoming the first female drama critic in New York. Over the years she whirled through countless hopeless love affairs, difficult marriages, and moments of deep despair and loss, to brief times of happiness and hope. "Three be the things I shall have till I die: / Laughter and hope and a sock in the eye."[7] She traveled, she wrote, she doubted, she worked hard, she was lazy. She produced verse, short stories, prose, reviews, film scripts. She loved to hate Hollywood as she sat beneath the palm trees complaining and having the time of her life. From wild parties in the Garden of Allah with her favorite people to establishing unions and anti-fascist organizations, she never stopped. *Union*, she insisted, is not a four-letter word. She had money, she spent it all. She wore ridiculously expensive hats and lingerie. She gave much away to political causes. Her activism got her into trouble and blacklisted. She ricocheted between Hollywood, New York, Europe, and Pennsylvania. She moved house *constantly*. She hated her mother-in-law passionately. She saw wars, she won awards, she loved and lost her husband. She approached her life with a wry eye and a hefty dose of melancholy. She was kind and cruel and glorious. "All the songs were ever sung, / All the words were ever said; / Could it be, when I was young, / Someone dropped me on my head?"[8] She ended up right back where she started, in New York, and died not very far from where she had lived as a child.

The funeral she never wanted was brief but celebratory. She was laid in her coffin wearing the pearl-encrusted gold brocade kaftan. The eulogy given by Lillian Hellman described Parker as "part of nothing and nobody but herself and it was this independence of mind and spirit that was her true distinction."[9] Flowers arrived at the Frank E. Campbell Funeral Chapel. The National Institute of Arts and Letters sent a wreath on an easel. the *New Yorker* sent white and yellow gladioli and poms. Sara Murphy, a vase of red roses.[10] All the people and places she had taken in throughout her life were represented at her funeral. That her ashes would then take fifty-three years to finally come to rest in Woodlawn Cemetery in the Bronx seems very Parkeresque. Even after death, she remained the hobo she wished to forever be.

But also, after death, she ensured that any legacy she did leave behind would be used to continue the work she felt most strongly about—the struggle to eliminate prejudice and injustice.

Her will, signed in a shaky hand on February 6, 1965, left her entire estate to Martin Luther King Jr., or, in the event of his death, the NAACP.[11] All proceeds from Parker's estate are still used today to fight these persistent social injustices.

And what of Parker herself? That she has a legacy is beyond doubt. Most people have heard of her; most people know something caustic she once allegedly said, or a witty verse or story. Perhaps fewer people know about her work in Hollywood, and despite her own unreliable judgment of it all, she *deserves* to be known for it. Her range was impressive and important—funny fluff for pleasure, serious issues, the corrosive nature of fame, the destructiveness of alcohol and addiction, lost love, doomed relationships, annoying friends, the complexities of marriage. The very fact that *A Star Is Born* has been remade so many times is testament to the power of the script devised by Parker, Campbell, and Robert Carson. It is time to take a fresh look at Parker and encompass the fullness of her achievements. She would hate receiving this credit, of course. She would scoff that anyone cared, insist that she never wrote anything of any worth. But it is also nice to think that on some level she could tolerate what for her would be the unbearable spectacle of her legacy.

And I imagine this legacy as the ending of a spectacular Hollywood film. A petite figure with dark hair and messy bangs, outlined in silhouette, is forever walking toward those blazing California forest fires that frightened her so much. Smoke billows. The magnificent flames crackle and fill the horizon. Everything is reaching toward the sky, and her brave, unflinching gaze takes it all in.

This list must be regarded as incomplete, since Parker worked uncredited on many more films than noted here, many of which never made it to production.

CREDITED

Suzy (1936)

Three Married Men (1936)

The Moon's Our Home (1936)

Lady Be Careful (1936)

A Star Is Born (1937)—Oscar nomination

Trade Winds (1938)

Sweethearts (1938)

The Little Foxes (1941)

Week-End for Three (1941)

Saboteur (1942)

Smash-Up: The Story of a Woman (1947)—Oscar nomination

The Fan (1949)

UNCREDITED

Here Is My Heart (1934)

One Hour Late (1934)

Mary Burns, Fugitive (1935)

Hands Across the Table (1935)

Paris in Spring (1935)

The Big Broadcast of 1936 (1935)

SHE ALSO SPONSORED TWO POLITICAL FILMS

The Spanish Earth (1937)

The 400 Million (1939)

There have been many reissues of Parker's work over the years by various publishers. Below is a list of the main collections and their original publication date.

STORY COLLECTIONS

Laments for the Living (1930)

After Such Pleasures (1933)

Here Lies: The Collected Stories of Dorothy Parker (1939)

Collected Stories (1942)

The Portable Dorothy Parker (1944)

Complete Stories (1995)

POETRY COLLECTIONS

Enough Rope (1926)

Sunset Gun (1928)

Death and Taxes (1931)

Collected Poems: Not So Deep as a Well (1936)

Collected Poetry (1944)

Not Much Fun: The Lost Poems of Dorothy Parker
     (UK title: *The Uncollected Dorothy Parker*) (1996)

Not Much Fun: The Lost Poems of Dorothy Parker
    (second edition, with additional poems; 2009)

PLAYS

Close Harmony, cowritten with Elmer Rice (1924)
The Coast of Illyria, cowritten with Ross Evans (1949)
The Ladies of the Corridor, cowritten with Arnaud d'Usseau
    (1953)

ACKNOWLEDGMENTS

The research for this book was carried out and completed during the COVID-19 pandemic, which offered a unique set of challenges. I did initially wonder how on earth this could happen. Luckily for me, I worked with some of the most amazing and talented archivists, who really are responsible for this book being written when it was. Many were working remotely and only spending one day a week in the archives, many of them fully masked, on a staggered schedule and socially distanced. They were working through the backlog of requests for materials and kept not only research but also writing alive during those early, terrible days of the pandemic. I could not be more grateful and in awe of:

Thom Davies at King's College, Cambridge; Martha O'Hara Conway and Juli McLoone at the Special Collections Research Center, University of Michigan; Amber Marie Kohl in Special Collections at the University of Maryland Libraries; Ursula Romero at Lilly Library, Indiana University; Kate Long at Neilson Library, Smith College; Cythnia Cathcart at the Condé Nast Library; the Houghton Library, Harvard University; the Harry Ransom Research Center at the University of Texas,

Austin; the Special Collections at the University of Penn State; the Howard Gotlieb Archival Research Center at the University of Boston Libraries; the Columbia Rare Book and Manuscript Library, Columbia University, and the Columbia Center for Oral History Research; Jane Klain of the Paley Center for Media in New York; Phil Gries of Archival Television Audio, Inc.; and Morex Arai at the Huntington Library.

Sebastian Doherty, my research assistant and Parker partner in crime, has been outstanding, saving my skin by spending time in the Rare Book and Manuscript Library at Columbia as soon as it reopened to researchers, letting me look over his WhatsApp shoulder, and filing and storing information so much better than I ever could. Thank you, thank you, Sebastian: cocktails at the Algonquin forthcoming, or, failing that, more cocktails at the Soho Grand.

So many other people have kindly provided me with essential information covering all aspects of the book, from missing audiotapes to interpreting photographs, to helping me understand the layout of Hollywood before I was able to actually visit: Anderson Cooper, Carl Rollyson, Al Deering, Muffy Bolding, Kevin Fitzpatrick, and Andrew Wilson.

Thank you, Jola Cora, for the tour of Hollywood and an enchanting night at Musso & Frank's imagining Dottie P in one of those booths with her martini(s).

Thank you, Karen Kukil, for drawing my attention to the script of *A Star Is Born* (1937) held in the Mortimer Rare Book Collection, Smith College.

As always, my family and friends have been the best:

Carole and Ces Crowther and Joanne and Peter Whiteside for unfailing support, love, and encouragement, as well as my regular meal scrounging. Rob Sanders for early reading and always championing. John Avery for our walks in the hills and chips at the pub afterward. Ella Cummins for delightful pictures of Oscar and his exploits. Solid, good friendship and wise advice from Cathy McKenna, Carolyn King, Suzanne Demko, and William Sigmund.

Thank you to Emily van Duyne for writerly solidarity, for always making me laugh, pertinent feedback, friendship, and generally sharing the experience of us writing our books together.

Thank you to Vanessa Curtis for *everything*: our daily support emails, mutual advice on skirts, snacks, and sofa dents, and drinking champagne and eating crisps on those rare, wonderful occasions when we are able to meet in real life.

Thank you, Kevin Cummins, for stunning photography, support, early reading, advice, champagne, a magical two-week Hollywood adventure, and a "first class" New York experience.

My agent, Carrie Kania at C&W Agency, always has the best ideas for books and this one is no exception. Thank you for everything: your support, friendship, and generally putting up with me.

And my editor at Gallery Books, Alison Callahan, is *the* perfect editor, giving me total freedom but the best guidance. Always wise, always kind, always fun.

And to the whole team at Gallery Books and Simon & Schuster, especially Taylor Rondestvedt for superb organization, and Dominick Montalto for exceptional copyediting. Any book is a team effort, and this is no exception.

ACKNOWLEDGMENTS

The life span of a book from start to finish lasts many years, and life passes during this time. I would like to pay tribute to a dear friend of decades, John Wood, who saved me from many scrapes over the years and will be sorely missed.

Finally, this book was always going to be dedicated to My George. He not only deserved it, but I figured Dorothy Parker would be delighted to have a book about her dedicated to the best dog in the world. It never crossed my mind that I would lose him while I was writing it. This one's for you, George, my sandy, snory, snack-guzzling, life-loving best boy. Thank you for everything you gave me. I miss you.

The upkeep of Dorothy Parker's grave in Woodlawn Cemetery is maintained by a memorial fund. If you would like to donate, please go to https://dorothyparker .com for more information.

NOTES

INTRODUCTION: OUT THERE

1. Dorothy Parker, interview by Mr. and Mrs. Robert E. Franklin, Popular Arts Project for the Oral History Research Project, June 1959, audio and transcript, Columbia Center for Oral History, Columbia University.

2. Ibid.

3. Dorothy Parker, *The Portable Dorothy Parker* (London: Penguin, 2006), 575.

4. Wyatt Cooper, "Whatever You Think Dorothy Parker Was Like, She Wasn't," *Esquire*, July 1, 1968, 57.

5. Parker, *The Portable Dorothy Parker*, 581.

6. This figure is approximate. Because she was often uncredited, it is difficult to establish exactly how many films she worked on. Eighteen are confirmed but almost certainly there are more. This list was compiled by Fred Lawrence Guiles, *Hanging On in Paradise* (New York: McGraw-Hill, 1975), 339.

7. Faye Hammill, *Women, Celebrity, and Literary Culture Between the Wars* (Austin: University of Texas Press, 2007), 3.

8. Dorothy Parker, "A Reputation Unearned and Unwanted," interview by Hubbard Keavy, *Evening Star* (Washington, DC), December 7, 1941, E-3.

9. Ibid.

10. Parker, interview, Oral History Research Project.

11. Ibid.

12. Ibid.

13. Parker, *The Portable Dorothy Parker*, 576.

14. Lillian Hellman, *An Unfinished Woman* (London: Quartet Books, 1977), 175.

15. Dorothy Parker to Albert Gross, telegram, January 2, 1939, Albert Gross Papers, University of Maryland.

16. My sincere thanks to Jane Klain at the Paley Center for Media, New York, and Phil Gries, Archival Television Audio, Inc., for their invaluable assistance and expertise on this matter.

17. My thanks to Anderson Cooper for confirming that he had tried to find the tapes, having been aware of their existence for years, but despite searching he could not find them in any of his mother's possessions. Anderson Cooper, email to author, March 3, 2021.

18. Lillian Hellman to Roderick Davis, letter, August 19, 1970, Lillian Hellman Papers, box 85.1, Harry Ransom Center, University of Texas, Austin.

19. Lillian Hellman to Thomas J. Hughes, letter, June 30, 1971, Lillian Hellman Papers, box 85.1, Harry Ransom Center, University of Texas, Austin.

20. Parker, interview, Oral History Research Project.

21. Please see the bibliography for a full list of existing biographies of Dorothy Parker.

22. Oscar Bernstien to Lillian Hellman, letter, March 16, 1970, Lillian Hellman Papers, box 85.1, Harry Ransom Center, University of Texas, Austin. There is also a letter dated November 2, 1967, indicating that Ferncliff Crematorium was billing the estate for six dollars, anticipating storing Parker's ashes from June 9, 1967, to January 9, 1968 (Folder 85.1). This suggests that the estate was paying about twelve dollars a year for Parker's ashes to be retained at Ferncliff Cemetery and Mausoleum.

23. Even during Parker's lifetime she was aware of this happening.

Witticisms were often ascribed to her that she never delivered. Unattributed stories, half-truths, and gossip all fill the gaps in those absences in Parker's story.

CHAPTER 1: GETTING THERE

1. Dorothy Parker, *The Uncollected Dorothy Parker*, ed. Stuart Y. Silverstein (London: Duckworth, 1999), 191.
2. Dorothy Parker, "A Reputation Unearned and Unwanted," interview by Hubbard Keavy, *Evening Star* (Washington, DC), December 7, 1941, E-3.
3. Dorothy Parker, interview by Mr. and Mrs. Robert E. Franklin, Popular Arts Project for the Oral History Research Project, June 1959, audio and transcript, Columbia Center for Oral History, Columbia University.
4. Dorothy Parker, a book review from 1941 posted on www.dorothy parkersociety.com, January 7, 2020, accessed December 13, 2021. https://dorothyparker.com/2020/01/700-dorothy-parker-words .html.
5. These figures have been reached using a 2021 online inflation calculator.
6. Parker, interview, Oral History Reserach Project.
7. Ibid.
8. Dorothy Parker, *Dorothy Parker: In Her Own Words*, ed. Barry Day (Lanham, MD: Taylor Trade Publishing, 2004), 1.
9. This is how Dorothy Parker described her father's business in Wyatt Cooper, "Whatever You Think Dorothy Parker Was Like, She Wasn't," *Esquire*, July 1, 1968, 57.
10. Marion Meade, *Dorothy Parker: What Fresh Hell Is This?* (London: Heinemann, 1987), 12.
11. Cooper, "Whatever You Think Dorothy Parker Was Like, She Wasn't," 57.
12. Dorothy Parker, *The Portable Dorothy Parker* (London: Penguin, 2006), 576.

13. Cooper, "Whatever You Think Dorothy Parker Was Like, She Wasn't," 57.

14. Ibid.

15. There were two schools next door to each other. The Blessed Sacrament Convent was at 168 West 79th Street, and next door at number 170 was the mirror-image Academy of the Blessed Sacrament. In Wyatt Cooper's article, which he based on recorded interviews with Parker, she states she attended the Blessed Sacrament Convent, though I have not been able to independently confirm this.

16. Meade, *What Fresh Hell Is This?*, 15.

17. Cooper, "Whatever You Think Dorothy Parker Was Like, She Wasn't," 57.

18. Parker, *The Portable Dorothy Parker*, 580.

19. Cooper, "Whatever You Think Dorothy Parker Was Like, She Wasn't," 57.

20. Parker, *The Portable Dorothy Parker*, 576.

21. John Keats, *You Might As Well Live: The Life and Times of Dorothy Parker* (London: Penguin, 1979), 23.

22. Meade, *What Fresh Hell Is This?*, 16.

23. All this information about these sketchy years in Parker's life is taken from the invaluable scholarship of Marion Meade in her Parker biography, *What Fresh Hell Is This?* Meade's research archive is held at Columbia University, New York.

24. Parker, *The Portable Dorothy Parker*, 573.

25. Faye Hammill, *Women, Celebrity, and Literary Culture Between the Wars* (Austin: University of Texas Press, 2007), 27.

26. Leslie Frewin, *The Late Mrs. Dorothy Parker* (New York: Macmillan, 1986), 19.

27. Parker, *The Portable Dorothy Parker*, 576.

28. Parker, *The Uncollected Dorothy Parker*, 81.

29. Parker, *The Portable Dorothy Parker*, 573.

30. Ibid.

31. Hammill, *Women, Celebrity, and Literary Culture Between the Wars*, 33.

32. Ibid., 34.

33. What's interesting to consider here is what Parker would have made of current versions of *Vogue* and *Vanity Fair*, which seem more closely linked with their mix of fashion, arts, and important cultural conversations, but also with increasing political consciousness. For example, under the editorship of Edward Enninful from 2017 to 2024, British *Vogue* seemed to perfectly reflect all social and political concerns shared by Parker. And in recent years *Vanity Fair* has been supporting Black Lives Matter, for instance, with a powerful front cover in 2020 depicting Breanna Taylor, murdered by the police.

34. Frewin, *The Late Mrs. Dorothy Parker*, 22.

35. Parker, *The Uncollected Dorothy Parker*, 197.

36. Ibid., 225.

37. Frewin, *The Late Mrs. Parker*, 23.

38. Meade, *What Fresh Hell Is This?*, 44.

39. Frewin, *The Late Mrs. Dorothy Parker*, 66.

40. Ian Hamilton, *Writers in Hollywood 1915–1951* (London: Faber & Faber, 2011), 3.

41. Hammill, *Women, Celebrity, and Literary Culture Between the Wars*, 25.

42. Dorothy Parker, *The Collected Dorothy Parker* (London: Penguin, 2001), 417.

43. Parker, *The Uncollected Dorothy Parker*, 205.

44. Parker, *The Portable Dorothy Parker*, 574.

45. Ibid.

46. Ibid.

47. Frank Crowninshield, "Crowninshield in the Cubs' Den," *Vogue*, September 15, 1944, 163.

48. Frank Crowninshield, "Crowninshield in the Cubs' Den (Part 2)," *Vogue*, November 1, 1944, 126.

49. Parker, *The Portable Dorothy Parker*, 575.
50. There are many excellent books that document the years of the Round Table and the events that took place there. Please see the bibliography.
51. Hamilton, *Writers in Hollywood 1915–1951*, 15.
52. Ibid., 18.
53. Ibid., 19.
54. Parker, *The Collected Dorothy Parker*, 418.
55. Ibid., 421.
56. Parker, *The Portable Dorothy Parker*, 574.
57. Ibid., 575.
58. Josephine van de Grift, "Humor's Sober Side," *Bisbee (AZ) Daily Review*, October 11, 1922, 4.
59. Ibid.
60. Ibid.
61. Parker, *The Uncollected Dorothy Parker*, 114.
62. Dorothy Parker to Robert Benchley [undated], box 12 C (#15), Robert Benchley Collection, Howard Gotlieb Archival Research Center, Boston University. This is also published under the title "Letter to Robert Benchley" in Parker, *The Uncollected Dorothy Parker*, 88.
63. Parker is making a witty biblical reference here to Genesis 38: 8–10, where the figure of Onan refuses to impregnate his widowed sister-in-law, Tamar, choosing instead to spill his seed on the ground.
64. Arthur F. Kinney, *Dorothy Parker* (Boston: Twayne Publishers, 1978), 40.
65. Ibid.
66. Finney, *Dorothy Parker*, 40.
67. Meg Gillette, "Modern American Abortion Narratives and the Century of Silence," *Twentieth-Century Literature* 58, no. 4 (Winter 2012): 664.

68. Meade, *What Fresh Hell Is This?*, 105. Meade also relates that Parker became convinced that the embryo's hands were already fully formed and that this made Parker feel even more wicked.

69. Ibid., 675.

70. Ibid.

71. Keats, *You Might As Well Live*, 93.

72. Hamilton, *Writers in Hollywood*, 19.

73. Ibid., 29.

74. Mankiewicz, like many writers, worked on numerous films for which his work went uncredited, the most famous being his contributions to *The Wizard of Oz*. However, he became most well-known for his fractious collaboration with Orson Welles on *Citizen Kane*. The story of this was made into its own film, *Mank* (2020).

75. Parker, *The Collected Dorothy Parker*, 96.

76. For a full, detailed account of Parker's European trip please see Meade, *What Fresh Hell Is This?*, 164–74. Meade covers in depth Parker's tense relationship with Hemingway (she liked him more than he liked her), more disastrous romantic escapades, and articles Parker was writing for the *New Yorker* and *Life*.

77. Finney, *Dorothy Parker*, 50.

78. Meade, *What Fresh Hell Is This?*, 183.

79. Ibid., 184. The outcome of the protest was not successful. Sacco and Vanzetti were both executed on August 23, 1927.

80. Parker, *The Collected Dorothy Parker*, 468.

81. Ibid., 503.

82. Ibid., 227.

83. Edwin Pond Parker II died January 7, 1933, after taking an overdose of sleeping powder. The coroner concluded that this was accidental.

84. Meade, *What Fresh Hell Is This?*, 194.

85. Parker, *The Collected Dorothy Parker*, 483.

86. Parker did start seeing a therapist about her drinking, Dr. Barach,

who encouraged her to cut down rather than abstain. But ultimately she refused to admit she had a problem, and the therapy did not last long.

87. Ellen Lansky, "Female Trouble: Dorothy Parker, Katherine Anne Porter, and Alcoholism," *Literature and Medicine* 17, no. 2 (Fall 1998): 212.

88. Parker, *The Portable Dorothy Parker*, 191.

89. Parker also wrote another short story tackling women and alcohol called "Just a Little One" about a character like Hazel Morse who loves animals and drinks too much. In denial about her problem, she repeats the refrain that she will just have a little one. See *The Portable Dorothy Parker*, 241.

90. Hamilton, *Writers in Hollywood*, 39.

91. Ibid., 33.

92. Anita Loos, *Kiss Hollywood Goodbye* (London: Quality Book Club, 1976), 119.

93. Mollie Merrick, "Movies and Movie People," *Evening Star*, January 4, 1929, 36.

94. Parker, interview, Oral History Research Project.

95. Merrick, "Movies and Movie People," 36.

CHAPTER 2: HOLLYWOODLAND

1. Dorothy Parker, "Dorothy Parker Discusses Her Plays and the State of Literature," interview by Studs Terkel, February 6, 1959, accessed December 17, 2021, https://studsterkel.wfmt.com/programs/dorothy-parker-discusses-her-plays-and-state-literature.

2. All quotes in this paragraph are taken from "In Lost 1953 Speech, Dorothy Parker Rips Hollywood," from a speech titled "Hollywood, the Land I Won't Return To," Dorothy Parker Society, March 6, 2017, accessed September 17, 2021, https://dorothyparker.com/2017/03/in-lost-1953-speech-dorothy-parker-rips-hollywood.html.

3. Marion Meade, *Dorothy Parker: What Fresh Hell Is This?* (London: Heinemann, 1987), 197.

4. Parker, "In Lost 1953 Speech, Dorothy Parker Rips Hollywood."

5. Dorothy Parker, "1966 Radio Interview with Dorothy Parker and Richard Lamparski," Dorothy Parker Society, August 13, 2021, accessed August 15, 2021, https://dorothyparker.com/2021/08/1966-radio-interview.html.

6. Faye Hammill, *Women, Celebrity, and Literary Culture Between the Wars* (Austin: University of Texas Press, 2007), 16.

7. Much of this information about the early days of Hollywood can be found on www.hollywoodsign.org along with some wonderful photographs, notably one showing Sunset Boulevard as a field. https://www.hollywoodsign.org/history-timeline.

8. Information taken from https://historynewsnetwork.org/blog/14513.

9. Meade, *What Fresh Hell Is This?*, 197.

10. MarriedAtTheMovies, "Grand Hotel: A History of the Ambassador Hotel & Cocoanut Grove," Medium.com, November 28, 2017, accessed September 15, 2021, https://medium.com/married-at-the-movies/grand-hotel-a-history-of-the-ambassador-hotel-cocoanut-grove-88d762b81e9e.

11. This is an example of the gaps and absences in Parker's life. When did she meet this couple? What did they mean to her? Why did she decide to move in with them?

12. Parker, "In Lost 1953 Speech, Dorothy Parker Rips Hollywood."

13. Ibid.

14. Ian Hamilton, *Writers in Hollywood 1915–1951* (London: Faber & Faber, 2011), 46.

15. Ibid.

16. Parker, "In Lost 1953 Speech, Dorothy Parker Rips Hollywood."

17. Mollie Merrick, "Movies and Movie People," *Evening Star* (Washington, DC), January 4, 1929, 36.

18. Leslie Frewin, *The Late Mrs. Dorothy Parker* (New York: Macmillan, 1986), 121.

19. Meade, *What Fresh Hell Is This?*, 200.

20. Statistic taken from https://www.encyclopedia.com/education /news-and-education-magazines/hollywood-1929-1941 #:~:text=Although%20the%20stock%20market%20crash, worsened%20nationwide%20Hollywood's%20apprehension %20grew.

21. Dorothy Parker, *The Portable Dorothy Parker* (London: Penguin, 2006), 588.

22. Ibid.

23. Ibid., 589.

24. Ibid.

25. Ibid., 601.

26. Ibid., 595.

27. Ibid., 594.

28. Hamilton, *Writers in Hollywood*, 59.

29. Marion Meade, *Bobbed Hair and Bathtub Gin: Writers Running Wild in the Twenties* (New York: Doubleday, 2004), 272.

30. Mary E. Barber, et al., "Aborted Suicide Attempts: A New Classification of Suicidal Behavior," *American Journal of Psychiatry* 155, no. 3 (March 1998): 385.

31. R. W. Maris quoted in Robin D. Everall, "The Meaning of Suicide Attempts by Young Adults," *Canadian Journal of Counselling /Revue canadienne de counseling* 34, no. 2 (2000): 113.

32. Dorothy Parker, *The Collected Dorothy Parker* (London: Penguin, 2001), 312.

33. Ibid., 304.

34. Dorothy Parker to Robert Benchley, October [illegible], 1930, 12:47 p.m., box 12 C, Robert Benchley Collection, Howard Gotlieb Archival Research Center, Boston University.

35. Dorothy Parker to Robert Benchley, October 24, 1930, box 12 C,

Robert Benchley Collection, Howard Gotlieb Archival Research Center, Boston University.

36. Hamilton, *Writers in Hollywood*, 50.

37. Ibid., 51.

38. Dorothy Parker, interview by Mr. and Mrs. Robert E. Franklin, Popular Arts Project for the Oral History Research Project, June 1959, audio and transcript, Columbia Center for Oral History, Columbia University.

39. It is worth noting, however, that Parker fit the classic model for such a woman that Hollywood welcomed—white and middle class. African American women writers did work in film but outside the Hollywood system. Zora Neale Hurston, for example, made films highlighting her social and political agenda and covering aspects of southern Black culture, such as *Logging* (1928), *Children's Games* (1928), and *Baptism* (1929). But there was seemingly no space in 1930s Hollywood for Black women writers despite the large number of people employed there.

40. Nancy Lynn Schwartz, *The Hollywood Writers' War* (Lincoln, NE: An Author's Guild Backinprint.com Edition, 2001), 20.

41. Dorothy Parker, *Dorothy Parker: In Her Own Words*, ed. Barry Day (Lanham, MD: Taylor Trade Publishing, 2004), 82.

42. Hamilton, *Writers in Hollywood*, 71.

43. Schwartz, *The Hollywood Writers' War*, 20.

44. Hamilton, *Writers in Hollywood*, 72.

45. Statistic taken from https://www.ipl.org/essay/The-Negative-Influence-Of-Film-In-The-FJ9YCWDSVYV.

46. Meade, *What Fresh Hell Is This?*, 220.

47. All quotations are taken from "Woman Writer Prefers Babies," *Bismarck (ND) Tribune*, April 29, 1932, 2.

48. In another depressing outcome for Parker, her beloved Robinson did not survive the attack.

49. The Preparedness Movement was an organization that advocated American entry into World War I.

50. Mooney was eventually pardoned in 1939. His mother had died in 1934 so did not live to see this day.

51. Milly S. Barranger, "Dorothy Parker and the Politics of McCarthyism," *Theatre History Studies* 26 (2006): 26.

52. Parker, interview, Oral History Reserach Project.

53. Schwartz, *The Hollywood Writers' War*, 25.

54. S. J. Perelman, *The Last Laugh* (New York: Simon & Schuster, 1981), 171.

55. Ibid., 172.

56. Parker, *The Collected Dorothy Parker*, 549.

57. Ibid., 550.

58. Meade, *What Fresh Hell Is This?*, 230.

59. Dorothy Parker to Alexander Woollcott, circa June 1934, box 17, MS. Am 1449, Houghton Library, Harvard University.

60. "Dorothy Parker Was October Bride," *Evening Star*, June 16, 1934, A-4.

61. Parker to Woollcott, circa June 1934.

62. Ibid.

63. Ibid.

64. Dorothy Parker to Alexander Woollcott [undated, 1934], box 17, MS. Am 1449, Houghton Library, Harvard University.

65. Ibid.

66. Ibid.

CHAPTER 3: A STAR IS BORN

1. Dorothy Parker, "1966 Radio Interview with Dorothy Parker and Richard Lamparski," Dorothy Parker Society, August 13, 2021, accessed August 15, 2021, https://dorothyparker.com /2021/08/1966-radio-interview.html.

2. Dorothy Parker, interview by Mr. and Mrs. Robert E. Franklin, Popular Arts Project for the Oral History Research Project, June

1959, audio and transcript, Columbia Center for Oral History, Columbia University.

3. Dorothy Parker, "In Lost 1953 Speech, Dorothy Parker Rips Hollywood," from the speech "Hollywood, the Land I Won't Return To," https://dorothyparker.com/2017/03/in-lost-1953-speech-dorothy-parker-rips-hollywood.html.

4. Ian Hamilton, *Writers in Hollywood 1915–1951* (London: Faber & Faber, 2011), 93.

5. Alma Whitaker, "Dorothy Parker, Our Only Woman Humorist Denies It," *Los Angeles Times*, September 13, 1934.

6. Sheilah Graham, *The Garden of Allah* (New York: Crown, 1970), 11.

7. Martin Turnbull, "About the Garden of Allah Hotel," accessed November 24, 2021, https://martinturnbull.com/about-the-garden-of-allah-series-of-books-by-martin-turnbull/about-the-garden-of-allah-hotel/.

8. The Garden of Allah became more and more run down as the years went by. It fell out of fashion and became increasingly seedy. It was eventually demolished in 1959. The goodbye party there was fitting. Hundreds of people turned up, there were high jinks in the pool, and Nazimova's *Salomé* was projected onto an exterior wall.

9. Graham, *The Garden of Allah*, 128.

10. Schwab's Pharmacy was located at 8024 Sunset Boulevard and was a famous hangout for actors and movie executives. It sold medicine, ice cream, light meals, and alcohol, and had a soda counter. Such was its fame that it even appeared in *Sunset Boulevard* (1950). It closed in 1983 and was demolished five years later.

11. Graham, *The Garden of Allah*, 76.

12. Nathaniel Benchley, *Robert Benchley: A Biography* (London: Cassell and Company, 1956), 245.

13. Graham, *The Garden of Allah*, 70.

14. Leslie Frewin, *The Late Mrs. Dorothy Parker* (New York: Macmillan, 1986), 191.

15. Parker, "1966 Radio Interview with Dorothy Parker and Richard Lamparski."

16. Ibid.

17. Graham, *The Garden of Allah*, 138.

18. Ibid.

19. Wyatt Cooper, "Whatever You Think Dorothy Parker Was Like, She Wasn't," *Esquire*, July 1, 1968, 59.

20. "I'll Get By" was written in 1928, with music by the New York–based composer Fred E. Ahlert and lyrics by Roy Turk. It was famously recorded by Ruth Etting and Billie Holiday.

21. Graham, *The Garden of Allah*, 161.

22. Ibid., 163.

23. Anita Loos (1888–1981) was one of the most successful Hollywood screenwriters. She wrote the novel (1928) and screenplay (1953) for *Gentlemen Prefer Blondes*.

24. Fred Lawrence Guiles, *Hanging On in Paradise* (New York: McGraw-Hill, 1975), 18.

25. Anita Loos, *Kiss Hollywood Goodbye* (London: Quality Book Club, 1976), 58.

26. Ibid., 120.

27. Dorothy Parker to Alexander Woollcott, circa late 1934/early 1935, box 17, MS. Am 1449, Houghton Library, Harvard University.

28. Ibid.

29. John Keats, *You Might As Well Live: The Life and Times of Dorothy Parker* (London: Penguin, 1979), 186.

30. S. J. Perelman, *The Last Laugh* (New York: Simon & Schuster, 1981), 186.

31. Ibid.

32. Parker, "1966 Radio Interview with Dorothy Parker and Richard Lamparski."

33. Parker to Woollcott, circa late 1934/early 1935.

34. Ibid.

35. All details about the housewarming party are from Marion Meade, *Dorothy Parker: What Fresh Hell Is This?* (London: Heinemann, 1987), 245.

36. Parker to Woollcott, circa late 1934/early 1935.

37. Keats, *You Might As Well Live*, 188.

38. Parker, "In Lost 1953 Speech, Dorothy Parker Rips Hollywood."

39. Dorothy Parker to Alexander Woollcott, circa June 1934, box 17, MS. Am 1449, Houghton Library, Harvard University. Wolf was Parker's Bedlington terrier. Flush refers to the dog of Elizabeth Barrett Browning, a poet who was often an invalid and had to take to couches.

40. Parker to Woollcott, circa late 1934/early 1935.

41. Ibid.

42. Dr. Robert Cornish controversially attempted (and succeeded) in bringing back to life two clinically dead dogs in 1934 and 1935 by using a seesaw to get blood flowing again and injecting them with adrenaline and anticoagulants. He wanted to try this experiment on prisoners after execution but was denied access on the grounds that if it worked, then the reanimated men could not be tried again due to the double jeopardy law.

43. Dashiell Hammett (1894–1961) is probably most well known for the fictional character Sam Spade, featured in *The Maltese Falcon*. In 1937 Hammett joined the Communist Party, and in 1951 he was sent to jail after refusing to name his collaborators in political activity. In 1953 he was called to give evidence in front of the House Un-American Activities Committee. Once again he refused to cooperate and was blacklisted.

44. It took until 2013 for all the Scottsboro Boys to be pardoned.

45. Helen Partridge, "The 'WOLF' at Dorothy Parker's Door," *Evening Star* (Washington, DC), February 24, 1935.

46. Andre Sennwald, "'Hands Across the Table' a Sprightly Romantic Comedy at the Paramount—'The Rainmakers,'" *New York Times*, November 2, 1935.

47. You can hear a recording of Billie Holiday here: https://www .youtube.com/watch?v=yD7b1ts2fUg.

48. Hamilton, *Writers in Hollywood*, 87.

49. It is worth noting that in 1934 William Randolph Hearst (1863– 1951) traveled to Berlin to interview Adolf Hitler and celebrated what he called the "great achievement" of the Nazi regime— the defeat of communism.

50. Hamilton, *Writers in Hollywood*, page 87.

51. Ibid., 89.

52. Parker interview, Oral History Reserach Project.

53. Arthur F. Kinney, *Dorothy Parker* (Boston: Twayne Publishers, 1978), 59. Harold Clurman was an American theater director and drama critic.

54. Ibid., 60.

55. Dorothy Parker, "Not Enough!" *New Masses* 30, no. 12, March 14, 1939.

56. Perelman, *The Last Laugh*, 173.

57. Ibid., 174.

58. Graham Greene, "Show Boat/The Moon's Our Home," *The Spectator*, June 26, 1936.

59. Frank S. Nugent, "'Suzy' at Capitol Clears Spelvin Mystery— Alex Botts Produces Earthquake at Roxy," *New York Times*, July 25, 1936.

60. Perelman, *The Last Laugh*, 175.

61. Dorothy Parker, *The Portable Dorothy Parker* (London: Penguin, 2006), 469.

62. Ibid., 176.

63. "Film Reviews: Three Married Men," *Variety*, September 1936.

64. Parker to Woollcott, circa late 1934/early 1935.

65. "Film Reviews: Miniature Reviews," *Variety*, October 1936.

66. Henry Hazlitt, "Books of the Times," *New York Times*, December 11, 1936.

67. Louis Kronenberger, "The Rueful, Frostbitten Laughter of Dorothy Parker," *New York Times*, December 13, 1936.

CHAPTER 4: THE DREARY IVORY TOWER

1. Dorothy Parker, *The Portable Dorothy Parker* (London: Penguin, 2006), 86.
2. E. V. Durling, "On the Side," *Los Angeles Times*, December 23, 1936.
3. John Keats, *You Might As Well Live: The Life and Times of Dorothy Parker* (London: Penguin, 1979), 208.
4. Marion Meade, *Dorothy Parker: What Fresh Hell Is This?* (London: Heinemann, 1987), 264.
5. Ibid.
6. All reactions to Parker's pregnancy are taken from Marion Meade's interviews.
7. Parker, *The Portable Dorothy Parker*, 468.
8. Ibid.
9. Ibid., 470.
10. Ibid.
11. "Writer Couple Will Be West-East Commuters," *Los Angeles Times*, November 8, 1936.
12. Sarah Clark Miller, "The Moral Meaning of Miscarriage," *Journal of Social Philosophy* 46, no. 1 (Spring 2015): 141.
13. Leslie Frewin, *The Late Mrs. Dorothy Parker* (New York: Macmillan, 1986), 210.
14. Wyatt Cooper, "Whatever You Think Dorothy Parker Was Like, She Wasn't," *Esquire*, July 1, 1968, 61.
15. Ibid., 57.
16. Parker, *The Portable Dorothy Parker*, 463.
17. Ibid.
18. David Welky, *The Moguls and the Dictators: Hollywood and the Coming of World War II* (Baltimore: Johns Hopkins University Press, 2008), 36.

19. Dorothy Parker, "1966 Radio Interview with Dorothy Parker and Richard Lamparski," Dorothy Parker Society, August 13, 2021, accessed August 15, 2021, https://dorothyparker.com/2021 /08/1966-radio-interview.html.

20. Parker, *The Portable Dorothy Parker*, 582.

21. Fred Lawrence Guiles, *Hanging On in Paradise* (New York: McGraw-Hill, 1975), 147.

22. The other nominations were Fredric March (Best Actor), Janet Gaynor (Best Actress), David O. Selznick (Outstanding Production), William A. Wellman (Best Director), Eric Stacey (Best Assistant Director), and William A. Wellman and Robert Carson (Best Original Story). Of these nominations only Wellman and Carson won.

23. Jay Carmody, "Long Awaited Modern Tale Now Told in Technicolor," *Evening Star* (Washington, DC), May 3, 1937, B-9. In an amusing aside, in a box to the right of this article is a tiny advertisement for the Ziegfeld Follies. Since it was Ziegfeld who got Parker fired from *Vanity Fair*, I am sure Parker would have appreciated the humor of her brilliance eclipsing him on this page.

24. Jay Carmody, "Script Writers Get Nods from Press Book Authors," *Evening Star* (Washington, DC), June 9, 1937, B-10.

25. There was also a television adaption in 1951 starring Kathleen Crowley and Conrad Nagel.

26. "No Cure for Curiosity," accessed January 19, 2022, http://www .virtualdavis.com/tags/dorothy-parker/.

27. Keats, *You Might As Well Live*, 220. Keats managed to interview the Beer family for his biography and their memories of Parker in Bucks County offer invaluable insight.

28. "Law in a Barber Shop," *Sunday Star* (Washington, DC), December 5, 1937, A-5. All information about this incident is taken from this source.

29. Ibid.

30. Meade, *What Fresh Hell Is This?*, 268.

31. Ibid.
32. Dorothy Parker to Alexander Woollcott, July 20 [no year], box 17, MS. Am 1449, Houghton Library, Harvard University.
33. Keats, *You Might As Well Live*, 218.
34. Lillian Hellman, *An Unfinished Woman* (London: Quartet Books, 1969), 173.
35. Parker, *The Portable Dorothy Parker*, 465.
36. Ibid.
37. Ibid., 462.
38. Parker, "1966 Radio Interview with Dorothy Parker and Richard Lamparski."
39. Ibid.

CHAPTER 5: A SOLDIER OF THE REPUBLIC

1. Dorothy Parker, *Dorothy Parker: In Her Own Words*, ed. Barry Day (Lanham, MD: Taylor Trade Publishing, 2004), 165.
2. Dorothy Parker, *The Portable Dorothy Parker* (London: Penguin, 2006), 464.
3. A later, rerecorded version of the film was narrated by Hemingway himself. And the French-language version by Jean Renoir. The version screened at the White House for the Roosevelts had Orson Welles narrating.
4. This figure is taken from Ian Hamilton, *Writers in Hollywood 1915–1951* (London: Faber & Faber, 2011), 109. Other sources list $13,000, but since one of these is Lillian Hellman this is to be taken with some caution (see next note).
5. Other details from this night described by Hellman, such as rancor between Hemingway and Scott Fitzgerald, who attended the screening, and the party afterward, were proved to be untrue. The general opinion of her contemporaries is that Hellman's stories were often stretched, exaggerated, or in some cases blatantly untrue.
6. Parker, *The Portable Dorothy Parker*, 462.

7. Ibid.

8. Ibid., 463.

9. Marion Meade, *Dorothy Parker: What Fresh Hell Is This?* (London: Heinemann, 1987), 281.

10. Ibid.

11. Parker, *The Portable Dorothy Parker*, 464.

12. Dorothy Parker, *The Collected Dorothy Parker* (London: Penguin, 2001), 589. This declaration did little to quiet gossip that she had joined the Communist Party.

13. Ibid.

14. It seems crucial to point out that although Parker felt humor was inappropriate in this context, socially and historically humor has often been used as a powerful and subversive tool to bring about change.

15. Dorothy Parker, *The Collected Dorothy Parker*, page 589.

16. Ibid.

17. Ibid., 593.

18. Ibid.

19. Ibid.

20. Ibid., 167.

21. Parker, *The Portable Dorothy Parker*, 464.

22. Ibid., 465.

23. Ed Ainsworth, "Can Laughter Die?" *Los Angeles Times*, February 5, 1939.

24. "Spanish War Takes Caustic Out of Her Poetry," *Los Angeles Times*, October 23, 1937.

25. John Keats, *You Might As Well Live: The Life and Times of Dorothy Parker* (London: Penguin, 1979), 229.

26. Parker, *The Portable Dorothy Parker*, 465.

27. Ibid., 464.

28. Ellen Lansky, "Female Trouble: Dorothy Parker, Katherine Anne Porter, and Alcoholism," *Literature and Medicine* 17, no. 2 (Fall 1998): 214.

29. Sheilah Graham, "Feminine Writers Discover Gold in the Scenario Hills," *Sunday Star* (Washington, DC), December 4, 1938, E-3.

30. S. J. Perelman, *The Last Laugh* (New York: Simon & Schuster, 1981), 187.

31. Frank S. Nugent, "The Screen," *New York Times*, December 23, 1938.

32. Parker, *The Collected Dorothy Parker*, 367.

33. Ibid., 368.

34. Ibid., 369. This story was rejected by the *New Yorker* much to Parker's fury.

35. Frank S. Nugent, "The Screen," *New York Times*, January 13, 1939.

36. "Miss Parker Never Poses," *New York Times*, January 8, 1939. All quotes and information in this paragraph are taken from this source.

37. "Henderson Tangles with Photographer at Parker Party," *Evening Star* (Washington, DC), January 7, 1939.

38. Parker, *The Portable Dorothy Parker*, 464.

39. Ibid., 465–66.

40. Meade, *What Fresh Hell Is This?*, 295.

41. Ibid., 295–96.

CHAPTER 6: SMASH-UP

1. "Eisler in Attendance at Reception for 19 in Hollywood Enquiry," *Evening Star* (Washington, DC), November 3, 1947.

2. "An Auction Event of Supreme Importance," *Los Angeles Times*, December 10, 1939.

3. Ibid.

4. Leslie Frewin, *The Late Mrs. Dorothy Parker* (New York: Macmillan, 1986), 236.

5. This pact fell apart in June 1941 when Germany invaded the Soviet Union.

6. "Jimmie Fidler in Hollywood," *Los Angeles Times*, November 27, 1939.

7. Marion Meade, *Dorothy Parker: What Fresh Hell Is This?* (London: Heinemann, 1987), 300.

8. Ibid., 301.

9. For more information on this see writers such as Warren J. Blumenfeld who argue that homophobia tends to manifest on four levels: personal, interpersonal, institutional, and cultural/societal.

10. Frewin, *The Late Mrs. Dorothy Parker*, 238.

11. Dorothy Parker, interview by Mr. and Mrs. Robert E. Franklin, Popular Arts Project for the Oral History Research Project, June 1959, audio and transcript, Columbia Center for Oral History, Columbia University.

12. Alan Campbell to Leonard Lyons, circa November/December 1939, item no. 70082123, Pennsylvania State University Library.

13. Alan Campbell to Leonard Lyons, telegram, November 16, 1940, item no. 70082123, Pennsylvania State University Library.

14. Dorothy Parker to Alexander Woollcott, circa December 1940, box 17, MS. Am 1449, Houghton Library, Harvard University. All quotations in this paragraph are taken from this source.

15. What appears to have happened is that Synder kidnapped Alderman from a radio station where he was working and demanded he take him to Etting. Then Synder held Etting and Alderman in the music room of the house while his daughter, Edith, was in another room. When Alderman tried to speak, Synder shot him and told Etting to call the police. Instead, she ran to her bedroom and grabbed her gun, which Synder then wrestled away from her. Seeing the gun fall to the floor, Edith, who had run in from another part of the house, picked it up and started shooting at her father. She missed.

16. Ian Hamilton, *Writers in Hollywood 1915–1951* (London: Faber & Faber, 2011), 156.

17. Dorothy Parker, *The Portable Dorothy Parker* (London: Penguin, 2006), 582.

18. Ibid.

19. Meade, *What Fresh Hell Is This?*, 308.

20. Dorothy Parker, *The Collected Dorothy Parker* (London: Penguin, 2001), 65.

21. Ibid., 67.

22. Hubbard Keavy, "A Reputation Unearned and Unwanted," *Evening Star* (Washington, DC), December 7, 1941. All information in this paragraph is taken from this source.

23. Meade, *What Fresh Hell Is This?*, 309.

24. Dorothy Parker to Alexander Woollcott, July 20, 1942, box 17, MS. Am 1449, Houghton Library, Harvard University. All quotations in this paragraph are taken from this source.

25. Dorothy Parker to Alexander Woollcott, September 2, 1942, box 17, MS. Am 1449, Houghton Library, Harvard University. All quotes and information in this paragraph are taken from this source.

26. Out of respect to Parker, who for the rest of her life hated her infamous two-line poem about how men view women in glasses, this book will not print it. It is easy enough to find online. Parker wished she had never written it.

27. This word is a jeering slur used against Jewish people.

28. "Says Wise-Cracks Taboo for Duration of War," *Monitor Leader* (Mount Clemens, MI), September 25, 1942.

29. Dorothy Parker to Leonard Lyons [undated, 1942], item no. 70082123, Pennsylvania State University Library.

30. The Alan Campbell Dorothy Parker Collection ([1930]–1949, bulk 1938–46) is held at the University of Michigan Library. Correspondence and financial papers are in box 1. Box 2 holds sepia photographs. I am indebted to the University of Michigan for allowing me access to this collection during the height

of the COVID-19 pandemic. In particular to Juli McLoone, who introduced me to my first ever Zoom archive visit so I could see the letters and get a feel for the collection. This was invaluable for the book. This was followed by rapid scanning of the entire collection during a very difficult time for archives.

31. Joshua Logan, *Movie Stars, Real People, and Me* (New York: Delacorte Press, 1978), 235.

32. Parker, *The Collected Dorothy Parker*, 595.

33. Ibid., 596.

34. Logan, *Movie Stars, Real People, and Me*, 236.

35. Meade, *What Fresh Hell Is This?*, 324.

36. Parker, *The Collected Dorothy Parker*, 597. Italics appear in the published version.

37. Logan, *Movie Stars, Real People, and Me*, 238.

38. Marie-Laure de Noailles (1902–70) was a French artist and patron of the arts. She associated with Dalí, Cocteau, and Man Ray. Her home was 11, place des États-Unis in Paris.

39. It is interesting to see Campbell using the European spelling "favourite" in this letter.

40. Alan Campbell to Dorothy Parker, circa late 1945/early 1946, box 1, Alan Campbell Dorothy Parker Collection ([1930]–1949, bulk 1938–46), University of Michigan Library.

41. Adela Rogers St. Johns, *Some Are Born Great* (New York: Doubleday, 1974), 107.

42. Alan Campbell to Dorothy Parker, November 25, 1945, box 1, Alan Campbell Dorothy Parker Collection ([1930]–1949, bulk 1938–46), University of Michigan Library.

43. Alan Campbell to Dorothy Parker, January 18, 1946, box 1, Alan Campbell Dorothy Parker Collection ([1930]–1949, bulk 1938–46), University of Michigan Library.

44. Alan Campbell to Dorothy Parker, circa late 1945/early 1946, box 1, Alan Campbell Dorothy Parker Collection.

CHAPTER 7: NO HAPPY ENDINGS

1. "California Committee Lists Noted Film Stars and Others as Reds," *Evening Star* (Washington, DC), June 9, 1949, A-3.

2. "Dorothy Parker Is Sued for Divorce by Campbell," *Evening Star* (Washington, DC), May 22, 1947.

3. "Dorothy Parker Wins Divorce from Campbell," *Evening Star* (Washington, DC), May 28, 1947.

4. Hedda Hopper, "Looking at Hollywood," *Los Angeles Times*, July 28, 1947.

5. Carl Erik Fisher, "It's Misleading to Call Addiction a Disease," *New York Times*, January 15, 2022.

6. Once again Parker did not win. She lost out to Valentine Davies for *Miracle on 34th Street*.

7. "The Greatest Story Never Told," *Voice of Freedom* 4, no. 1 (Spring 1951).

8. Quote taken from a note in the Marion Meade Papers, series IV, box 8, folder 9, Rare Book and Manuscripts Library, Columbia University Library.

9. Dorothy Parker to Orson Welles, telegram, March 13, 1947, boxes 1–4, correspondence M-P, Welles mss, Lilly Library, Indiana University.

10. "Eisler in Attendance at Reception for 19 in Hollywood Inquiry," *Evening Star* (Washington, DC), November 3, 1947, A-4.

11. Ibid.

12. Ibid.

13. Shawn Levy, *The Castle on Sunset* (London: Weidenfeld & Nicolson, 2020), 5. Levy's book is an engaging history of the hotel from its inception to the current day with some wonderful archival photographs.

14. Ibid., 99.

15. Ibid., 161.

16. "'Fan' Made Modern for Picture," *Los Angeles Times*, August 29, 1948.

17. "Comment of Those Named in Inquiries," *Los Angeles Times*, June 9, 1949.

18. Ibid.

19. "California Committee Lists Noted Film Stars and Others as Reds."

20. Ibid.

21. Office memorandum from director of FBI to SAC New York, May 18, 1950.

22. FBI file on Dorothy Parker, page titled "<u>DOROTHY PARKER (NY-100 98708)</u>."

23. "Team Again: Miss Parker to Remarry Ex-Husband," *Los Angeles Times*, August 15, 1950.

24. Wyatt Cooper, "Whatever You Think Dorothy Parker Was Like, She Wasn't," *Esquire*, July 1, 1968, 111.

25. Ibid., 112.

26. FBI file on Dorothy Parker, "<u>DOROTHY PARKER (NY-100 98708)</u>."

27. Ibid.

28. Marion Meade, *Dorothy Parker: What Fresh Hell Is This?* (London: Heinemann, 1987), 341.

29. FBI file on Dorothy Parker, page titled "<u>ADMINISTRATIVE PAGE LA 100-32635</u>."

30. Dorothy Parker, *The Portable Dorothy Parker* (London: Penguin, 2006), 582.

31. Ibid.

32. Dorothy Parker on Norman Mailer quoted by Noel Pugh in Marion Meade Papers, transcripts folder 1, Rare Book and Manuscripts Library, Columbia University Library.

33. Telegrams and letters exchanged between the University of Michigan and Dorothy Parker, 1934, in Marion Meade Papers, folder 3, box 8, Rare Book and Manuscripts Library, Columbia University Library.

34. E. M. Forster to Dorothy Parker, May 15, 1957 (unsent), EMF 18/419, King's College Library, Cambridge.

35. Parker took every possible opportunity to criticize the Beat poets. In *The Portable Dorothy Parker*, her published speech "The Function of the Writer, Address," given at the *Esquire* symposium in October 1958, is heavily edited. The final part of the speech deals briskly and firmly with the Beat poets, who receive some classic Parker treatment. A full copy of the speech is among the Robert Gorham Davis papers at Columbia University Library. The observations quoted here are taken from Dorothy Parker, "Dorothy Parker Discusses Her Plays and the State of Literature," interview by Studs Terkel, February 6, 1959, accessed December 17, 2021, https://studsterkel.wfmt.com/programs/dorothy-parker-discusses-her-plays-and-state-literature.

36. Ibid.

37. Hedda Hopper, "Entertainment," *Los Angeles Times*, September 14, 1961.

38. Dorothy Townsend, "The Queen of Wisecracks Marshals Her Subjects: Dorothy Parker Sets Up L.A. Shop," *Los Angeles Times*, June 18, 1962.

39. Ibid.

40. Interview with Nina Foch in folder 1, box 8, Marion Meade Papers, Rare Book and Manuscripts Library, Columbia University Library.

41. Dorothy Parker, *The Portable Dorothy Parker*, 613.

42. Ibid.

43. Cooper, "Whatever You Think Dorothy Parker Was Like, She Wasn't," 57.

44. Ibid., 111.

45. The three stories were "The Lovely Leave," "A Telephone Call," and "Dusk Before Fireworks." They appeared on the series *The*

Festival of Performing Arts and were dramatized by Margaret Leighton and Patrick O'Neal.

46. Murray Schumach, "Dorothy Parker Discuss TV," *New York Times*, May 6, 1962.

47. Cooper, "Whatever You Think Dorothy Parker Was Like, She Wasn't," 61.

48. Incidentally, this hotel had been used as a filming location for *Some Like It Hot* in 1958.

49. Dorothea McCall, "Dorothy Parker Leaves Librarians Breathless," *Coronado Eagle & Journal* 49, no. 44, November 1, 1962.

50. Ibid.

51. Mary Ann Callan, "Students Appalling to Dorothy Parker," *Los Angeles Times*, April 28, 1963. All information and quotes in this paragraph are taken from this article.

52. Interview with Frederick Shroyer in folder 1, box 8, Marion Meade Papers, Rare Book and Manuscripts Library, Columbia University Library.

53. Cooper, "Whatever You Think Dorothy Parker Was Like, She Wasn't," 111.

54. Meade, *What Fresh Hell Is This?*, 392.

55. Dorothy Parker, "1966 Radio Interview with Dorothy Parker and Richard Lamparski," Dorothy Parker Society, August 13, 2021, https://dorothyparker.com/2021/08/1966-radio-interview.html.

56. Interview with John Carlyle in folder 1, box 8, Marion Meade Papers, Rare Book and Manuscripts Library, Columbia University Library.

57. Dorothy Parker, *Dorothy Parker: In Her Own Words*, ed. Barry Day (Lanham, MD: Taylor Trade Publishing, 2004), 127.

EPILOGUE

1. Dorothy Parker, *The Portable Dorothy Parker* (London: Penguin, 2006), 571.

2. This essay was published in March 1965.

3. Sadly, Parker does not name any names here, though stars of the time who would fit the bill are Elizabeth Taylor, Richard Burton, and Audrey Hepburn. But Parker also took an interest in prominent New York socialites and high society. She was an avid reader of the fashion writer and columnist Eugenia Sheppard.

4. Wyatt Cooper, "Whatever You Think Dorothy Parker Was Like, She Wasn't," *Esquire*, July 1, 1968, 114.

5. Adela Rogers St. Johns, *Some Are Born Great* (New York: Doubleday, 1974), 109.

6. Parker, *The Portable Dorothy Parker*, 571.

7. Ibid., 97.

8. Ibid., 235.

9. "Dorothy Parker Recalled as Wit," *New York Times*, June 10, 1967.

10. Copies of funeral flower receipts are held in the Lillian Hellman Papers, box 85.2, Harry Ransom Center, University of Texas, Austin.

11. A copy of Parker's will is held in the Lillian Hellman Papers, box 85.2, Harry Ransom Center, University of Texas, Austin.

BIBLIOGRAPHY

DOROTHY PARKER

Parker, Dorothy. *The Uncollected Dorothy Parker*. Edited by Stuart Y. Silverstein. London: Duckworth, 1999.

Parker, Dorothy. *The Collected Dorothy Parker*. London: Penguin, 2001.

Parker, Dorothy. *Dorothy Parker: In Her Own Words*. Edited by Barry Day. Lanham, MD: Taylor Trade Publishing, 2004.

Parker, Dorothy. *The Portable Dorothy Parker*. New York: Penguin, 2006.

Parker, Dorothy, and Arnaud d'Usseau. *The Ladies of the Corridor*. London: Penguin, 2008.

GENERAL BIBLIOGRAPHY

Anger, Kenneth. *Hollywood Babylon*. London: Arrow Books, 1975.

Barbas, Samantha. *Movie Crazy: Fans, Stars, and the Cult of Celebrity*. New York: Palgrave, 2001.

Barber, Mary E., Peter M. Marzuk, Andrew C. Leon, and Laura Portera. "Aborted Suicide Attempts: A New Classification of Suicidal Behavior." *American Journal of Psychiatry* 155, no. 3 (March 1998): 385–89.

Barranger, Milly S. "Dorothy Parker and the Politics of McCarthyism." *Theatre History Studies* 26 (2006): 7–30.

Benchley, Nathaniel. *Robert Benchley: A Biography*. London: Cassell and Company, 1956.

Dean, Michelle. *Sharp: The Women Who Made an Art of Having an Opinion*. London: Fleet, 2018.

Donaldson, Scott. "Scott and Dottie." *Sewanee Review* 124, no. 1 (Winter 2016): 40–61.

Dyer, Richard. *Heavenly Bodies*. 2nd ed. London: Routledge, 2004.

———. *Stars*. 2nd ed. London: BFI Publishing, 1998.

Everall, Robin D. "The Meaning of Suicide Attempts by Young Adults." *Canadian Journal of Counselling/Revue canadienne de counseling* 34, no. 2 (2000): 11–25.

Feibleman, Peter. *Lilly: Reminiscences of Lillian Hellman*. New York: William Morrow, 1988.

Fitzpatrick, Kevin C. *A Journey into Dorothy Parker's New York*. Berkeley, CA: Roaring Forties Press, 2005.

Fowles, Jib. *Starstruck: Celebrity Performers and the American Public*. Washington and London: Smithsonian Institution Press, 1992.

Frewin, Leslie. *The Late Mrs. Dorothy Parker*. New York: Macmillan, 1986.

Gillette, Meg. "Modern American Abortion Narratives and the Century of Silence." *Twentieth-Century Literature* 58, no. 4 (Winter 2012): 663–87.

Graham, Sheilah. *The Garden of Allah*. New York: Crown Publishers, 1970.

Guiles, Fred Lawrence. *Hanging On in Paradise*. New York: McGraw-Hill, 1975.

Hallam, Elizabeth, and Jenny Hockey. *Death, Memory and Material Culture*. Oxford and New York: Berg, 2001.

Hammill, Faye. *Women, Celebrity, and Literary Culture Between the Wars*. Austin: University of Texas Press, 2007.

Hellman, Lillian. *An Unfinished Woman*. 2nd ed. London: Quartet Books, 1977.

Hoffman, Nancy Jo. "Reading Women's Poetry: The Meaning and Our Lives." *College English* 34, no. 1 (October 1972): 48–62.

Jaffe, Aaron. *Modernism and the Culture of Celebrity*. Cambridge: Cambridge University Press, 2005.

Keats, John. *You Might As Well Live: The Life and Times of Dorothy Parker*. London: Penguin, 1979.

King, Florence. "Dorothy Parker, Uncompassionate Liberal." *American Enterprise* 6, no. 3 (May–June 1995): 93.

Kinney, Arthur F. *Dorothy Parker*. Boston: Twayne, 1978.

———. "Dorothy Parker's Letters to Alexander Woollcott." *Massachusetts Review* 30, no. 3 (Autumn 1989): 487–515.

Krystal, Arthur. "Slow Fade: F. Scott Fitzgerald in Hollywood." *New Yorker*, November 19, 2009.

Lamparski, Richard. *Manhattan Diary*. Albany, GA: BearManor Media, 2006.

Lansky, Ellen. "Female Trouble: Dorothy Parker, Katherine Anne Porter, and Alcoholism." *Literature and Medicine* 17, no. 2 (Fall 1998): 212–30.

Levant, Oscar. *The Memoirs of an Amnesiac*. New York: G. P. Putnam's Sons, 1965.

Levy, Shawn. *The Castle on Sunset: Love, Fame, Death and Scandal at Hollywood's Chateau Marmont*. London: Weidenfeld & Nicholson, 2019.

Lewis, Lisa. *The Adoring Audience: Fan Culture and Popular Media*. London: Routledge, 1992.

Logan, Joshua. *Movie Stars, Real People, and Me*. New York: Delacorte Press, 1978.

Loos, Anita. *Kiss Hollywood Goodbye*. London: Quality Book Club, 1976.

McCall, Dorothea. "Dorothy Parker Leaves Librarians Breathless." *Coronado Eagle & Journal* 49, no. 44, November 1, 1962.

Meade, Marion. *Bobbed Hair and Bathtub Gin: Writers Running Wild in the Twenties*. New York: Doubleday, 2004.

———. *Dorothy Parker: What Fresh Hell Is This?* London: Heinemann, 1987.

Miller, Sarah Clark. "The Moral Meanings of Miscarriage." *Journal of Social Philosophy* 46, no. 1 (Spring 2015): 141–57.

Perelman, S. J. *The Last Laugh*. New York: Simon & Schuster, 1981.

Rojek, Chris. *Celebrity*. London: Reaktion Books, 2001.

Rollyson, Carl. *Lillian Hellman: Her Life and Legend*. London: Endeavour Media, 2017.

Schwartz, Nancy Lynn. *The Hollywood Writers' War*. Lincoln, NE: Authors Guild Backinprint.com, 2001.

Skeggs, Beverley. *Feminist Cultural Theory: Process and Production*. Manchester, UK: Manchester University Press, 1995.

Stacey, Jackie. *Star Gazing: Hollywood Cinema and Female Spectatorship*. London: Routledge, 1994.

St. Johns, Adela Rogers. *Some Are Born Great*. New York: Doubleday, 1974.

Sudjic, Deyan. *Cult Heroes*. London: Andre Deutsch, 1989.

Thomas, Lyn. *Fans, Feminisms and 'Quality' Media*. London: Routledge, 2002.

Vanderbilt, Gloria. *It Seemed Important at the Time: A Romance Memoir*. New York: Simon & Schuster, 2004.

Young-Bruehl, Elisabeth. *Subject to Biography: Psychoanalysis, Feminism and Writing Women's Lives*. Cambridge, MA, and London: Harvard University Press, 1998.

NEWSPAPER ARTICLES

Ainsworth, Ed. "Can Laughter Die?" *Los Angeles Times*, February 5, 1939.

Associated Press. "Dorothy Parker Was October Bride." *Evening Star* (Washington, DC), June 16, 1934.

———. "This Is Personal: So Said Poet When Asked of Romance." *Evening Star* (Washington, DC), June 18, 1934.

———. "Heir Is Expected by Dorothy Parker, Her Friends Say." *Evening Star* (Washington, DC), December 15, 1936.

———. "Sergeant Looks for Oculist in M's, Campbell Pays $100." *Sunday Star* (Washington, DC), December 5, 1937.

———. "Their Salaries Among Highest Paid During 1936." *Sunday Star* (Washington, DC), January 9, 1938.

———. "Henderson Tangles with Photographer at Parker Party." *Evening Star* (Washington, DC), January 7, 1939.

———. "Dorothy Parker Is Sued for Divorce by Campbell." *Evening Star* (Washington, DC), May 22, 1947.

———. "Dorothy Parker Wins Divorce from Campbell." *Evening Star* (Washington, DC), May 28, 1947.

———. "Eisler in Attendance at Reception for 19 in Hollywood Inquiry." *Evening Star* (Washington, DC), November 3, 1947.

———. "Ten Authors to Face Quiz in New Phase of Book Controversy." *Sunday Star* (Washington, DC), June 28, 1953.

Bismarck (ND) Tribune. "Women Writer Prefers Babies." April 29, 1932.

Callan, Mary Ann. "Students Appalling to Dorothy Parker." *Los Angeles Times*, April 28, 1963.

Carmody, Jay. "Script Writers Get Nods from Press Book Authors." *Evening Star* (Washington, DC), June 9, 1937.

———. "'Sweethearts' Hits New Level in Beauty and Melody." *Evening Star* (Washington, DC), December 30, 1938.

Detroit Times. "Dorothy Parker Here for Rally." October 8, 1944.

Durant (MS) News. "Broadway Limited." May 6, 1937.

Durling, E. V. "On the Side." *Los Angeles Times*, December 23, 1936.

Evening Star (Washington, DC). "California Committee Lists Noted Film Stars and Others as Reds." June 9, 1949.

Fisher, Carl Erik. "It's Misleading to Call Addiction a Disease." *New York Times*, January 15, 2022.

Graham, Sheilah. "Feminine Writers Discover Gold in the Scenario Hills." *Sunday Star* (Washington, DC), December 4, 1938.

———. "Royalty Sees Hollywood on a Busy Schedule." *Evening Star* (Washington, DC), March 11, 1939.

Grimes, William. "Dorothy Parker Breakfast: Tasty but Indigestible." *New York Times*, October 15, 1994.

Hopper, Hedda. "Looking at Hollywood." *Los Angeles Times*, July 28, 1947.

———. "Entertainment." *Los Angeles Times*, September 14, 1961.

James, Caryn. "Critic's Notebook: At Wits' End; Algonquinites in Hollywood." *New York Times*, January 8, 1993.

Jaynes, Gregory. "About New York; 90 Subdued Years of Funerals for the Famous." *New York Times*, June 8, 1988.

Kaplan, Morris. "Dorothy Parker's Will Leaves Estate of $10,000 to Dr. King." *New York Times*, June 27, 1967.

Keavy, Hubbard. "A Reputation Unearned and Unwanted." *Evening Star* (Washington, DC), December 7, 1941.

Los Angeles Times. "Writer Couple Will Be West-East Commuters." November 8, 1936.

———. "Spanish War Takes Caustic Out of Her Poetry." October 23, 1937.

———. "Jimmie Fidler in Hollywood." November 27, 1939.

———. "An Auction Event of Supreme Importance." December 10, 1939.

———. "Film Colony Speakers Attack Dies' Committee Charges." February 22, 1940.

———. "Chinese War Film Will Be Presented." April 5, 1942.

———. "'Fan' Made Modern for Picture." August 29, 1948.

———. "Team Again: Miss Parker to Remarry Ex-Husband." August 15, 1950.

———. "Writer Parker Remarried to Former Spouse." August 18, 1950.

Merrick, Mollie. "Movies and Movie People." *Evening Star* (Washington, DC), January 4, 1929.

Michigan Chronicle. "Dorothy Parker Scores Dewey with Deadly Wit." November 4, 1944.

Monitor Leader (Mount Clemons, MI). "Says Wise-Cracks Taboo for Duration of War." September 25, 1942.

New York Times. "Vanity Fair's Editors Out." January 13, 1920.

———. "Dorothy Parker, Farmer." August 24, 1936.

———. "Miss Parker Never Poses." January 8, 1939.

———. "$488 Party No Joke to Dorothy Parker." March 16, 1939.

———. "Dorothy Parker's Husband Is Found Dead on Coast." June 15, 1963.

———. "Dorothy Parker Recalled as Wit." June 10, 1967.

Nugent, Frank S. "The Screen." *New York Times*, July 25, 1936.

Parker, Dorothy. "Not Enough!" *New Masses*, March 14, 1939.

Partridge, Helen. "The 'WOLF' at Dorothy Parker's Door." *Evening Star* (Washington, DC), February 24, 1935.

People's Voice. "'Book Burning' Is Arousing Nationwide Protests." July 3, 1953.

Schumach, Murray. "Dorothy Parker Discusses TV." *New York Times*, May 6, 1962.

Sorel, Edward. "The Literati: Mr. and Mrs. Dorothy Parker's Arrival in Hollywood." *New York Times*, September 7, 2018.

Stroock, Mark. "Letter to the Editor: Dorothy Parker; Just Part of the Story." *New York Times*, December 11, 1994.

Sunday Star (Washington, DC). "Dorothy Parker Recovering." February 28, 1932.

Townsend, Dorothy. "The Queen of Wisecracks Marshals Her Subjects: Dorothy Parker Sets Up L.A. Shop." *Los Angeles Times*, June 18, 1962.

Van de Grift, Josephine. "Humor's Sober Side." *Bisbee (AZ) Daily Review*, October 11, 1922.

Whitaker, Alma. "Dorothy Parker, Our Only Woman Humorist Denies It." *Los Angeles Times*, September 13, 1934.

Whitman, Alden. "Dorothy Parker, 73, Literary Wit, Dies." *New York Times*, June 8, 1967.

Winchell, Walter. "The Press-Box." *Daily Record*, May 29, 1952.

Wolfert, Ira. "At Last There's a Nickname That's Worthy of Hepburn." *Evening Star* (Washington, DC), October 9, 1941.

ONLINE SOURCES

Anderson, Hephzibah. "Dorothy Parker's Stunning Wit and Tragic Life." *BBC Culture*, June 7, 2017. https://www.bbc.com/culture/article/20170605-dorothy-parkers-stunning-wit-and-tragic-life.

Brown, JPat. "Throughout the '50s, the FBI Hung on Dorothy Parker's Every Word." *Muckrock*, May 3, 2018. https://www.muckrock.com/news/archives/2018/may/03/dorothy-parker-fbi-file/.

Columbia Center for Oral History. "Dorothy Parker: Hollywood." Soundcloud. https://soundcloud.com/ccoh/dorothy-parker-hollywood?in=ccoh/sets/from-the-archive-1.

Cooper, Wyatt. "Whatever You Think Dorothy Parker Was Like, She Wasn't." *Esquire*, July 1, 1968. https://classic.esquire.com/article/share/3189e551-05f0-4dac-983c-902558a09682.

Dorothy Parker Society. https://dorothyparker.com/.

Esotouric Podcast. "Episode #45: Mrs. Parker & Friends in the Garden of Allah." November 25, 2013. https://esotouric.com/2013/11/25/canteatsunshine45/.

Finding Lost Angeles. "The Ambassador Hotel & Cocoanut Grove." December 13, 2017.

Fitzpatrick, Kevin. "Dorothy Parker—Marion Meade Interview." Soundcloud. https:/soundcloud.com/k72ndst/dorothy-parker-marion-meade.

———. "A Conversation with Marion Meade." Dorothy Parker Society, March 15, 2006. https://dorothyparker.com/gallery/a-conversation-with-marion-meade.

———. "Dorothy Parker Happy in Los Angeles." *Huffpost*, December 6, 2013, updated December 6, 2017. https://www.huffpost.com/entry/dorothy-parker-los-angeles_b_4399844.

The History Chicks. "Episode 56: Dorothy Parker Part Two." August 30, 2015. http://thehistorychicks.com/episode-56-dorothy-parker-part-two/.

Hitchens, Christopher. "Rebel in Evening Clothes." *Vanity Fair*, October 1999. Digitized October 10, 2006. https://www.vanity fair.com/magazine/1999/10/hitchens199910.

Horder, Mervyn. "Dorothy Parker: Political Activist, Melancholic, Bootleg Scotch Drinker." *Literary Hub*, May 1, 2019. https:// lithub.com/dorothy-parker-political-activist-melancholic-boot -leg-scotch-drinker/.

Karr, Christopher. "Why Faulkner, Fitzgerald and Other Literary Luminaries Hated Hollywood." *Highbrow Magazine*, August 13, 2012. https://www.highbrowmagazine.com/1469-why-faulkner -fitzgerald-and-other-literary-luminaries-hated-hollywood.

Longworth, Karina. "The Blacklist Part 3: Dorothy Parker." WBEZ Chicago, February 16, 2016. https://www.wbez.org/stories/the -blacklist-part-3-dorothy-parker/bf9f16f3-3075-4a09-b198 -b555c95dcd3d.

———. "Dorothy Parker Goes to Hollywood." *Slate*, February 26, 2016. https://slate.com/culture/2016/02/the-hollywood-career-and -blacklist-experience-of-dorothy-parker.html.

MarriedAtTheMovies. "Grand Hotel: A History of the Ambassador Hotel & Cocoanut Grove." November 28, 2017. https://medium .com/married-at-the-movies/grand-hotel-a-history-of-the -ambassador-hotel-cocoanut-grove-88d762b81e9e.

Meade, Marion. "An Interview with Marion Meade." By Ellen Meister. *Bookslut*, July 2014.

Palmer, Iva-Marie. "In Their Shoes: The Round Table's Los Angeles." *Condé Nast Traveler*, June 11, 2014. https://www.cntraveler .com/galleries/2014-06-11/los-angeles-attractions-to-cele brate-the-round-table-anniversary?fbclid=IwAR2XkDKG DkOA5oyLHh_zfJLO0uzG4TnhwpLpl6axhOncpq216I BKYopTklQ.

Parker, Dorothy. "In Lost 1953 Speech, Dorothy Parker Rips Hollywood." From a speech titled "Hollywood, the Land I Won't Re-

turn To." Dorothy Parker Society, March 6, 2017. https://dorothy
parker.com/2017/03/in-lost-1953-speech-dorothy-parker-rips
-hollywood.html.

―――. "Dorothy Parker Discusses Her Plays and the State of Literature." Interview by Studs Terkel. Studs Terkel Radio Archive,
February 6, 1959. https://studsterkel.wfmt.com/programs/dorothy
-parker-discusses-her-plays-and-state-literature.

―――. "1966 Radio Interview with Dorothy Parker and Richard
Lamparski." Dorothy Parker Society, August 13, 2021. https://
dorothyparker.com/2021/08/1966-radio-interview.html.

Rozzo, Mark. "Secrets of the Chateau Marmont." *Vanity Fair*, February 4, 2019. https://www.vanityfair.com/style/2019/02/secrets-of
-the-chateau-marmont.

Shapiro, Laurie Gwen. "The Improbable Journey of Dorothy Parker's Ashes." *New Yorker*, September 4, 2020. https://www.new
yorker.com/culture/culture-desk/the-improbable-journey-of
-dorothy-parkers-ashes.

Silsbee, Kirk. "This Hotel Kept All the Secrets of the Rich and Famous
. . . Until Now." *GQ*, June 23, 2015. https://www.gq-magazine
.co.uk/article/garden-of-allah-the-secret-life-of-celebrities.

Sorel, Edward. "Inside the Trial of Actress Mary Astor, Old Hollywood's Juiciest Sex Scandal." *Vanity Fair*, September 14, 2016.
https://www.vanityfair.com/hollywood/2016/09/inside-the
-trial-of-actress-mary-astor-hollywoods-juiciest-sex-scandal
?fbclid=IwAR0e4RcIERZGtDWM1G7Xfjg054IZigOidUL
KmYNeKsR61rGGX8Ml67L_Qds.

Southern Bookman (blog). "Dorothy Parker and F. Scott Fitzgerald
Drank the Same Wine." March 16, 2006. https://louismayeux
.typepad.com/southern_bookman/2016/03/dorothy-parker-and
-f-scott-fitzgerald-drank-the-same-wine.html.

The Ten-Year Lunch; Wits & Legends of the Algonquin Round Table
(Complete). 1987. YouTube. https://www.youtube.com/watch?v=_
ObXzrP4wdc&t=234s.

Turnbull, Martin. "About the Garden of Allah Hotel." https://martin
turnbull.com/about-the-garden-of-allah-series-of-books-by
-martin-turnbull/about-the-garden-of-allah-hotel/.
VirtualDavis. "No Cure for Curiosity." http://www.virtualdavis.com
/tags/dorothy-parker/.

ARCHIVES CONSULTED
Columbia Center for Oral History Research, New York
Columbia University Libraries Archival Collections, New York
Harry Ransom Center, University of Texas, Austin
Houghton Library, Harvard University, Cambridge, Massachusetts
Howard Gotlieb Archival Research Center, Boston University, Boston
Huntington Library, San Marino, California
King's College, Cambridge, England
Lilly Library, Indiana University, Bloomington, Indiana
Penn State University Library, State College, Pennsylvania
University of Maryland Archival Collections, College Park
University of Michigan Library (Special Collections Research Center),
    Ann Arbor

G ail Crowther is a freelance writer, researcher, and academic. She is the author of *Three-Martini Afternoons at the Ritz: The Rebellion of Sylvia Plath and Anne Sexton*. Gail divides her time between the north of England and London.